"Authoritative and accessible . . . Coleman's evenhanded history . . . effectively combines tributes to the valor of the soldiers and air crews who participated."

—*Kirkus Reviews*

ATTACK OF THE "CHARLIE BLUES"

Within seconds, seven more Claymores scythed through the North Vietnamese. The Charlie Blues blazed away with M-16s and M-79 grenades. The violence of the fire detonated grenades and ammunition on the bodies lying in the trail. Rifle and machine gun fire from the eastern flank security position blasted the trail edge of the enemy's lead element. As bright as it was in the moonlight, the sky was further lit up by the violent ambush fire. So complete was the surprise, so total the devastation, that not one single NVA weapon was fired in exchange.

Pennington, who had the right flank security mission, fired M-79s and M-16s at the trail to the west. There wasn't a North Vietnamese soldier left alive for fifty meters along the trail; those on either side of the trap had vanished. Knowlen, recognizing that he was probably in the middle of a much larger force, signaled his force to break back for the rendezvous point. There they formed up and prepared to head back to LZ Mary.

"Coleman has done a splendid job of telling the story of that bloody testing time. This is no dry dissection from the vantage point of two decades gone. Coleman was there. He celebrates the victories, mourns the defeats—and pulls no punches in his meticulous re-creation of both."

—Joseph Galloway, *U.S. News & World Report*;
former UPI reporter at Pleiku

CHOPPERS

Previously Published as *PLEIKU*

J.D. COLEMAN

St. Martin's Paperbacks

Choppers was previously published in hardcover and paperback as *Pleiku.*

CHOPPERS

Copyright © 1988 by J.D. Coleman.

Cover photograph by J.D. Coleman.

All rights reserved. No part of this book may be used or reproduced in any manner whatsoever without written permission except in the case of brief quotations embodied in critical articles or reviews. For information address St. Martin's Press, 175 Fifth Avenue, New York, N.Y. 10010.

Library of Congress Catalog Card Number: 88-1940

ISBN: 0-312-96635-0

Printed in the United States of America

St. Martin's Press hardcover edition published 1988
St. Martin's Paperbacks edition/March 1989

St. Martin's Paperbacks are published by St. Martin's Press, 175 Fifth Avenue, New York, NY 10010.

10 9 8 7 6 5 4 3

To those brave soldiers of the First Team
who paid the ultimate price to win one
for Garry Owen

CONTENTS

FOREWORD

An army consists of individuals, organizations, and equipment. *Seldom* in the long history of armies have these three ingredients been so ingenuously intermixed as they were in the creation of the first air assault division. *Never* in the history of armies has such a new concept been committed to combat on such short notice and with so many questions still unanswered.

This book is the history of the development of the airmobile concept and the ultimate testing of that concept in the crucible of combat. It is the history of equipment, and how new equipment can be introduced into a military organization without costly and time-consuming processes. It is a history of organizations and of the trade-offs that must be made in putting a combined arms team on the battlefield.

But above all it is a history of soldiers—soldiers with vision, soldiers with courage, soldiers with candor, soldiers with confidence, soldiers with humor, and soldiers with compassion. It is a history of soldiers of every rank, from general to private, an extraordinary group of soldiers who breathed life into a concept and whose own lives ultimately were dependent on the success of that concept.

The integration of aircraft into the combat structure of

the U.S. Army had been going on since the first airplanes and helicopters were produced for the War Department. For years, innovative soldiers of all ranks had worked with helicopters and fixed-wing aircraft toward integrating them into the various combat and support functions of the Army. But not until the creation in 1962 of the U.S. Army Tactical Mobility Requirements Board, chaired by General Hamilton Howze, did the Army turn the functional pieces into a conceptual whole.

From the time the Howze Board recommended the creation of an airmobile division until that division was tested in the Vietnam highlands near Pleiku, the man who orchestrated this unique organization was General Harry W. O. Kinnard. The Army could not have selected a better individual to transfer concept into reality. General Kinnard was an experienced combat veteran of World War II who made his mark as an airborne commander and staff officer. As the operations officer he had played a critical role in the successful defense of Bastogne. In addition to his combat experience, he had a broad background as a commander and as a staff officer in several valuable research and development assignments. General Kinnard brought these experiences to the new airmobile division. For the officers and noncommissioned officers that he selected for the testing of this concept, he created an environment that unfettered them from the more conventional thought processes and encouraged them to think in a new dimension—a dimension free from the ageless restrictions and tyranny of terrain.

This was not an easy task. He was forcing change on the Army. Entrenched segments of large bureaucratic organizations fight change because change challenges long-held views and ideas. How he overcame this obstacle is a paradigm for those trying to create change in any hierarchical structure. But the Army was changed by General Kinnard and his sky troopers.

The division passed, with colors and aircraft flying, all of the tests outsiders could design. Meanwhile, events halfway around the world were about to thrust this nascent division into the ultimate testing ground for man, machine, and organization: combat. In the summer of 1965, President Lyndon Johnson directed that the 1st Cavalry Division (Airmobile) be the first U.S. Army division to be deployed to Vietnam.

Moving the new division to Vietnam on short notice was another challenge. The Army hadn't moved a full division and all of its equipment overseas since the Korean War. And the Army had never moved a division with over four hundred aircraft. From the time the division arrived in Vietnam until the Pleiku Campaign occurred was another period of learning and experimentation for the soldiers of the First Team. They had been tested since the day the decision was made to create an air assault division. The ultimate test would take place in the central highlands of South Vietnam.

The confluence of events that brought this division into the central highlands just as North Vietnamese regular army forces were preparing to launch an attack to seize the provincial capitals in that region would seem to be straight out of fiction. But the battles that took place were not fiction.

Until now, no book about Vietnam has managed to couple the mundane aspects of organizations and equipment with the highly charged interactions of men in combat. J. D. Coleman, who was involved with the 1st Cavalry Division from start to finish, has managed to create a book that might have been as interesting to read as an army field manual or an after-action report, but instead is a highly readable primer on many facets of how the American Army functions.

The most important facet he highlights is how dependent the success of this division was on people. Mr. Coleman brings history to life with his vignettes of soldiers under stress. He reminds us of the fog of war that forces commanders to make decisions with limited and often incorrect information. He poignantly reminds us of those who died.

The history of the campaign in the highlands of Vietnam

is a testament to all those involved in the creation of the airmobile concept. But above all it is a testament to the soldiers of the 1st Air Cavalry Division who fought so courageously and who proved through their actions that the concept would work.

This book is a history—a history of soldiers. Thank God there were soldiers such as these.

—*E. C. Meyer*
General, U.S. Army,
Retired
Arlington, Virginia

PREFACE

Throughout this narrative of the Pleiku Campaign, the movements, activities, and battles of the North Vietnamese Army (NVA) forces will be interspersed with the concurrent actions of the American forces.

Obtaining information on the movements and actions of the U.S. and allied forces is relatively easy for a historian. The archives of the Army abound with source material. Additionally, the author, who wrote the official after-action report of the Pleiku Campaign as well as the recommendation for the Presidential Unit Citation for the 1st Cavalry Division (Airmobile), came into possession of a number of documents and photographs not available to the general public.

But information on NVA activities is not so readily available. Hanoi has not yet seen fit to open its archives to historians, so the best method of tracking NVA units is to use the same information intelligence officers used to track those units during the Vietnam War. The debris littering the battlefield after every engagement—diaries, battle plans, infiltration unit identification, and so on—inevitably yielded information of some intelligence value. Interrogating captured NVA soldiers also provided valuable insights into their units' histories, travels, key command figures, and battle plans.

In the case of the three NVA regiments that play a role in this narrative, both Army of the Republic of Vietnam (ARVN) and American intelligence officers began obtaining information about them from the time the 32nd Regiment entered Kontum Province. Initial information came from agent reports, but after the 32nd Regiment began engaging in combat operations, additional information flowed into the allied intelligence banks. Prisoners taken following the 32nd's operations against the Duc Co Special Forces camp in August yielded specific information about unit identities, infiltration data, and battle plans.

And so it went, through the two months in the battle covered in this book. More than 150 prisoners were questioned and intelligence elicited. The 1st Cavalry Division units captured more than three duffle bags of documents during the battle, all of which added to the total picture of the enemy force.

Additionally, during a campaign by the 196th Light Infantry Brigade north of Saigon in 1966, what appeared to be the headquarters of Vietcong Military Region II was overrun. Among the hundreds of pounds of documents taken from the site was an after-action report of the battles in the Ia Drang Valley, accompanied by a map of the actions (which is reproduced in appendix III).

For some units we have a fairly complete dossier; for others, whose documents evaded capture, we have some blanks. Nevertheless, our picture of the NVA division that fought and bled in the central highlands in the autumn of 1965 is complete enough to make a credible story. In no case have accounts been fictionalized to improve the story line. What you will read is what happened, and it is portrayed with as much historical accuracy as is humanly possible.

ACKNOWLEDGMENTS

The acknowledgments for this book properly begin with with Major General Harry Kinnard, Colonel George Beatty, and Major Charles Siler, who, twenty-two years ago, thought enough of the researching and writing talents of an infantry captain to entrust to him the history of the just-completed Pleiku Campaign. Out of a three-month effort came a combat operations after-action report unlike any produced before or after in Vietnam and a recommendation for a Presidential Unit Citation, which is reproduced in appendix IV. Copies of those documents, plus dozens of transcriptions of interviews, maps, pictures, and other pieces of information, lay in a foot locker for nearly twenty years, until the idea of doing this book took shape.

To those three officers who gave me this opportunity goes my profound gratitude. A special thanks also to Lieutenant General Richard Knowles for his patience with me in those initial interviews twenty-two years ago and, more recently, in hours of consultation on the aspects of the campaign that didn't appear in the after-action report. Thanks are due also for help during that period with the advisory people at II Corps Headquarters in Pleiku. My particular gratitude goes to Major William P. Boyle, the assistant intelligence advisor for II Corps, who shared with me a draft of a monograph entitled "Lure and Ambush" which aided materially in the writing of my after-action report.

The Office of the Chief of Military History, Department of Army, provided enormous help by making available the transcripts of interviews done by Captain John Cash for his monograph on LZ (Landing Zone) XRAY. My thanks also to the Department of Army's Research Assistance Branch and to the Military Field Branch of the National Archives.

Many of the pictures in this volume were taken by Associated Press photographers. I am especially grateful to Horst Faas, who gave me a bundle of his wire photos those many years ago to illustrate the Presidential Citation recommendation. And thanks must now go to James M. Donna, director of Wide World Photos, for having granted permission to use those pictures in this volume.

Adding immeasurably to the narrative flow of this book are the recollections of the many who took part in the campaign, especially those who took the time to dig through their memory banks for names, dates, and places that often helped unlock a seemingly insolvable riddle.

A very special note of gratitude goes to General E. C. Meyer for years of friendship and for taking the time from an extremely busy schedule to pen the foreword to this book. An acknowledgment of contribution must certainly go to Ethan Ellenberg, my agent, whose early suggestions on pacing and content helped convince St. Martin's Press of the importance of this campaign. Thanks also to Jared Kieling of St. Martin's and his associate, Jesse Cohen, for the editing skills that honed and polished the manuscript.

And, finally, I would be remiss if I did not acknowledge the contributions of my wife Madeline. It was her drive and determination that got the material dug out of the foot locker to begin with, directed a pair of hands toward the keyboard, and then acted as editor and critic as the manuscript took shape.

—J. D. Coleman
Atlanta, Georgia

CHOPPERS

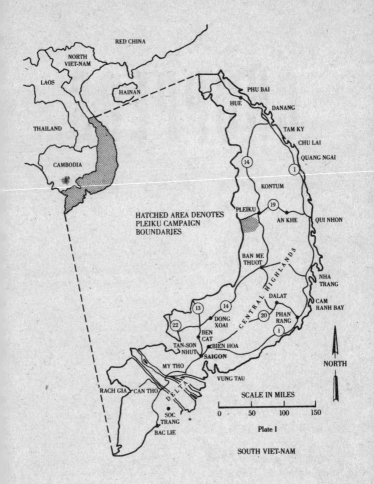

RED CHINA

NORTH
VIET-NAM

LAOS

HAINAN

THAILAND

CAMBODIA

PHU BAI

HUE

DANANG

TAM KY

CHU LAI

QUANG NGAI

(14)

(1)

KONTUM

HATCHED AREA DENOTES
PLEIKU CAMPAIGN
BOUNDARIES

PLEIKU

(19)

AN KHE

QUI NHON

BAN ME
THUOT

C E N T R A L   H I G H L A N D S

NHA
TRANG

DALAT

CAM
RANH BAY

(13)

(14)

(20)

PHAN
RANG

(22)

DONG
XOAI

(1)

BEN
CAT

TAN-SON-
NHUT

BIEN HOA

SAIGON

NORTH

MY THO

D E L T A

VUNG TAU

RACH GIA

CAN THO

SCALE IN MILES

0   50   100   150

SOC
TRANG

Plate I

BAC LIE

SOUTH VIET-NAM

PROLOGUE

In the fall of 1965 in the plateau country west and south of Pleiku City in the Republic of Vietnam, there occurred a series of battles, firefights, skirmishes, and engagements which became known as the "Pleiku Campaign" or, sometimes, the "battles in the Ia Drang." What separated this series of battles from those before and after was that it was the first time in history that a North Vietnamese regular army division and an American Army division met on the battlefield. That the American division was the newly organized and still untested airmobile division made the campaign precursory. Its impact on the Vietnam War and beyond was substantial.

The accepted dates for the Pleiku Campaign are October 19 to November 25, 1965. But the crucial political and military decisions that led to this historic confrontation actually occurred months, even years, before.

That there were any North Vietnamese regular units in the south at all stemmed from a momentous decision made in August 1964 in Hanoi by the Lao Don politburo. The best analysis of that decision, which historians now believe was *the* key North Vietnamese decision of the entire conflict, is by Dave Richard Palmer, in his book *Summons of the Trumpet*.

Palmer argues persuasively that Ho Chi Minh and his lieutenants had become aware by late summer 1964 that they were losing the insurgency in the south—that the pendulum had begun to swing toward the other side. The Vietcong were losing their effectiveness; the Saigon regime had stabilized after a series of coups and counter-coups and its armed forces were improving; outside nations, particularly the United States, were rallying to the cause of South Vietnam; and, finally, the population of the south, numbed after a decade of revolutionary terror, had begun to move away from the cause of insurgency.

So Ho Chi Minh made a decision that ran counter to communist doctrine; he would retrieve his fading chances by sending regular army units southward, with the hope of a major victory—capturing a provincial capital, destroying a large South Vietnamese force, and/or slicing the country in half at its most vulnerable spot. That spot was the highlands, the axis of action running from Duc Co on the Cambodian border through Pleiku City, the provincial capital of Pleiku Province, through An Khe in the central part of the country, and terminating in Qui Nhon, a city on the South China Sea.

On the American side, the political decisions that led to U.S. involvement are well known. Less familiar are the key decisions leading to the employment of helicopters in battle in general, and to the creation and employment of the air-mobile division in particular. The ubiquitous role of the helicopter in Vietnam doubtless has led many to believe that airmobility was the product of the war, rather than the war being the crucible in which were tested concepts and theories that had evolved since World War II.

Airmobility had its roots in both the airborne and glider techniques of World War II and the concepts for the use of aviation in direct support of Army ground forces. After World War II, Army thinkers realized that parachutes and gliders were a terribly inefficient and costly means of getting troops and equipment into battle. They also recognized that the newly independent U.S. Air Force was more concerned with jets and rockets than with troop transport and organic fire support.

Lieutenant General John J. Tolson, in his 1973 monograph on airmobility, notes that the precursory decision for airmobility occurred in 1952, when the Army proposed forming twelve helicopter battalions. This decision was made even though a practical troop-carrying helicopter was still unproven and helicopter tactics and techniques existed only in the minds of a few visionaries.

The mid-fifties were the gestational years for embryonic tactics and techniques. Both the Army and helicopter industry observers closely scrutinized the French and British helicopter operations in Algeria and Malaysia. While chief of operations for the Army in 1954, General James M. Gavin, the legendary World War II paratroop commander, ordered a series of staff studies to design hypothetical cavalry organizations around the potential of the helicopter. General Tolson, then a colonel, was General Gavin's chief of doctrine and combat developments as well as the principal architect of airmobility doctrine during those formative years.

Development of troop-carrying helicopter doctrine coincided with early experiments in arming helicopters to provide suppressive fires during the critical approach phase of a combat assault. But as yet there was no official U.S. Army policy on the development of airmobility; too many Army agencies were pursuing separate programs in isolation of one another, too often with a tendency toward parochialism. The Army started to get its house in order in the late fifties, and in January of 1960 established the Army Aircraft Requirements Review Board, chaired by Lieutenant General Gordon B. Rogers. The Rogers Board, as it became known throughout the Army and the aircraft industry, sorted through some 119 design concepts submitted by 45 aircraft manufacturing companies and evaluated them in terms of both technical and operational feasibility.

The Rogers Board, when viewed in retrospect, had a limited charter. Later it was obscured by the Howze Board and the tests of the 11th Air Assault Division. But it did represent some significant milestones in the development of army aviation, particularly in the fields of development, procurement, and personnel planning.

During this period, the most significant technological advancement was the development of the gas turbine engine, to replace the reciprocal engines in use in all U.S. Army helicopters of that era. The aerial platform chosen for the turbine was the Bell XH-40 Utility Helicopter. It became the HU-1, then the UH-1B and UH-1D, and, to the millions of soldiers in Vietnam, the "Huey." Eventually it replaced the noisy, inefficient, and maintenance-demanding H-19, H-21, and H-34. The Boeing Vertol HC-1B Chinook, powered by twin gas turbines, was then on the drawing boards to replace the piston-powered Sikorsky H-37.

The country's "real" flying service, the U.S. Air Force, looked upon these developments with growing alarm. An October 1951 memorandum of understanding between the Army and Air Force declared that the Army could use organic aircraft for the purposes of expediency and improving ground combat and logistics procedures within the combat zone. When the Korean War began, the Army owned 668 light airplanes, mostly artillery spotters, and 57 light helicopters. By 1960 the Army had acquired more than 5,000 aircraft of many varieties and had become the acknowledged leader in the tactical and logistical use of the rotating airfoil.

Two exceptions to the 1951 agreement on weight limitations for Army fixed-wing aircraft were the OV-1 Mohawk and the Caribou. The Caribou was a logical follow-on to the earlier birds produced by the deHaviland Aircraft Corporation—the Beaver and the Otter. The Caribou, a twin-engine, short-takeoff and landing aircraft with a rear-end loading door, carried thirty-two passengers and was envisioned by the Army as the natural bridge between the Army's capabilities and the C-130s of the Air Force.

The Mohawk, another twin-engine bird, was originally thought of as a pure surveillance aircraft. But its design, initially a joint effort of the Army and the Marines, brought about an aircraft that had far greater potential than simple visual reconnaissance. Eventually it became capable of carrying sophisticated sensor systems, such as infrared cameras and side-looking airborne radar. It also had hard points upon which armament could be slung.

As General Tolson noted in his airmobility monograph, the development of the Mohawk and Caribou "threw down a gauntlet to Air Force strategists." These two aerial systems were the two major symbols of U.S. Army–Air Force disagreement over roles and missions, and "more time was devoted to these systems than to the entire airmobility concept itself."

The decade of the sixties arrived with the Army rapidly expanding its aircraft inventory, but without a clear sense of direction. Not only did the Army have its scraps with the Air Force, but internecine warfare within the Army hierarchy was hobbling the development of a comprehensive airmobile concept. The old, established branches of the Army—Infantry, Artillery, Armor (Cavalry)—all wanted to be proponents of the concept. The Transportation Corps viewed the helicopters as flying jeeps and trucks; the Medical Corps wanted absolute control of air evacuation aircraft, the training of the pilots, and so on.

Then, in 1961, the first Army aviation units, both fixed-wing and helicopter, arrived in Vietnam. Three H-21 helicopter companies and one Otter company were used in the advisory effort throughout each of the four tactical zones. In early 1962, the 45th Transportation Battalion, a command and control unit, deployed from Fort Sill, Oklahoma, followed by two more light-helicopter companies. The first UH-1 "Huey" unit in Vietnam was the 57th Medical Detachment, a medevac unit which arrived in early 1962. It was followed by the 23rd Special Warfare Aviation Detachment, a Mohawk outfit that carried the new battlefield surveillance sensors.

Even as these units began receiving their baptisms of fire, learning the lessons of combat and developing air mobility doctrine on a trial and error basis, momentous events were occurring in the Department of Defense. Secretary of Defense Robert NcNamara asked the Army to review its entire aviation procurement program, particularly the program dealing with the new Bell utility helicopter. He wanted a final report by mid-November 1961.

The report was submitted on time and with a predictably conservative and disjointed approach. McNamara's whiz kids ripped the report apart, and on April 19, 1962, he sent the now famous memorandum to the Secretary of the Army declaring that the Army had not fully explored the opportunities offered by technology to break its traditional ties to surface mobility. The analysts at the Office of the Secretary of Defense (OSD) believed that air vehicles operating close to the ground offered a quantum increase in effectiveness and moreover, air transportation was probably less costly than rail or ship transport, even in peacetime.

The secretary urged the Army to reexamine its aviation requirements with a "bold new look" at land warfare mobility. This reexamination, his memo said, could come only through testing; more studies of the same subject would not suffice. Moreover, McNamara directed that the testing and reporting be divorced from traditional viewpoints and policies and free from veto or dilution by conservative staff review. And then, in a stunning departure from usual OSD protocol, he suggested a number of officers and key civilians, headed by Lieutenant General Hamilton H. Howze, to manage the Army's efforts.

Secretary McNamara summed up the emphasis he placed on the Army reexamination of tactical mobility: "I shall be disappointed if the Army's reexamination merely produces logistically oriented recommendations to procure more of the same, rather than a plan of fresh and perhaps unorthodox concepts which will give us a significant increase in mobility."

Tolson's comments on McNamara's charge to the Army hints at the myriad crosscurrents within the Army establishment:

> This benchmark in airmobility history resulted from the fortunate confluence of several trends: first, the personal dissatisfaction of the Secretary of Defense with the Army's failure to exploit the potential capabilities of airmobility; secondly, an undeniable attitude of many Office of the Secretary of Defense civilian analysts who looked upon the service staffs and most officers as reluctantly being dragged into the twentieth century; third, there was a nucleus of Army aviation-oriented officers both in the office of the Secretary of Defense and Army Staff who recognized the possibility of capitalizing on Mr. McNamara's attitude to sweep aside ultraconservative resistance within the Army itself. Finally, there was an opportunity to present to the Secretary of Defense for his signature directives that would cause the Army to appoint an evaluation by individuals known for their farsightedness and to submit recommendations directly to the Secretary of Defense in order to avoid intermediate filtering.

The Army immediately appointed a board of officers and senior civilians, headed, obviously, by Lt. Gen. Hamilton Howze, then the commander of the XVIII Airborne Corps at Fort Bragg, North Carolina. The official name for the ad hoc board was the U.S. Army Tactical Mobility Requirements Board, but to the Army in general and to history, it simply was known as the "Howze Board."

The basic board membership was thirteen general officers and five civilians. But eventually, more than 3,200 military personnel and nearly a hundred civilians participated in the tests, war games, exercises, and operational research—all aimed at the investigation, testing, and evaluation of the organizational and operational concepts of airmobility.

The final report of the Howze Board, submitted August 20, 1962, had three major recommendations: first, the creation and testing of three baseline airmobile organizations—an air assault division, an air transport brigade, and an air cavalry brigade. The second recommendation involved a series of programs that would modernize the Army force structure by replacing conventional forces with airmobile forces. Third, the board suggested a requirement for an increased acquisition and training of aviators, including warrant officer pilots.

Of the three organizations recommended, the air assault division was the principal tactical innovation. It would have 459 aircraft, as compared to less than one hundred in a standard infantry division. The trade-off would come from making do with fewer ground vehicles—1,100 as compared to 3,452. Fire support was provided by three 105-mm towed howitzers and a battalion of Little John rockets, which was capable of firing both conventional and nuclear-tipped rounds. This was fairly conventional, given that all guns and rockets would be transported by helicopters.

What marked this division as truly innovative and raised the hackles of the Air Force was the fire support augmentation—twenty-four Mohawks armed with machine guns and rockets and thirty-six B-model Huey helicopters armed with forty-eight 2.75-inch rockets, called aerial rocket artillery.

Two battalions of D-model Hueys provided lift for the infantry elements. The medium lift battalion, for which the Chinooks were earmarked, would assist in tactical lift and logistical lift within the division's area of operations.

The planners had developed on paper a unit that had all the essential elements of combat power—maneuver forces, reconnaissance, firepower, communications, and service support. Because the concept of an air assault division had been given only a cursory testing by the Howze Board, the final report recommended a continuing program of field tests, using the first units to become operational under the activation schedule.

The Howze Board completed its mission in ninety days, from the original assignment to the finished report. As Tolson recalls, "In view of the enormous staffing task involved, and the sheer size of the analytical task, such alacrity has few parallels in staff work, in or out of the military service."

In mid-September of 1962, Howze and another member of the board worked out of the office of the Chief of Staff of the Army, preparing rebuttals for the various attacks that were coming from all directions.

Throughout the fall of 1962, Tolson recalls, it appeared at times that the work of the Howze Board was going to be studied to death and finally filed away for historians. "The fact that it survived attacks by members of Congress, the Air Force, and conservative elements within the Army was a tribute both to the soundness of its basic conclusions and to the dedicated officers within the Army who believed that airmobility was the wave of the future," Tolson wrote.

On January 8, 1963, the Chief of Staff of the Army, General Earl K. Wheeler, summoned a brigadier general from his post as assistant division commander of the 101st Airborne Division. He briefly outlined the recommendations of the Howze Board and then said: "Harry, I want you to determine how far and how fast the Army can go and should go in embracing the airmobile concept."

Brigadier General Harry William Osborne Kinnard recalled his response to General Wheeler's mission order: "Yes, Sir." The experimental air assault division had its first commander.

The Army had chosen well, although few could have predicted on that January day that Brigadier General Harry Kinnard would go on to fashion an operational reality from a vision and a dream and then command it in combat. Not even in the heyday of the birth and development of the airborne divisions in World War II did one individual accomplish a similar feat. The men who dreamed the dreams of airborne tactics did not get to prove them in combat as division commanders.

Kinnard's ultimate success with the air assault/airmobile

concept resulted in a number of senior officers claiming that they had recommended him for the job. Kinnard suspected that an airmobile demonstration he put on for General Wheeler in early October 1962, when the 101st was preparing to invade Cuba, was what prompted Wheeler to think of him.

Kinnard had never served on the Howze Board; in fact, he was attending senior officer flight school when the board was in session. And obviously he was not a part of the old-line Army aviation clique.

But he was a warrior, a thinker, and an innovator. Although a smallish man, standing less than six feet, Kinnard was a strong commander, exerting leadership through a steely will cloaked by a soft-spoken demeanor and a genuine concern for his people. He was fiercely loyal to his subordinates—perhaps even to a fault, some have said—but in return, he commanded unquestioned loyalty.

Kinnard was a 1939 graduate of West Point, commissioned as a second lieutenant of infantry. After a stint in the Hawaiian Islands with the 27th Infantry, he reported to Fort Benning, Georgia, to attend the parachute school. After earning his wings in November 1942, he became the S-3 (operations officer) of the 501st Parachute Infantry Regiment. When the regiment was deployed to England, he became the regimental executive officer.

The 501st was assigned to the 101st Airborne Division and was part of the airborne assault on Normandy. Kinnard parachuted into Normandy on the night of June 5–6, taking command of the 1st Battalion, 501st, on June 12. His next operation was the airborne invasion of Holland on September 17, when he jumped in still as commander of the 1st Battalion, 501st.

In his four-plus months of combat command, Kinnard won a Distinguished Service Cross, the second-highest medal for valor, as well as a Silver Star. On September 30, General Maxwell Taylor chose him to become the division G-3 (operations officer). He became a full colonel at the age of twenty-nine, one of the youngest in the Army. In the Battle of the Bulge, as G-3 of the 101st at Bastogne, he coined the "hole in the doughnut" phrase and suggested to Brigadier General McAuliffe that the general's initial response to the German surrender ultimatum, "Nuts," was an appropriate formal reply.

After the war, temporarily reduced back to the grade of lieutenant colonel, Kinnard headed the Airborne Test Section of the Army Field Forces Board at Fort Bragg. In 1950 he was selected to attend the Air Command and Staff College. There, with a sort of prescience, he wrote a paper on the tactical uses of helicopters.

After graduation from the school, Kinnard went to England as the airborne member of a group of American officers working with the British on the standardization of military equipment. For three years, from 1952 to 1955, he was an instructor in airborne operations at the Armed Forces Staff College. During this period he got his eagles back.

His next assignment was the Army War College at Carlisle Barracks, and after that a coveted assignment as commander of the 1st Battle Group, 501st Infantry, the modern counterpart of his wartime regiment. He also had the unique experience, as an infantryman, of commanding the 101st Division Artillery for almost a year.

He was selected for another school, the national War College at Fort Lesley McNair, in Washington, D.C., from which he graduated in June 1959. He was assigned to the Office of the Deputy Director of Defense, Research and Engineering (DDRE) in the Office of the Secretary of Defense, where he served for nearly two years. His next assignment was as executive to the Secretary of the Army, until July 1962, when he was promoted to Brigadier General and assigned as assistant division commander of the 101st Airborne Division at Fort Campbell, Kentucky.

So, from 1942 until 1963, a period of more than twenty-one years, every nonschool assignment that came the way of this doughty little Texan had involved the jumping out of airplanes. The spirit of the airborne, with its élan, its can-do philosophy, its flexibility, and, above all, its "lightweight" state of mind were to figure significantly in command decisions made by Kinnard in the air assault division.

It didn't hurt that the Army decided that the division to be activated as the test unit would be the 11th Airborne Division, which had fought in the Pacific theater in World War II and spun off the 187th Airborne Regimental Combat Team for combat in Korea. By the simple expedient of placing an "Air Assault" tab over the basic patch, which featured a winged numeral eleven in red and white on a blue background, the Army was able to capture all of the spirit of an old-line airborne division to go with the experimentation of the soon-to-be-tested airmobile concept.

1

BUILDING THE DIVISION

Hurricane Isabelle, out in the Atlantic, was influencing the weather in the Carolina operational area. Low-flying scud and rain blanketed the landscape and the humidity and wind made the mid-fifties temperatures seem even colder. The damp chill was more than enough to bring fires to light in tent stoves. Plumes of smoke from hundreds of newly erected general purpose, command post, and mess tents drifted in the mist.

The 11th Air Assault Division (Test), augmented by elements of the 2nd Infantry Division, had completed the administrative phase of its movement from Fort Benning as well as a series of tune-up division maneuvers. The division now lay bivouacked in woods, next to open fields, in an area north of Columbia and south of Rock Hill, South Carolina, generally along the west bank of the Catawba River.

At 11:00 P.M., most of the troops were in their tents, but the commanders and staff officers were burning the midnight oil. The following day, October 14, 1964, the 11th Air Assault Division was to go to war: AIR ASSAULT II—a play war, to be sure, but deadly serious in its intent.

Some 11,000 miles to the west, at a different latitude, rain showers from the northwest monsoon soaked the jungle trail.

Colonel To Dinh Khan, commander of the 32nd Regiment of the North Vietnamese 325th Division, stood with his staff as elements of his regiment's 635th Battalion slipped into the wetness of the jungle and headed into Laos, following the lead of the 334th Battalion, which had started south two weeks earlier. Shortly, Colonel Khan's headquarters would follow and, later in the month, the last battalion, the 966th, would start south. The destination of the 32nd Regiment was Kontum Province in the central highlands of South Vietnam. The 32nd also was going to war, a very real war.

AIR ASSAULT II was the final test of the experimental airmobile division. Three of the Army's biggest commands put together an organization called "Project TEAM" to direct the testing and evaluation of the division and its supporting 10th Air Transport Brigade. Not only was the exercise the major test for airmobility, it also was the largest post–World War II maneuver ever held in the United States. A maneuver area of more than six thousand square miles had been staked out, from Columbia, South Carolina, in the south to well past Fayetteville, North Carolina, encompassing the drainages of the Catawba, Lynches, and Peedee rivers. Project TEAM had drawn up scenarios that would confront the division with every known spectrum of warfare, from counterinsurgency through mid-intensity to nuclear conflict. For the next thirty days, the theory of airmobility would receive its acid test, with elements of the division almost always in contact with some part of the aggressor forces, played by the 82nd Airborne Division and reinforced by the tank and mechanized infantry battalions of the 2nd Infantry Division.

The theories that led to the formation of the air assault division had many champions; but they also had their share of debunkers, not only from the Air Force, but also from within the Army. And for them, at last, AIR ASSAULT II was a chance to smash the concept and put an end to the nonsense that soldiers ought to fly their own aircraft into combat. Particularly the armored and mechanized infantry types were licking their chops at the opportunity to put this upstart in its place. So when, on the morning of October 14, in absolutely miserable weather, elements of the 11th's 1st Brigade climbed aboard the UH-1D lift choppers and flew across the Catawba River into the maneuver area, and then, at breathtaking treetop altitudes, roared south to mock battlefields at Kershaw and Camden, South Carolina, it was more than just another helicopter ride for the sky troopers of the 11th.

The first phase of the testing called for finding, fixing, and destroying guerrilla elements. The glass-bubbled scout birds buzzed around like angry dragonflies, and the guerrillas soon revealed their positions. Just as quickly, they were surrounded, as dozens of lift birds arrived with startling suddenness to disgorge sky troopers at all points of the compass. The umpires and evaluators were impressed. They recalled the previous exercises in these Carolina maneuver grounds— SWIFT STRIKE II and III—where the many farms with fences required troops to either travel by circuitous road nets or dismount and laboriously move on foot to their objectives. With the airmobile division, fences, roads, and streams were simply no obstacle. The guerrillas never had a chance. Round one went to the 11th.

The next phase, defending against a conventional attack, pitted the two brigades of the 11th against two brigades of the 82nd and a composite armored brigade from the 2nd Division. Now, at last, the detractors thought, the air assault division would get its comeuppance. It was one thing to whip up on some raggedy-ass guerrillas, but quite another to tangle with what many considered the finest foot soldiers in the U.S. Army—the paratroopers of the 82nd Airborne. But the airmobile division in the defense in a mid-intensity environment went about its work far differently than would standard infantry outfits. The attacking aggressor forces never got a solid target; light defensive works to their front would melt away, sucking in and stretching out their formations, only to have them struck violently from the flanks by heliborne infantrymen. Tanks and armored personnel carriers didn't fare any better, as highly mobile troops pinned down the armor with standard infantry anti-armor weapons and then had rocket-launching helicopters and twin-engine Mohawks swoop in for the finishing strokes. The sky troopers blew bridges across the unfordable rivers, then finished off trapped columns piecemeal.

In the offense, the 11th vaulted across the river barriers to strike in the rear areas of the aggressor forces. There were deep penetration raids, carried out with helicopters roaring at nearly 100 knots in what the airmobile warriors called "nap of the earth" flying. In the deep forest, the quarry could hear noise but never could pinpoint the precise direction of attack until it was too late. Over and over the 11th slashed and hit and fell back, moving in battalion leaps of forty and fifty miles to hit and hit again. Never before in the history of warfare had a maneuver force been able to marshal forces so quickly and so repeatedly at points of decision.

Nor was the activity entirely tactical. Soldiers have to be fed and resupplied with ammunition; their mobility merely compounds the problem. Helicopters have strict maintenance schedules and an insatiable thirst for JP-4 fuel, and aviators have to eat, too. The scenario required the testing of the 10th Air Transport Brigade. With Fort Benning established as the main logistical base for the 11th, the logistical side of the house had its work cut out for it. The airmobile division had developed a theory of supply that called for the Air Force to "wholesale" logistical support to a log base using the large, fixed-wing transport. The twin-engine, short-takeoff and -landing Caribous would then begin the "retailing" portion of the logistical train, flying supplies to dirt strips in the operational area. There, the mobile forward support elements of the division's support command would break down the supplies into unit increments and load them out on Chinooks for movement to the battalions. At the battalions, the Huey would be converted into an airmobile truck to get the supplies forward to a rifle company. Logistics were as airmobile as tactics. The impact on controllers and evaluators was dizzying.

After thirty days of racehorse scrimmaging, the test ended, and while the official verdict would be a long time coming, there was no doubt in anyone's mind that the 11th Air Assault Division had made the same case for airmobility in a maneuver that the tank outfits in the 1940 Louisiana maneuvers had done for armored doctrine in the Army. The division was good—damn good—and the troops knew it. As one veteran noncommissioned officer remarked, "That dog can flat hunt."

It all started on February 15, 1963, when the 11th Air Assault Division was activated along with the 10th Air Transport Brigade, an organization utilizing both fixed- and rotary-wing transport aircraft. The 11th was headquartered in the old Harmony Church area of Fort Benning, while the 10th Air Transport Brigade moved into available space at Lawson Army Airfield.

The first man on the air assault division's morning report on February 15 was Brigadier General Harry W. O. Kinnard. The number two man was Colonel Elvy B. Roberts. Both had been in the 101st Airborne Division at Fort Campbell, Kinnard as assistant division commander and Roberts as a battle group commander, and they had served together with the 101st in combat.

It was only a month earlier that General Kinnard had been told by the Army Chief of Staff to go out and form an airmobile division. Kinnard recalls his feelings when he received General Wheeler's mission. The moment he walked out of the chief's office he started thinking about all the things he had to do, and on his way back to Fort Campbell came up with some sixty items he believed would be critical in the success or failure of the air assault concept.

When I got back to Fort Campbell I persuaded my good friend

and division commander, Charlie Rich, of the importance of what I was doing, and even talked him into letting me steal a lot of his good people when I went over to Fort Benning . . . people like Colonel Elvy Roberts, who was to become my Chief of Staff . . . and like Lieutenant Colonel Tom Nicholson, who was the signal officer of the 101st and turned out to be a wonderful signal officer in both the 11th and later in the 1st Cav.

Kinnard also got a lot of good noncommissioned officers from the 101st. But that wasn't the limit of the raiding that went on in the formative stages of the division. In the first place, the division did not become full-blown as the result of the Department of Army general order that activated it.

It was an evolutionary, modular development in which the unit started with a single battalion combat team, the main maneuver element being the 1st Battalion, 187th Infantry, commanded by Lieutenant Colonel John Hennessey, the man who had commanded the ad hoc battle group that had worked with the Howze Board at Fort Bragg. The battalion grew to a brigade combat team and eventually, with the loan of 2nd Infantry Division battalions, to a full division.

This growth came out of the hide of the rest of the Army. The very best officers, including rated aviators, noncommissioned officers, and even private soliders, slated for duty at some other station, suddenly found their orders changed and themselves diverted to Fort Benning and the 11th Air Assault Division. The aviation battalion of the 4th Division at Fort Lewis, Washington, provided enough aircraft and pilots to form A and B companies of Lieutenant Colonel John B. Stockton's 227th Assault Helicopter Battalion, the fledgling division's first lift unit. Stockton was destined to become one of the most controversial figures in the division, both at Fort Benning and in Vietnam.

In the case of the 3rd Missile Command at Fort Bragg, the unit found itself deactivated, with all personnel and equipment transferred to Fort Benning. Colonel Richard T. Knowles, the commander of the 3rd Missile Command, was destined to become the one-star task force battle commander of the Pleiku Campaign.

In January 1964, the 2nd Brigade of the 2nd Infantry Division, commanded by Colonel William R. "Ray" Lynch, garrisoned at the Kelley Hill cantonment area at Fort Benning, for all intents and purposes became a brigade of the 11th Air Assault Division. Troops of the brigade still wore the Indianhead shoulder patch of the 2nd Division, but they also wore on the right breast pocket of their fatigues the red, white, and blue patch of the 11th Air Assault Division.

Kinnard gave his subordinate leaders their head in formulating airmobile tactics and doctrine as well as developing mechanical things that would help the concept work. Tom Nicholson's signal battalion reduced its equipment and vehicle requirements so that there was no vehicle larger than a jeep in the whole battalion.

Colonel George Beatty's 1st Infantry Brigade was charged with the mission of coming up with what ultimately became a lightweight ladder for disembarking troops from a hovering CH-47 tandem-rotor Chinook. The designer of the "hook ladder" was Lieutenant Colonel Harlow Clark, the deputy commander of the brigade. The engineer battalion, commanded by Lieutenant Colonel Robert J. Malley, worked on sectionalizing engineer equipment so that the largest single piece could be lifted by a Chinook.

And Kinnard formed the division "Idea Center," where any man, enlisted or officer, could come in with an idea and where that idea would receive a full evaluation. If necessary, he was given help in making drawings or otherwise putting his idea onto paper. Nothing like it had ever happened before in the Army, and the Idea Center gave birth to a number of techniques that made the air assault division unique. Some of these innovations were highly technical, such as a radio-wire integration kit which permitted commanders in the air to talk directly by tactical radio to ground telephones. The first kit was assembled in a .50-caliber ammunition box.

Other ideas that were implemented included the use of plastic water jugs in lieu of metal cans and a rubber attachment to the fuel nozzle that prevented JP-4 from sloshing back out of the fill pipe on the helicopter. The prototype was made from a plumber's helper.

A man and a good idea are one thing, but the assets to put that idea to work are another. And a special fund for the 11th was something else that made it unique in the Army. Kinnard said the money was made available by some of the people he knew well who still held key jobs on the civilian side of the Army—notably, the Assistant Secretary for Installations and Logistics and the Assistant Secretary of Research and Development. During the early days of the division, they came down to Fort Benning and asked Kinnard what they could do to help. His reply was: "Well, if you can get me a slush fund, by whatever name you want to call it, of a million or two bucks, so I can play around with different ideas, it would be the greatest thing you could do." They bought the idea and came up with a fund of about $1.2 million, with which Kinnard's procurement folks could go out and buy items off the shelf.

The 11th went directly to civilian suppliers and made purchases of lightweight equipment—plastic water jugs, lightweight tents, blivits (rubber fuel drums), rough-terrain vehicles which became known as "Mules," lightweight fuel pumps, small radio packs, and even the ladder for the Chinook.

It also helped create a state of mind among the men of the division—sky soldiers, they were called—as they came to believe in the airmobile concept. One of the crucial aspects of the airmobile concept was that it had to do more than merely provide infantry troops with helicopters for rides to and from a combat area. Throughout 1963 and into 1964, the division trained its ground elements in conjunction with its air elements to create a well-honed combat team.

The training took place in the vastness of the back reservation of Fort Benning, to which had been added some specially leased land on the southern and eastern boundaries. The additional land was necessary; what was adequate for mechanized and motorized infantry training was inadequate for airmobile tactics. The division also used the sprawling reservation at Fort Stewart, Georgia, located near Savannah.

Ground elements began thinking in terms of air vehicles; commanders and staffs substituted space and distance measurements with time intervals. Aviators became familiar with problems faced daily by ground troops. New concepts in supply and evacuation were developed; techniques in communications and the control of widely dispersed units were perfected. Thousands and thousands of actions were designed to forge the unit into a finely tuned mesh of men and machines.

In the air assault division, every member of a rifle squad knew the position he would take upon loading onto a UH-1 helicopter. There was no milling about, no wasting of precious seconds in the pickup zone. Upon landing, every man knew the correct way to exit the aircraft to provide maximum dispersion on the landing zone. Every man in the division learned how to quickly rig sling loads and how to lash down cargo in the CH-47 Chinook helicopters or the twin-engine, fixed-wing Caribou.

And, in order to qualify for the coveted Air Assault Badge, each man had to successfully rappel from a helicopter— thrice from 60 feet and twice from 120 feet. Many a veteran paratrooper allowed that it was a whole lot scarier hanging from a rope from a hovering helicopter than it ever was just jumping out of an airplane.

There were a lot of paratroopers in the 11th Air Assault Division. A significant slice of the 1st Brigade had been designated officially as airborne; ultimately, the entire 1st Brigade would be airborne. But, additionally, General Kinnard had a thing about paratroopers: "I made it a strong point to bring in airborne types, and I also did my best to get all the combat arms of the division to be parachutists," he says. This philosophy manifested itself in a division policy: all battalion commanders or special unit commanders had to be parachutists or aviators. This created a problem when the battalions of the 2nd Division joined the 11th. In one instance, the commander of the 2nd Battalion, 38th Infantry, Lieutenant Colonel A. J. Millard, a very competent, but nonairborne, commander, was removed and replaced by Lieutenant Colonel Robert Tully, who had made two combat jumps in Korea. The arbitrary removal caused some resentment within the battalion, but ultimately, Tully's leadership and charisma restored the unit's morale.

Kinnard's justification for his rule was that parachutists have a certain mentality that he thought could adapt admirably to the kind of thing he believed the division ought to be doing with helicopters. "Airmobility is a state of mind," he said, "and I found that, by and large, parachutists are more able to adapt to that state of mind than other people."

Kinnard spent a great deal of time talking to men of the 11th about this "state of mind." He preached the importance of downsizing, of squeezing the excess weight out of the division. He told his troopers that the air assault division was the Army's next logical step. There was a time when the Army carried cavalry horses up to the front in trucks so as not to tire them. Then it stopped carrying the horses and simply used the trucks. "Now, in this stage," he told the sky troopers, "we are leaving behind the jeeps and trucks and seeing how far we can go by aircraft."

Troops began learning a new language; every soldier was issued an air assault handbook and a brevity codebook called *Quick Fox*. The squad-carrying Hueys became "Alloys"; the tandem-rotor Chinooks were known as "Acrobats." Aviation formations such as "heavy right" and "heavy left" became as well known to the infantry soldier as the care and cleaning of his M-14.

The lift battalions identified their birds with colored markings—a triangle for Company A, a square for Company B, and a circle for Company C. The colors of the circles denoted the unit—blue for the 229th and green for the 227th, both assault helicopter battalions that provided the troop-lift choppers, and yellow for the cavalry squadron, which also had some lift helicopters. Within the Huey companies, each platoon was given a color—yellow, white, orange, red—and each of the four aircraft within the platoon was given a number. A plate corresponding to the platoon designation was affixed to the aircraft, usually on the pilot's door.

All of this made it easy for a ground commander to get his troops lined up for a pickup. It would work like this: The incoming lift commander, with the call sign "Snake Yellow One," would radio the ground commander the number of ships in his lift and the formation, such as heavy left. So the ground commander would know that Yellow One was in the lead, with Yellow Two on his right and Yellow Three and Four echeloned to the left and rear. The trailing platoons, White, Orange, and Red, each with four birds, would be in the same formation. Ground leaders then would designate specific lift ships for each element of the ground force and deploy these elements around the PZ (pick-up zone) to be in position to move directly to their assigned aircraft as soon as the skids touched down. There would be no flailing about; no lost soul running wildly around the pickup zone looking for a ride. On a 16-ship PZ a rifle company could be picked up and the entire formation not be at risk on the ground for more than a minute. Going into a landing zone, the lift ships would barely get heavy on their skids before the troops had charged off the birds into prearranged assault patterns. It was a rare occurrence for an air assault in the 11th to have lift ships on the ground for more than thirty seconds and the bulk of that time was taken for the last man out on each side of the aircraft to slide the door shut. This was, after all, still a training environment; the doorless status of the choppers in Vietnam was still to come.

Many pieces of military hardware that were destined to become standard items of issue in the Army were tested along with the airmobile concept to determine compatibility. After having determined that the match was optimum, there was the problem of convincing the Army's "elders."

Colonel Dick Knowles, an artilleryman and veteran of World War II and Korea, was the first division artillery (divarty) commander of the 11th. After the breakup of the 3rd Missile Command, Kinnard asked Knowles to take over the 11th's artillery. As the Army had chosen well with Kinnard, Kinnard's choice of Knowles was equally fortuitous. A tall, lanky Midwesterner, Knowles was a superb commander. But, more important, he immediately understood the nuances of the airmobile concept. He was, of course, a parachutist, but soon qualified as an Army aviator. He also was cunning and resourceful with a great sense of humor—attributes made necessary by the "us against the Army" posture in which the 11th so often found itself.

Knowles recalls the battle to get the experimental M-102, a lightweight, 105-mm howitzer, adopted as the Army standard. The Army had the standard howitzer and the self-propelled howitzer, but no gun with a decent range that was light enough to be lifted by a Huey. The research and development people came up with a howitzer—the M-102—that seemed to fill the bill, but everybody was against it. The brass at Fort Sill, the home of the artillery, were opposed to it, as was the commandant of the Army's Command and General Staff College, also an artilleryman. And, when a four-star general, Dwight Beach, of the Army's Materiel Command, weighed in against the gun, it appeared doomed. Finally, to settle the issue for good, the army's chief of staff, General Wheeler, sent Barksdale Hamlett, his four-star vice-chief, down to Fort Benning to hear the arguments of the 11th.

Knowles recalls the day:

We put on a dog and pony show. The demonstration went

well, but I had a feeling that it wasn't entirely conclusive. The Chinook used as a prime mover could carry the standard howitzer as easily as it could the M-102. So while everybody went off to lunch, I called Colonel Senneff (commanding the Aviation Group) and said, "Hey, I'm losing this battle and I need some of your famous support. Can you get a new bird with a 48-foot rotor?" He said he could. Then I called my exec. and told him to get one of the M-102s down to the airfield.

So when General Hamlett goes out to the airfield to get on his T-39 and go back to the Pentagon, I told him there was one other reason why we needed this howitzer . . . to give us the capability of employing our "skinny battery" concept. When we got to the plane, one of Senneff's Hueys was flying by with the howitzer slung beneath. The timing was perfect. I told Hamlett, "General, there's no other howitzer in the world that can do this. We need it." He responded simply, "Dick, you've got it." And that's how the Army got the M-102. It was that close.

There is more to the story, according to Knowles and Senneff. It seems that when the Huey first tried to sling up the M-102, it wouldn't budge. There was just too much weight for the density altitude, which is aviator talk for a condition of heat and humidity that cuts a helicopter's lift capability. So Senneff and his people began stripping the gun of everything but its working parts and the bird of everything and everybody but the pilot. It worked, but the clinching flyby was made on a wing and a prayer.

It was that kind of outfit, made up of people who seemingly could work miracles. It also was made up of some genuine characters—in professional sports they would be known as "flakes." One of them was John B. Stockton. He had moved over from the 227th Assault Helicopter Battalion to command the 3rd Squadron, 17th Cavalry. This air cavalry unit was true cavalry—totally airmobile, with every man having a seat in some organic aircraft. By its very nature, the unit bred a swashbuckler attitude. This natural propensity was aided and abetted by its commander. Stockton, balding, rawhide-lean, and just under six feet tall, had the handlebar mustache of the old time cavalryman. When viewed without his headgear, he looked a lot like a Yul Brynner with facial hair. Years later those who knew him during his days with the 11th and 1st Cavalry swore that he must have been the model for the air cavalry commander depicted in the movie *Apocalypse Now*.

He sent a man to a supply depot in Philadelphia to get black cavalry hats for everyone in the squadron. That the hats were unauthorized headgear didn't faze "Bullwhip-6," as Stockton called himself. He made wearing the black hat mandatory for special occasions, including squadron retreat formations. He also ordered all of his men to wear cavalry-style mustaches—in an era when a clean-shaven face was definitely the mode—and had all of his officers, regardless of basic branch, wear the crossed sabers of the cavalry.

Dick Knowles, by that time the assistant division commander and Stockton's immediate superior, has some vivid memories of John Stockton and those days at Fort Benning:

> He used to run those retreat ceremonies out there, all decked out in the black hats, which was against all regulations and customs of the service. The Chief of Staff of the Army saw some sort of news story with all those characters in their black hats and sent a sharp note down to Harry Kinnard about it. So Harry called me and told me to take care of it. The reason was that Stockton was my guy and Kinnard believed in the use of the chain of command.

Knowles called in Stockton and told him, "Stockton, take off those cotton-picking black hats." Stockton was sharp, though, and he loved the challenge. He came right back with, "How about special occasions?" Knowles conceded the point, considering the morale of the men, because Stockton's unit really did have a superior esprit de corps. He said special occasions would be okay, but that special permission would be necessary.

Knowles recalled that later, Stockton and part of his squadron were sent up to Fort Knox, Kentucky, for some special training. When he got back, he went to see Knowles, telling him, "Boss, I got some bad news," and proceeded to inform Knowles that while he was at Fort Knox, some event came up that he believed qualified as a special occasion. Because he couldn't immediately contact the general, Stockton made the decision on his own. Unfortunately, someone took pictures, one of which was printed in the *Army Times*. Said Knowles, "Well, I could just see Harold K. Johnson when he saw that picture. I told Kinnard and we braced ourselves for a blast . . . but I guess he never saw it, or didn't care any more, because it passed without notice."

This was typical Stockton behavior—to bend a rule to the breaking point—and it would be a thorn in Knowles's side until Stockton left the division after the Pleiku Campaign.

In early 1964, the Grover E. Bell Award, given annually for research and experimentation in the field of helicopter development, was awarded to the 11th Air Assault Division. At the honors banquet of the American Institute of Aeronautics and Astronautics, the 11th was cited for its pioneering work in the application of the rapid mobility and firepower provided by the helicopter to extend the Army's ground combat capabilities.

And the testing went on. On the heels of the earlier EAGLE STRIKE, EAGLE CLAW, and AIR ASSAULT I came HAWK ASSAULT I, HAWK ASSAULT II, HAWK STAR I, and then HAWK FLASH, most of them on the sprawling military reservation at Fort Stewart. The tests were administered by the Test, Evaluation and Control (TEC) Group of the Army's Combat Developments Command. TEC Group was commanded by Brigadier General Robert Williams, a veteran aviator with whom Kinnard had had a sort of running battle during the testing process.

Kinnard said he felt that Williams was more concerned

with hard data on the division's performance than on the things Kinnard believed were vital.

> I felt . . . that the things that can be measured and put into numbers are not the critical things that will decide whether a unit is really a good operational unit or not; that the really important things were much more apt to be determined by intuitive military judgment of people with a lot of balance and background. And in that regard, therefore, I felt that probably the feelings of people who came to visit us meant more in the long run than how many Caribous could land per "square hour."

And the visitors were plentiful; it became virtually a who's who of the Departments of Defense, Army, and Air Force. Oh yes, the blue suiters came to see what kind of threat this division posed to the Air Force and its sovereignty over the air. Kinnard recalled that handling visitors was really one of the hardest parts of his job, because of the tremendous volume. Actually it was one of the sixty items he had made note of just after receiving his first mission order from General Wheeler. He asked for and got help from the Fort Benning commander and from the TEC Group. He also made sure that the division was staffed with competent public information and protocol people.

But most of all, he impressed upon all members of the division that, like it or not, the visitors were going to be there and, like it or not, their opinions of the division were apt to bear very, very heavily on the final decision of the worth of the airmobile concept—particularly visitors like Generals Creighton Abrams, H. K. Johnson, Earle Wheeler, and Secretary of Defense McNamara. "So we did our best," he recalled, "not to look upon it as an onerous chore, but as an important part of what we were doing."

Nevertheless, the intense, unrelenting flow of visitors and strap hangers led Kinnard at the time to quip, "Never have so few been observed so often by so many," paraphrasing the famous quote by Churchill.

The attitude of most of the Air Force observers, from Chief of Staff Curtis LeMay on down, was generally hostile. But Knowles remembers one exceptional visit by LeMay, who had served in the horse artillery before entering the Army's flying service. After one particularly spectacular demonstration of tactical mobility, LeMay pulled his cigar from his mouth, turned to Knowles, and growled, "Dick, that beats the shit out of horses."

The summer of 1964 was spent preparing for the big division tests in the Carolina maneuver area. This was to be the payoff—the demonstration to hundreds of critical eyes that airmobility was here to stay. The 11th, even with the augmentation from the 2nd Division, still had only six maneuver battalions which operated for the most part under the 1st and 2nd Brigade headquarters. The 3rd Brigade, commanded by Colonel Thomas W. "Tim" Brown, working with a planning headquarters, was allocated two maneuver battalions for an operation late in the Carolina tests.

It was one of the paradoxes of this development of airmobility that the main thrust of the tests was within the parameters of a medium- or high-intensity combat environment, not in a counterinsurgency situation. The division's test tables of organization and equipment (TOE's) reflected this thrust. For example, at one time the division artillery boasted a Little John rocket battalion, which had a battlefield nuclear weapon delivery capability, in addition to three 105-mm howitzer battalions and an aerial rocket artillery (ARA) battalion, the airmobile answer to the 155-mm medium-artillery battalion in a conventional infantry division. The primary weapon in each of the three firing batteries was the B-model Huey, armed with twin forty-eight tube rocket pods firing 2.75-inch aerial rockets. The B-models were shorter, stubbier versions of the H-model, which was a main troop lift aircraft—sort of like comparing a two-door and a four-door sedan. Nevertheless, with ninety-six rockets aboard, each bird packed a formidable punch.

The organization of the lift units was influenced by the need to maintain the tactical integrity of infantry units. Thus, a lift platoon would be able to carry a rifle platoon and a lift company would be able to carry a rifle company. Of course this was before the Hueys sprouted door guns and pilot armor for protection in an insurgency environment. But even before these additions, there was a substantial defect in the division's TOE. The original TOE called for only two assault helicopter battalions, with one medium-lift helicopter battalion. In theory, based on the long-standing Army doctrine of two up and one back, two battalions of a brigade would be used in an assault. The reserve battalion could be hauled by the Chinooks of the medium-lift unit. In practice, it never quite worked out that way; the two assault lift battalions constantly were piecemealed back and forth between the brigades. There just never seemed to be enough lift, which placed heavy requirements on the Aviation Group headquarters as well as the division staff to insure that flying assets were parceled out correctly. This defect was never corrected, most likely because of the ultimate costs of adding a third lift unit, and the division learned to make do with what it had.

Throughout AIR ASSAULT II, regardless of the situation, the division's elements performed superbly. The sight of a battalion of fifty or so Hueys in tight formation, roaring over the Carolina countryside at treetop level, was breathtaking. It was also costly to the government. It seems that the poultry business, particularly the raising of turkeys, was a major part of the economy in the Carolinas. And turkeys are notoriously high strung; keeling over in a faint—or worse—if startled. Chickens also have been known to do strange things, like smother themselves. The low-flying helicopters of the 11th left in their wake thousands of dead turkeys and chickens and the undying enmity of the overworked claims officers.

As the tests progressed, everyone in the division, from

Kinnard to the lowest-ranking soldier, knew they were a success. Regardless of the tactical situation, the division proved conclusively that its elements could seek out an enemy over a very wide area, fix him, and then rapidly bring together the necessary firepower and troops to destroy him. In a low-intensity war, the division would be ideally suited for controlling large areas; in a medium- or high-intensity conflict, it would serve superbly as a screening force or mobile reserve that could deliver a decisive blow to an enemy by swiftly concentrating maximum force at a vulnerable spot.

After the test, the division returned to Fort Benning to await the official verdict. On November 15, 1964, Kinnard told his sky soldiers,

> Our reward is the knowledge that we have accomplished a very tough mission, ahead of the rugged original schedule, and in a manner which has won the admiration and thanks of the Army's top leaders. With airmobility, the soldier has been freed forever from the tyranny of terrain.

While awaiting word from the top that the Army would adopt an airmobile division into its permanent structure, the troops were kept busy training in the Fort Benning area. In early 1965, some aviation units and supporting elements of the division were deployed to the Dominican Republic. The task force, composed primarily of elements of the 229th Assault Helicopter Battalion, stayed in the "Dom-Rep" during the summer.

Those early months of 1965 at Fort Benning were a time of anxiety for Kinnard and his staff. In a written report that ultimately would be read by McNamara, Kinnard strongly recommended that the air assault division be added to the regular force structure of the Army. He also recommended that the 101st Airborne Division be named as the Army's first airmobile division and that all combat arms units be parachute-qualified. Kinnard and his staff also had recommendations about organizational strengths, equipment, and weapons. One of the weapons systems the division badly wanted to keep was the battalion of twenty-four Mohawks, each armed with five-inch Navy "Zuni" rockets. The Mohawks were fast enough to fly escort for the lift helicopters, using figure eight patterns above and below the formations and then, at the precise moment, darting ahead to lay heavy suppressive fire on the landing zone.

The recommendations were strongly endorsed by Lieutenant General Charles Rich, the commander of the Third Army at Fort McPherson, Georgia, and the Test Director. Continental Army command at Fort Monroe, Virginia, gave the recommendations a less warm, but still positive, endorsement. Then the paperwork hit the Army staff and bogged down. Kinnard recalls:

> I never really, to this day, knew what specific action the Army staff took on my piece of paper. It seemed as if they were going through a love dance with the OSD . . . as if they were trying to find out what OSD was thinking before they thought it, and so on.

When McNamara finally saw the recommendations, he recognized that the Army had done all he had asked of it in terms of wringing out the airmobile concept. And he approved—in fact, directed—the inclusion of an airmobile division into the Army's permanent force structure.

Kinnard and his staff had kept their ears close to the ground and, in the interim, were inventing things the division could do to keep the Army's attention—such as long-range tanks for Caribous so they could be flown across the Pacific, aerial refueling of helicopters, *anything* the commanders and staff could come up with to show how much capability the organization had.

By early 1965, it was apparent that Army ground troops would be committed to Vietnam. It was also apparent, at least

33

at the senior staff level, that either the 11th Air Assault Division or the 2nd Infantry Division would be very much involved in any major troop deployments to Southeast Asia. Because the divisions were so intermixed a decision would have to be made by Department of Army about which one would be tabbed as the new airmobile division. But even as the decision process progressed in Washington, the division, brigade, and battalion staffs began war-gaming situations pegged on a Vietnam mission. Because of specific top secret guidance provided the division staff by Department of Army, primary emphasis was placed on the central highlands of Vietnam: the II Corps Tactical Zone.

June 16 was set as the date that Secretary of Defense McNamara would make the formal announcement about the authorization of an airmobile division. In a nationally televised press conference, McNamara announced that an airmobile division had been authorized for the Army's force structure. This was no surprise. Every sky trooper had been expecting it.

What did come as a surprise to most of the division was McNamara's announcement that the famed 1st Cavalry Division had been chosen to carry the banner of airmobility beyond the test stage. The 11th Air Assault Division colors were to be retired; the 2nd Infantry Division colors (no men or equipment to be involved) were to be transferred to Korea; and the colors of the 1st Cavalry Division were to be brought back to U.S. soil for the first time in twenty-two years. Appropriately, Kinnard was chosen to command the new division. McNamara then said the airmobile division would have only eight weeks to reach REDCON-1, the highest combat readiness condition.

What McNamara did not say in his announcement, but what the division learned quickly enough in the follow-up paperwork, was that the brutal trade-offs with the Air Force in the Pentagon had cost Kinnard his beloved armed Mohawk battalion. Additionally, since the writing was on the wall that the division was headed for an insurgency environment, the Little John battalion was eliminated from the TOE.

The decision about the identity of the bearer of the airmobile standard was not without some bloody internecine battling within the Army family. Each of the various "establishments" within the Army wanted its favorite arm or service or division to carry the standards of airmobility. Kinnard very much wanted the 101st Airborne Division, his World War II outfit, to be named the airmobile division. Major General John Chiles, the commander of the 2nd Infantry Division, headquartered in the Sand Hill sector of Fort Benning, who had "loaned" a good portion of his division to the 11th for the air assault tests, wanted the 2nd to become the airmobile division, with himself as the division commander. He had commanded in combat a platoon, a company, a battalion, and a regiment of the 2nd Division and desperately wanted to lead the full division in Vietnam. Chiles was indiscreet enough to discuss the situation and his yearnings for command with Joe Treaster, a reporter from the command newspaper, *The Indianhead* (actually an insert in the Fort Benning paper *The Bayonet*). Treaster, a recent draftee more accustomed to the city room of the *Miami Herald*, ran the interview, embarrassing Chiles enormously. There were some in the Army who wouldn't have minded if the 11th had been chosen to rejoin the ranks of the Regular Army divisions. So everyone, regardless of grade or position, had a strong opinion about what kind of shoulder patch would be worn by the sky soldiers.

But what really ensured the designation of the 1st Cavalry Division as the airmobile division was the fact that there were a lot of cavalrymen, either in terms of original branch or in terms of service in the 1st Cavalry Division, then in positions of power in the Pentagon, plus some who were recently retired. It rankled them that the famed 1st Cavalry had been reduced to a common infantry division, pulling picket-line guard duty in Korea. Horses were long gone from the cavalry inventory. The cavalrymen (actually armor branch types now) who once had been hostile toward the airmobility concept now embraced the helicopter as the way to get the cavalry mobile again. It was simply a version of "golden rule" (he who has the gold, rules); in this case, it was "star rule." And there were far more stars on the side of the 1st Cavalry Division than on the side of the 101st, the 2nd, or the 11th, which apparently no one wanted very much anyway.

And so the 1st Cavalry became the bearer of the Army's airmobile standard. The division had carved out an enviable combat record, first in the Pacific in World War II and then during the Korean War. It was acknowledged to have been "First in Manila," "First in Tokyo," and "First in Pyongyang," and from General Douglas MacArthur it had earned the sobriquet, the "First Team." So the men of the division began sewing on the big gold and black shoulder patch and settling into the nomenclature of a cavalry outfit with the smugness of knowing they were in the first airmobile division in the world. Only a very few in the Army could have visualized then what other firsts lay ahead for the famous First Team.

2

ORGANIZATION
AND
DEPLOYMENT

In Quang Ninh Province, North Vietnam, the week of July 22 to 25, 1965, marked the end of some forty-five days of pre-infiltration training for the 33rd Regiment of the North Vietnamese Army (NVA) and the beginning of its movement south. Its infiltration route crossed from North Vietnam into Laos, continued south through Laos, and entered South Vietnam via Kontum Province. Its final destination was in southwestern Pleiku Province.

July 28 was a typically hot July day in southwestern Georgia. Around Fort Benning, down on main post and over on Sand Hill, it was business as usual. But in those parts of the post that housed the soldiers of the Army's new airmobile division, the sweaty brows came from anxiety, not the heat.

President Lyndon B. Johnson was to address the nation in a radio and television speech, and speculation was rife on what he would say. In the division's information office, the speculation was over. Just minutes before President Johnson's speech, the Atlanta bureau of the Associated Press called and asked for an official reaction to the president's announcement. The text of Johnson's speech had been advanced to wire services with an embargo. But no one said the bureau chief couldn't start some advance digging.

Wherever they could, officers, noncommissioned officers, and soldiers gathered around radios and television sets, waiting expectantly for their commander in chief to speak. The day was significant also in that it was the date that the 1st Cavalry Division (Airmobile) had reached REDCON-1. In the nationwide address, President Johnson said he had decided, because of the "lessons of history," to make a major effort in Vietnam. Then he announced what every trooper in the division had been waiting for: "I have today ordered to Vietnam the airmobile division. . . ."

The announcement touched off a tidal wave of media contacts, the first batch of the thousands that would ultimately cover the division's activities. In an ad hoc news conference held for newsmen who swarmed to the division's Harmony Church headquarters following the announcement, General Kinnard said: "I have no misgivings whatever about the ability of this division to perform superbly in Vietnam in any way that may be required. I believe we will make the Army and the country proud of us."

But as important as the president's message was, more important was what he did not say. There had been a general anticipation among those in the know that the president would also announce a state of emergency and authorize call-up of U.S. Army Reserve and National Guard units. That he failed to do so was, in the minds of many historians, *the* key American decision of the Vietnam War. But it also had an immediate effect on the division.

General Kinnard was distinctly unhappy about that turn of events, because had a state of emergency been declared, the division could have deployed every man with the idea that he could have stayed in Vietnam until wounded, killed, or evacuated, or until some standard rotational program had been set up. But in the absence of an emergency declaration, the rules then in effect about the soldier completing his enlistment were still valid. If a man deployed with the division and after he got to Vietnam his enlistment was up, even if it were only a week after he got there, he was free to go back to the United States. And there were other ground rules that had to be observed, such as those concerning a soldier's return to a combat zone within a certain period of time. "The net impact of all this on the division," Kinnard recalled, "was that we had to strip out a great many highly trained men at exactly the worst time, namely, just as we were preparing to go to war."

For example, the division had to turn loose five hundred highly trained pilots, crew chiefs, and mechanics from the aviation units, replace them with personnel unfamiliar with the new doctrine of airmobile warfare, and then put the replacements through a grueling training program to enable them to play catch-up.

It had been a very hectic time from the date the 11th Air Assault Division closed on Fort Benning at the conclusion of the AIR ASSAULT II test on November 15 until this July day. While waiting for word from the top that the Army would adopt into its permanent structure an airmobile division, the 11th kept reasonably busy with training in the Fort Benning area, some of it low-level and classified preparation for ultimate deployment to Vietnam.

But after the McNamara announcement on June 16, the activity became frenzied. To be sure, the preparations for deployment still had a "secret" label attached, but there were thousands of other tasks that had to be accomplished simply to get the division reorganized into the airmobile structure that had been authorized by the Army.

The original, organic units of the 11th Air Assault Division had to prepare for deactivation, while simultaneously being reactivated into a 1st Cavalry Division organization. The attached elements of the 2nd Infantry Division had to do the same, boxing up unit emblems, memorabilia, and heraldic items for shipment to Korea and preparing for receipt of like items from the troops on the demilitarized zone (DMZ). (See appendix I for unit designations on the exchange, i.e. 3rd Squadron, 17th Cavalry, to 1st Squadron, 9th Cavalry.)

Amazingly, the changeover took place without major glitches, and for the troops in the line units, switching allegiance to new units was not particularly troublesome. In fact, General Knowles, when advising General Kinnard not to fight the brass about the designation of the 1st Cavalry, said he told Kinnard that troops have short memories when it comes to unit designations, and that after the first battle, the heritage of the 11th Air Assault would merely become another chapter in the glorious history of the 1st Cavalry Division.

But other problems facing the division were nearly insurmountable. As of the reorganization date, the division was short a substantial number of officers, warrant officers, and enlisted men. Part of this was because many officers, particularly aviators, were nondeployable under the announced criteria. Another complication was the major increase in the number of airborne spaces brought about by a TOE change calling for the entire 1st Brigade and a proportionate slice of the division support to be airborne-qualified. Many experienced noncommissioned officers were "borrowed" from the 101st and 82d airborne divisions, and in a special jump school, 659 fledgling troopers won their silver wings at Fort Benning's Fryar Field.

The aviation school at Fort Rucker, Alabama, conducted two special classes—a UH-1 transition class for eighty-nine aviators who had been flying other aircraft, and a Huey gunship aerial weapons firing course for another 120 men. The latter was to provide crew members for UH-1B gunships, which had to be used as lift ship escorts in lieu of the armed OV-1 Mohawks the Army had bargained away in order to get the airmobile division. The 1st Cavalry was permitted to retain six OV-1 aircraft for use as infrared surveillance and photo-reconnaissance birds.

Another herculean task was the requirement to relocate the nearly 7,500 families of division members. Of course, advance planning was done in secret, but in the final stages, the job was accomplished by the Infantry Center's Army Community Service Agency in conjunction with the division's own family assistance groups, which received substantial help from the wives of senior officers and noncommissioned officers in the division.

The official changing of the colors ceremony took place on July 3, 1965, in Fort Benning's Doughboy Stadium. The colors of the 11th Air Assault Division were cased and retired, and then, to the strains of the traditional cavalry song "Garry Owen," John Stockton, wearing the uniform of a 1930s cavalryman and mounted on a cavalry charger, marched the colors of the 1st Cavalry Division onto the stadium floor. There was scarcely a dry eye among the special visitors—old cavalrymen invited by Kinnard to attend the ceremony. One of the special guests was now-retired General Hamilton Howze. The idea his study board had recommended had become a reality.

During the early days of July, despite the obvious preparations, personnel who were aware of the mission ahead were unable to divulge the classified nature of that mission. A story is told of a captain who had been waiting for nearly two years for on-post housing. In early July, when a four-bedroom unit on the main post of Fort Benning opened up, he had to assure his family that the stories about the division being deployed to Vietnam were nothing more than rumors. And so they moved from their off-post housing—only to move again in just four weeks.

Once the cat was out of the bag, however, work began in earnest. What once was considered a frenetic schedule was looked upon fondly as a rest time, compared to the last three weeks before deployment. The announcement came on July 28: the lead brigade was to board its troop ship on August 13!

The division instituted a unique system of concurrent centralized and decentralized preparations. While Preparation for Overseas Movement processing was handled at a central location, using the county-fair system of stations to handle 850 men daily in the big field house at Harmony Church, the vast training requirement for the entire division was accomplished by means of centralized direction and decentralized execution.

Operational planning was conducted apart from normal division functions; ultimately, five operational plans were developed. The division was fortunate in this area in that, since General Johnson had told General Kinnard earlier in the year that the division would eventually be deployed to Vietnam, its G-2 (intelligence) and G-3 (operations) sections had been war-gaming with studies based on the very area of Vietnam into which the 1st Cav was most likely to be deployed.

During this period, the chiefs of all but one of the G-sections changed over. The sole hold-over was Lieutenant Colonel Robert McDade, the G-1 (personnel). In the operations shop, Lieutenant Colonel Earl Buchan, coming in from command of the 229th Assault Helicopter Battalion, took over from Lieutenant Colonel Robert Shoemaker, who took command of the 1st Battalion (Airborne), 12th Cavalry.

The new G-2 was Lieutenant Colonel Bobby Lang, who replaced Lieutenant Colonel Frederick Ackerson, posted as the commander of the 1st Battalion, 5th Cavalry. The logistics side of the house (G-4) was handled by Lieutenant Colonel Raymond Kampe.

Decisions were made daily that were to have long-reaching effects on both the division and the Army. Most were in the areas of tactics and doctrine, but some of the more notable were not. The men of the division, accustomed to the requirements of garrison life, sported blazing yellow cavalry patches and white name tags on their fatigues. Underwear and handkerchiefs were position-revealing white. Many of the fatigue uniforms were wash-faded to a near gray.

The new jungle fatigues were still not being produced in division-size quantities; the Cav would deploy and fight initially with what it had on its back. So the division headquarters passed out an order: dye all uniforms, underwear, and handkerchiefs a dark green. Much of the burden was assumed by the quartermaster laundry at Fort Benning, but many sky troopers bought the dye and did it themselves, at home or in laundromats.

Practically every packet of green-and-black dye in Georgia was snapped up. The sewage in Columbus, Georgia, and Phenix City, Alabama, was said to have turned green and stayed that way for weeks afterward. But the division's uniforms toned down. White name tapes were further dulled by felt-tip marker. The division ordered the Cav patches cut off, although not everyone got the word. General Knowles recalls having seen troopers on the trains leaving Fort Benning wearing not only Cav patches, but also the patches of the 11th Air Assault Division.

Those who dyed their fatigues with the patches still attached ended up with green-and-black patches. That, combined with the stencil outline patch used by John Stockton's 9th Cavalry, gave some folks at division headquarters a bright idea: manufacturing black-and-green patches along with rank and branch insignia.

The origin of the idea is attributed to several folks—Kinnard, Knowles, and even George Beatty, the 1st Brigade commander who had just changed places with Chief of Staff Elvy Roberts. Regardless, a Vietnamese tailor in Saigon made some prototypes for members of the advance party, but these were judged unsatisfactory. Kinnard ordered a better brand from a Japanese manufacturer and had them issued shortly after the division arrived in Vietnam. The trend swept the division like wildfire, eventually spreading to other units in Vietnam and, ultimately, to the entire Army.

The loss of the bright yellow on the patch met with some resistance. Mrs. Ben Dorcy, the widow of a 7th Cavalry regimental commander in the 1920s, had, with the help of her husband, designed the original patch when the division was first formed in 1921. She said the patch had been made large and bright so that it could be seen across the parade fields at Fort Bliss, Texas, and because it would be worn by "big men who would do big things." At the time of the Cav's preparation for Vietnam, Mrs. Dorcy, known by several generations of cavalrymen as "Mother Dorcy," was living in the Distaff Home in Washington, D.C. She objected strenuously to the patch's colors being changed, but finally acquiesced when General Kinnard patiently explained to her that it was necessary in order to save young lives.

The Cav also became, albeit reluctantly at first, the champion of the new M-16 rifle. Earlier, during some testing with the air assault division, the M-16, known then as the AR-15, had been tested against the standard infantry weapon, the M-14. Dick Knowles remembers that after some severe field testing, nearly everyone, particularly Kinnard, was convinced that the M-16 was inferior to the M-14.

The AR-15 was manufactured by Colt. It was light—only 6.3 pounds empty—and fired a 5.56-mm (.223-caliber) cartridge with a muzzle velocity of 3,250 feet per second. On full automatic, it had a cyclic rate of fire of between 700 and 900 rounds per minute. In contrast, the standard M-14 was heavier, longer, and slower. It also carried much of the recoil kick of its predecessor, the M-1. But its standard NATO cartridge of 7.62mm endeared it to military purists.

Then, in July, during the preparations for deployment, the division sent a select group of officers to Vietnam to visit U.S. troops in contact then—the 173rd Airborne Brigade and the Special Forces elements—to obtain first-hand battle information on tactics and techniques as well as to assess opinions of the commanders on equipment and tactics. What they learned was that the standard, peacetime weapons tests do not measure the worth of a weapon in combat, and that the M-16 was exactly the rifle the troops needed to match up the AK-47, the standard infantry weapon of the main force Vietcong and the NVA.

When the team returned to Fort Benning, Knowles was acting division commander while Kinnard was on a short break with his family at the Third Army's recreation area at Lake

Allatoona, northwest of Atlanta. The team briefed Knowles in detail and recommended that the division be equipped with M-16s prior to deployment. Knowles recalls: "Knowing our test results and General Kinnard's strong feelings against the M-16, I balked at making a decision on the spot. Nevertheless, it had to be made quickly because the Army had to ship thousands of rifles to us and we were extremely limited in training time."

Knowles arranged for a chopper and flew to where Kinnard was taking his break and briefed him on all of the division's activities, saving the toughest recommendation for last. Finally, Knowles sprung the M-16 issue.

Kinnard's first comment was, "You have got to be kidding!" But Knowles hung in there, with all the rationale and persuasiveness he could muster plus the comments of Bob Shoemaker, the G-3 who had been with the Vietnam visitation team. After intense questioning and a long, awkward pause, General Kinnard made his decision. "Okay, Dick," he said, "under one condition. You take on the responsibility for training the entire division in the firing, care, and maintenance of the M-16."

Knowles readily accepted the challenge, flew back to Fort Benning, and set the machinery in motion. But that was not the end of the problem. A few days later, Knowles got a call from Lieutenant General L. J. Lincoln, the deputy chief of staff for logistics in the Pentagon. He got right to the point: "Dick, I have four or five carloads of M-16s that I understand you ordered. Knowing how Kinnard feels about that weapon, I can't release them to you." But Knowles did some fast talking and persuaded Lincoln that the division really wanted the weapons and that Kinnard had given his personal okay.

Knowles said that on the training of the troops, the weapons department of the Infantry School at Fort Benning responded magnificently. They made the finest instructors available, and the Army brought additional experts in from all corners of the world. No unit ever had better training in its basic arm as it prepared for war than did the 1st Cavalry, and it paid off handsomely.

When President Johnson made his announcement on July 28, the division already had begun to slack off slightly on routine training in order to begin packing its equipment and supplies. General cargo and aircraft were to depart from eastern seaboard and Gulf Coast ports. In fact, many of the aircraft had already been ferried to the ports of embarkation. Most of the ships to be used for the movement were U.S. naval ships, operated with civilian crews by the Military Sea Transport Service (MSTS). But one vessel, the aircraft carrier USS *Boxer*, was still a ship of the line of the U.S. Navy and had a military crew.

The *Boxer*, loading out of Jacksonville, carried more than 220 aircraft, mostly the CH-47 Chinooks and the four CH-54 Flying Cranes from the attached 478th Aviation Company. It also carried a mule.

The saga of Maggie the mule was but one chapter in the turbulent life of John Stockton, the 9th Cavalry's colorful commander. When the air assault division was in the Carolinas on maneuvers the previous October, some of the officers in Stockton's squadron talked a farmer out of his old gray mule and gave it to Stockton as a gag birthday gift. Stockton didn't look on it as a gag, however, and ordered his staff to make sure that the mule got back to Fort Benning. No one is quite sure how the squadron acquired permanent title to the mule, named Maggie by Stockton in honor of his wife, but somehow it did end up at Benning.

After the division got its Vietnam marching orders, Kinnard put out an order that there would be no pets taken to Vietnam. And, to make sure that the word reached the guy Kinnard intended to get the message, he called Knowles in and told him, "Dick, it's your responsibility to see that that mule and that little dog John runs with do not get to Vietnam." It was a case of too little, too late.

In front of witnesses, Knowles passed on the order to

Stockton: "Did you get the word on pets?" "Yessir," said Stockton. But as with all orders given to Stockton, it had to be made explicit. Knowles had not asked Stockton whether he had already made arrangements to ship Maggie.

A few days later, Stockton went to division headquarters to tell Knowles the sad story. It seems that one of his captains, who had been sent to supervise the loading of the 9th Cavalry's helicopters, had been to dinner with the skipper of the *Boxer* and, in the course of the evening, the Navy captain had apparently had more than his share of cocktails. According to the captain, when the party got back to the ship that night, some reporters were hanging around and asked the skipper what his mission was. He replied, "I can't tell you what my real mission is, but I can tell you I'm taking the 1st Cav's mule to Vietnam." Stockton had, of course, waited until the *Boxer* had set sail before relaying the story to Knowles.

Knowles rushed over to Kinnard's office to give him the bad news and was told to have the mule taken off at the first port of call. Knowles suggested to Kinnard that, since the eyes of the world seemed to be focused on the 1st Cavalry, a better course of action might be to declare the mule an exception to policy, make it the division's mascot, and forget about the whole thing. But the saga of Maggie the mule was far from over.

During the first week of August, commanders tried to give every man a few days' leave before departure, a few days to spend with their families before the long, hard time ahead. For the troopers and families both, the leave provided a tremendous boost in morale before the men were to leave their country and their loved ones for at least a year—or, for some of them, forever.

Movement of personnel was accomplished in three increments. An advance liaison planning detachment of thirty-two key officers and men, led by Brigadier General John S. Wright, the assistant division commander for support, departed on August 2 by commercial air.

An advance party of 1,030 officers and men and 152 tons

of cargo was deployed by the Air Force Military Airlift Command from Robbins Air Force Base, just south of Macon, Georgia, over a six-day period, beginning August 14.

The bulk of the division moved by MSTS troop ships. The first ship, with the 2nd Brigade headquarters, two infantry battalions, and one artillery battalion, left Charleston, South Carolina, on August 15. The ship was combat-loaded, as opposed to being administratively loaded, the premise being that the division might have to land fighting and wouldn't have the luxury of time on the beach to sort itself out.

A total of six troop carriers, four aircraft carriers, and seven cargo vessels were employed in the over-water movement. The 1st Brigade loaded out on the USNS *Geiger,* the 2nd Brigade on the *Buckner,* the 3rd Brigade on the *Rose.* The remainder of the division loaded on the *Darby,* the *Patch,* and the *Upshur.* The division's aircraft were crowded on to the carriers USNS *Kula Gulf, Croaton,* and *Card* and the USS *Boxer.* Kinnard and his staff saw everybody off, then boarded a plane for Vietnam.

During the same week that the 1st Cav Division loaded out on ships, the last regiment of the NVA division it was destined to meet, the 66th, departed Thanh Hoa Province in North Vietnam. Its destination: the Chu Pong (Pong Mountain) complex, a longtime Vietcong secret base along the Cambodian border in southwestern Pleiku Province. Thus, from different starting points in the north and at different times, the regiments moved south to converge ultimately in the central highlands of South Vietnam.

This, of course, was the physical manifestation of the critical North Vietnamese decision made in the late summer of 1964 when the politburo escalated its war strategy from one of reinforcement of National Liberation Front (NLF) forces, popularly called "Vietcong," with weapons, supplies, and individual replacements, to a commitment of North Vietnamese regular army units.

In the minds of the men who made the march from the

north, the first stages of their infiltration, departing their homeland by truck and, on one occasion, by train, were the easiest and most exciting. Once they entered Laos, however, the tough part began. From there, all movement was on foot over rugged mountain trails, across swift-flowing rivers, and through the jungle. Heat, hunger, and sickness became their constant companions. The way stations were of some assistance and comfort, but only for the barest of essentials. There were fifty of these along the routes from the 17th parallel in Laos and in Cambodia to where the regiments were to leave the trail and set up operational headquarters in Pleiku Province. Each of the way stations was manned by an NVA unit which provided guides, food, and some protection.

Fortunately for the infiltrating regiments, the U.S. Air Force had not yet begun in earnest the incessant bombardment of the infiltration trail, an interdiction operation that, although never closing the trail, did cause casualties in the infiltrating units. In actuality the incidence of malaria probably caused as many casualties as did the bombs. All three regiments arrived with ranks depleted by illness.

By contrast the move of the 1st Cavalry by ship was almost luxurious. To be sure the four weeks at sea provided little idle time; but each night troops had a safe, dry place to sleep. They had plenty to eat; in fact the food was so good and plentiful that despite a daily physical exercise session on deck many of the men put on weight during the voyage.

Commanders used the time to provide additional training and preparation for jungle combat. Skull practice in counterguerrilla tactics, patrolling, jungle navigation, and other pertinent subjects kept skills sharp. Familiarization with firing of weapons was carried out from the after decks of the troop carriers. On the *Buckner*, for example, the ship's veteran chief engineer, Anthony Guezuraga, rigged up a floating target that demonstrated amazing stability despite the turbulence of the ship's wake.

Before Kinnard left for Vietnam, he had one last meeting with the Army's chief of staff, General Harold K. Johnson. In recalling the meeting, Kinnard said he probably received all sorts of generalized instructions, but the thing he remembered vividly was a mission-type order in which General Johnson said, "Harry, your job with your division is to prevent the enemy from cutting Vietnam in two through the Vietnamese highlands." Like his original mission order to organize the division, Johnson's mission order for the 1st Cavalry in Vietnam fit the way Kinnard liked to operate.

Once in Vietnam, Kinnard recalls, he immediately had a problem with the field commander, General William C. Westmoreland. Kinnard felt that Westmoreland, who had been in Vietnam since January 1964 and thus was out of touch with the thrust of the airmobility tests, did not understand the nature of the airmobile division.

> When I arrived with my staff I found General Westmoreland had an entirely different idea for the division. He said he wanted to break it up into three brigades and station them all over the country. I was able to make a very strong counter argument to General Westmoreland and based a lot of it on the fact that the Chief of Staff had told me what I was supposed to do and there was no way I could do that under his plan.

Kinnard recalls that he also used the argument that the division was tailored for employment as a whole.

> I told him that we only had two lift battalions and the name of this game is to be able to concentrate your lift assets to give a high degree of mobility to as many of your people as possible at one time. If you penny-packet them all over the country, you have lost it. Fortunately, I was able to convince him of that.

While it is likely that Westmoreland might have toyed with

the idea of making fire brigades of the 1st Cavalry and that the thought of all of those helicopter assets spread out to aviation-poor units probably made members of his staff salivate, it is just as likely that he did not seriously consider it for long. The immediate threat to the western highlands was too real. Moreover, it is doubtful that General Johnson's desires alone would have been persuasive. Westmoreland was running a subunified command, directly under Commander in Chief of the Pacific Admiral U. S. Grant Sharp. And Admiral Sharp took his direction from the Joint Chiefs of Staff and the National Military Control Authority. General Johnson, while powerful enough to dictate the designation of the 1st Cavalry Division as the airmobile standard bearer and, as a member of the Joint Chiefs, a framer of strategic direction, did not, in fact, command the Army and certainly did not dictate troop employments in Southeast Asia.

In his book *A Soldier Reports*, Westmoreland recounts the struggle he had with Admiral Sharp over his plan to station the airmobile division at An Khe, some thirty-five miles inland from the coastal enclave of Qui Nhon:

Since the most serious and immediate enemy threat was in the Central Highlands, I deemed it essential as one of my first moves, which I had pointed out on several occasions in asking for the airmobile division, to deploy an American force there. I intended that a battalion of American Marines temporarily secure Qui Nhon for the safe landing of the division. Although I anticipated using Route 19 to supply the division, supplies could go by air, which the airmobile division with its large numbers of organic helicopters was uniquely equipped to accomplish. No exponent of the enclave strategy, Admiral Sharp nevertheless objected to deploying the airmobile division inland. He wanted to base the division itself at Qui Nhon and clear Binh Dinh province before moving inland, thus insuring a solid base for supply by road. He still was concerned also lest the enemy score a psychological victory against American troops *à la* Groupement Mobile 100.

Westmoreland prevailed, and the Cav was assigned to an area just north of Route 19 where it passes through the village of An Tuc. The map location was called An Khe, and it became the new home of the 1st Cavalry Division (Airmobile). The advance party, arriving at Cam Ranh Bay in C-141 airlift aircraft, staged there until the entire party closed, then boarded C-130s for the flight to the Military Assistance Command, Vietnam (MACV) strip by the Special Forces camp at An Tuc.

General Wright assembled his men shortly after their arrival and told them they were going to create a base and that it was going to be done without the use of bulldozers or power equipment. This was because earth-moving equipment stripped the land of its protective grasses and bushes and, with 435 helicopters soon to arrive, the base would quickly become a vast dust bowl or, depending on the season, a gigantic mud pie. What Wright did not tell the advance party was that he had learned this the hard way, as a Japanese prisoner of war forced into hard labor clearing a Japanese air strip. The general then tied a cloth about his forehead, picked up a machete, and, to the horror and chagrin of the assemblage, led the way into the scrub jungle to carve out a base that would be, as he put it, "as clean as a golf course." The name stuck, and the helipad—the largest in the world—was soon world-famous as the "Golf Course." And for several months afterward, veterans of that advance party, colonels and privates alike, could be distinguished by the callouses on their palms.

As a sort of footnote to the selection of An Khe as the base, Kinnard recalls that he also pitched a proposal to Westmoreland that the Cav be based in Thailand and operate exclusively against the Ho Chi Minh Trail in Laos and Cambodia. By having a totally secure base in Thailand, the division could concentrate all of its combat assets on the interdiction of the trail. Westmoreland was intrigued by the idea, but said political opposition to the tactic might be too much to overcome. He nevertheless gave permission for Kinnard to visit General Richard Stillwell, commander of the Military Assistance Group in Thailand. Stillwell confirmed that the Thais were very nervous about the increasing number of American soldiers in Thailand and would not permit basing a combat division whose purpose was to strike against supposedly neutral Laos and Cambodia. Another problem was trying to run operations in Laos; Ambassador William Sullivan simply was not about to permit it. And the whole thing became more or less moot by the increasing pressure the NVA was creating in the western highlands.

The troops celebrated the division's forty-fourth anniversary, September 13, on the high seas. But the following day, the *Buckner*, with the 2nd Brigade, dropped anchor in Qui Nhon harbor. Two days earlier, the *Boxer* had arrived and the Cav birds already were flying to shore.

Kinnard and a small staff, in a launch, began visiting all of the troop ships as they arrived in the harbor. He also paid a visit to the *Boxer*, not only to talk with the commander of troops, Lieutenant Colonel Benjamin Silver, who also was the commander of the 228th Assault Support Helicopter Battalion (CH-47 Chinooks), but also to ask the skipper of the *Boxer* to spring a couple of his seamen from the brig.

They were incarcerated after having sneaked onto the fantail of the ship, where a stall had been set up for Maggie the mule. Armed with a hot iron, they seared the initials USN on the haunch of the unfortunate beast. Knowles had learned of the incident while visiting the ship the previous day, and had suggested to Kinnard that he make a personal appeal to the skipper of the *Boxer* for clemency for the two sailors.

When the unloading started, it suddenly occurred to Knowles that Stockton was going to have to transport that mule somehow to An Khe. So he summoned Stockton and asked him what his plan was to get Maggie to An Khe. Stockton started to say, "I talked to Ben Silver . . ." Knowles stopped him in mid-sentence. "John, I am going to give you an order. I do not want that mule to go up in a Chinook." Knowles said he could just visualize the mule getting excited and kicking a hole in the side of a Chinook, costing the division an aircraft and a crew because of a dumb mascot. "Do you understand?" he emphasized to Stockton. "Yessir," was Stockton's reply.

"It wasn't but thirty minutes later when I looked up and saw the mule slung under Stockton's command chopper," Knowles said. "It was typically Stockton; he would obey the letter of the order, but make his own decisions about the spirit."

Combat elements of the division closed on the An Khe base on September 14, and the Vietcong wasted little time in probing the base defenses. While the valley and the route into the base was secured by the 1st Brigade of the 101st Airborne Division, the responsibility for base defense remained with the division. The green troops expended a lot of ammunition early on, firing mostly at shadows. During the early days at An Khe, the saga of Maggie the mule ended tragically. She wandered too far outside the perimeter one cloudy night and was shot by a spooked picket guard. The flailing about on the perimeter revealed a fundamental truth about the division for anyone who was perceptive enough to see it: the 1st Cavalry Division (Airmobile) that had just arrived in Vietnam was *not* an elite unit. True, the concept of airmobility was elite, but the troopers who were to provide the sinew for making the concept a reality were typical of the American infantry, artillery, and engineer soldiers the U.S. Army was providing to all of its line outfits in 1965.

So a lot of ammunition was fired off in those first days on the perimeter, until inexperienced troops began recognizing shadows for what they were and leaders began exercising the kind of control and fire discipline that was expected of a first-rate outfit. Step by step, the division began reaching a true wartime readiness; not the paper brand of readiness, but that special kind of discipline marked by proficiency and dependability and automatic habits of combat not taught in any school. The division was striving to reach an elite status. The question was, would the enemy allow it the time?

3

SETTING
THE STAGE

It was the summer of 1965. John Wayne was still making movies (*The Sons of Katie Elder*). So was Andy Warhol (*Hedy*, about the shoplifting trial of Hedy Lamarr). The Oscar-winning picture that year was *The Sound of Music*, and the Grammy-winning song was "The Shadow of Your Smile." And somewhere beyond the sea, four mop-tops were busy making their own brand of music—the score for *Help*, the second Beatles film feature.

Even farther beyond the sea, in Vietnam, the score of another version of "Help" was being fashioned. General William C. Westmoreland, commander of U.S. Military Assistance Command, Vietnam (COMUSMACV), presiding over a steadily deteriorating situation, had repeatedly badgered the Joint Chiefs of Staff for reinforcements. Of particular concern was the situation in the highlands which, from the days of the Vietminh, had been a choice target of the insurgents. The advisory compounds at Camp Holloway near Pleiku and in Qui Nhon City had been struck by the Vietcong early in the year, with a great loss of American lives. A crack ARVN regiment had been mauled by two NVA battalions near Dak To in Kontum Province. The major east-west road, National Highway (QL) 19, and north-south route, QL 14, had been cut by the Vietcong, and no government traffic flowed in or out of the highlands.

These battles in the vulnerable western plateau region were not accidental engagements generated by local decisions or circumstances. Rather, they were the outgrowth of a master plan devised by General Nguyen Chi Thanh, a member of the People's Republic Central Committee and the field commander of all NVA and VC forces in the South. He envisioned not only liberation of huge chunks of the South, but also head-to-head combat with the Americans. General Thanh believed he could inflict so many casualties on the American forces that political pressure in the United States would end the troop buildup. The debate in Hanoi indicated that General Vo Nguyen Giap had some doubts about all phases of the strategy, but permitted Thanh to proceed with his plan because it was consistent with the overall policy decision of the politburo in August 1964, which was to engage in the dual strategies of *dau tranh vu trang* (armed struggle) and *dau tranh chinh tri* (political struggle). One of the arms of political struggle was *dich ban* (action among the enemy), which involved the manipulation of public opinion throughout the world, particularly in the United States.

Thanh's plan took the shape of a campaign with the ultimate goal of securing and dominating a major portion of the Republic of Vietnam. It was to be known as the Dong Xuan (Winter–Spring) Campaign 1965–66. An army corps of three field fronts, or divisions, was given the task of executing this campaign. The corps was to operate in an area bounded on the north by the 17th parallel; on the south by a line running generally along the southern boundaries of Pleiku, Phu Bon, and Phu Yen provinces; on the east by the South China Sea; and on the west by the Laotian and Cambodian borders. Control of the corps was in the hands of General Thanh and the high command in Hanoi rather than under Military Region V, which for years had controlled Vietcong operations in this area.

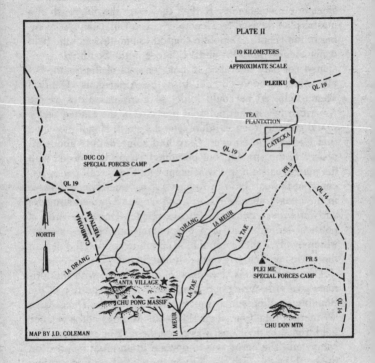

PLATE II

10 KILOMETERS
APPROXIMATE SCALE

PLEIKU   QL 19

TEA
PLANTATION

CATECKA

QL 19

DUC CO
SPECIAL FORCES CAMP

PR 5

QL 14

QL 19

CAMBODIA
VIETNAM

IA DRANG

IA MEUR

IA TAE

IA DRANG

NORTH

IA DRANG

PLEI ME
SPECIAL FORCES CAMP

PR 5

ANTA VILLAGE

IA TAE

IA MEUR

IA TAE

CHU PONG MASSIF

CHU DON MTN

QL 14

MAP BY J.D. COLEMAN

Within the framework of the Dong Xuan Campaign, the three field fronts were to conduct a series of lesser campaigns. One of these was the "Tay Nguyen (Western Plateau) Campaign," which had as its objective the seizure of Kontum and Pleiku Provinces and parts of Binh Dinh and Phu Bon Provinces. Specific objectives of the Tay Nguyen Campaign were the Special Forces Camps in Pleiku and Kontum Provinces, long a thorn in the side of the communist high command; the city of Kontum, where the 24th Special Tactical Zone headquarters was located; Le Thanh District headquarters; and the city of Pleiku itself, with its II Corps headquarters and the reserve forces for all of the western highlands.

During the month of July, while the 1st Cavalry Division was frantically getting ready for deployment, the 32nd Regiment, the lead element of the North Vietnamese division targeting the highlands, was busy in the deadly business of preparing itself for bigger battles that lay ahead. Already it had registered minor triumphs at Polei Kleng in March and at Le Thanh District headquarters in June. During the latter two weeks of July, the 32nd surrounded the Duc Co Special Forces camp, located on Highway 19, thirteen kilometers from the Cambodian border and fifty-five kilometers west of Pleiku City, the provincial capital. Almost daily, the camp was harassed by fire from small arms, automatic weapons, and recoilless rifles as well as from numerous squad- and platoon-sized probes of the camp's defenses. Intelligence sources available to the ARVN and to the American advisers indicated a force of at least regimental size. They determined that it was either an NVA unit or a main force VC unit with a sizable North Vietnamese augmentation. An all-out attack on the camp appeared imminent.

The camp's garrison consisted of Captain Richard B. Johnson's Special Forces Detachment A-215, with a dozen men; its Vietnamese Army counterpart, the Luc Luong Dac Biet (LLDB), which, literally translated, means airborne-ranger; two hundred Montagnard irregulars; and two hundred Nuong tribesmen. The Nuongs were descendants of Chinese refugees who settled in Vietnam in past centuries; they first engaged in river pirating and general banditry, then realized that hiring out as professional soldiers was a more reliable, if not legal, source of income. The Nuongs were the highest-paid non-American troops in Vietnam. They were used as scouts, ambush specialists, and bodyguards and whenever especially skillful and tough professional killers seemed to be indicated. Despite all of this, the garrison was no match for what lurked outside the wire.

To counter this threat, the ARVN high command sent one of its strategic reserve units from Saigon. The Airborne Brigade, with a strength roughly comparable to an NVA regiment, was helicoptered into the camp on August 3, with the mission to conduct search-and-destroy operations west and south of the camp defenses to relieve enemy pressure and drive them from the area. Concurrently, the ARVN II Corps commander, Major General Vinh Loc, ordered the 3rd Armored Task Force (ATF) to move from its staging area in Pleiku City to the Le Thanh District headquarters near the village of Thanh Binh, located on Highway 19, roughly half the distance between Pleiku City and Duc Co. After several days of fierce but futile fighting against a well entrenched and determined force west and southwest of the camp, the Airborne Brigade was ordered to move back and secure the airstrip adjacent to the camp to permit resupplying by fixed-wing aircraft. A resupply airdrop had gone awry and resulted in helping the enemy more than it did the friendlies. Meanwhile, the ATF—whose strength included an M-41 tank company, an M-113 armored personnel carrier company, an ARVN ranger battalion, a platoon of artillery consisting of two towed 105-mm howitzers, and an engineer platoon—reached Thanh Binh village unopposed. There, it was reinforced by an ARVN Marine task force of two battalions, whose senior U.S. adviser was the legendary U.S. Marine Corps Major William G. Leftwich, Jr. The ARVN Marines had just completed reestablishing the Le Thanh District Headquarters, which had been overrun in June by the 32nd NVA Regiment and temporarily abandoned by the government forces.

According to Lieutenant Colonel Edward B. Smith, Jr., Pleiku sector adviser and detailed as the operations officer of the 24th Special Tactical Zone, the ATF was ordered on August 9 to attack west on Highway 19 and link up with the Airborne Brigade at Duc Co. The task force proceeded without opposition until it reached a point about seven kilometers east of the camp, where the road made a sharp turn to the north. The column was strung out along about six kilometers of road and was struck, first at the nose of the column and, within minutes, at the center of the column. The 32nd Regiment used two battalions, reinforced with some automatic weapons and rocket launchers from a third battalion, which had stayed around Duc Co to keep pressure on its defenders. It was the prototype of the lure-and-ambush tactic.

The two battalions hammered at the armored column during the afternoon. A two-company pincer attack, striking at the middle of the column, effectively split the task force into two sectors. A lesser attack hit the rear of the column, pinning that force down and preventing it from breaking through to reinforce the more heavily engaged sector. When the odds were right, this ambush tactic had generally produced high rates of success in annihilating the ambushed force. But in this case, where the force being attacked was equal or greater in strength, the tactic, while punishing, did not obtain the results the NVA sought. By nightfall, it became obvious to Colonel Dinh Kanh, the regimental commander, that his forces were insufficient to wipe out the ARVN column. Nevertheless, shortly after daybreak on August 10, Kanh ordered a coordinated four-company assault on the lead elements of the task force. The attack was beaten off by a heavy volume of tank and armored personnel carrier fires, and the NVA force withdrew, leaving patrols to maintain harassing contact with the task force. On the 11th, the ATF linked up with the Airborne Brigade at Duc Co and conducted fruitless sweeps to the west and southwest of the camp. The task force then returned to Pleiku City without incident.

The tune-up period was over for the NVA 32nd Regiment, and the Field Front (division command) learned some valuable lessons, even though the cost was more than one hundred killed during the month-long operation at Duc Co. The campaigns of the 32nd Regiment had made it very clear that while the regiment could handle the district headquarters at Le Thanh, defended by Regional and Popular Force troops (RuffPuffs), the strength of the ARVN in conventional forces within reinforcing distance of the Special Forces camps required additional manpower. That manpower was on the way.

On September 10, the first elements of the 33rd Regiment crossed into Pleiku Province from Cambodia, and by October 2, the entire regiment had closed on a village known to the NVA as ANTA. The regimental staging area was on the eastern slope of the Chu Pong Massif, a 450-square-kilometer mountain mass that lay, for the most part, just east of the Cambodian border. Its peaks rose more than four hundred meters off the floor of the rolling plateau country that stretched in unbroken waves the sixty or so kilometers to Pleiku City. ANTA Village was convenient for the Field Front planners in that it was nearly equidistant between the Plei Me and Duc Co Special Forces camps. The division's third regiment, the 66th, which left the north in mid-August, was not due to arrive in the Chu Pong assembly area until late October or early November.

The Field Front designated to conduct the Tay Nguyen Campaign, in addition to the three regiments, also was assigned the H-15 Vietcong main force battalion, a battalion of 120-mm mortars and a battalion of 14.5-mm antiaircraft guns. The latter two were on the infiltration trail behind the 66th Regiment and not due to arrive until mid-November. Each regiment had an authorized strength of 2,200 men and consisted of three 550-man battalions, organized along the lines of the Chinese People's Army, with four 120-man companies of light infantry. The basic infantry weapon was the Kalashnikov assault rifle, better known as the AK-47, considered by experts to be the most successful assault rifle ever made. It fired a 7.62-mm rimless cartridge that had a muzzle velocity of 2,700 feet per second. The AK-47 had a cyclic rate of fire of seven hundred rounds per minute. It was infinitely superior to anything the GVN forces could field and better than the U.S. Army's standard infantry weapon, the M-14, but was matched in firepower volume by the Army's new M-16. The AK-47 was suited to the tactics of the NVA which favored the offensive and assault with high volumes of fire on a narrow front. Despite its capability for automatic fire, however, it also could be a formidable single-shot weapon for aimed fire. This permitted NVA leaders to have each man in a squad or platoon assigned a point target in an ambush situation or in the assault, rather than having them blaze away in the best Hollywood tradition.

Other weapons in the NVA battalions were the Ruchnoi Pulyemet Degtyarova (RPD), a modern and efficient machine gun fed from a fifty-round drum. Weighing only sixteen pounds with a rate of fire of seven hundred rounds per minute, it was far better than any comparable weapon produced by the U.S. Army or the ARVN. The M-60 machine gun, the U.S. counterpart, was a belt-fed weapon introduced in the 1950s. The M-60 was superior to the RPD in a defensive situation but less effective in the offense. The NVA also equipped their weapons platoons with the RPG-2 rocket launchers (sometimes identified by allied forces as the B-40). Like many Soviet weapons, it was an improved version of a captured German Wehrmacht weapon, the famous Panzerfaust. It consisted of a lightweight 40-mm tube with a pistol grip and a simple bar sight. An 82-mm or 90-mm warhead was mounted on a 40-mm rocket body and had an effective range of about 150 meters. Although designed as an antitank weapon with a shaped-charge warhead, the RPG was used largely as a company assault weapon and GI's often mistakenly reported RPG detonations as incoming mortar rounds. Each NVA soldier carried from three to five Chicom "potato masher" grenades, which were used effectively in close-in combat. All soldiers carried an entrenching tool, either a shovel or a pickaxe, and used it habitually. Even when pausing for no more than two hours on a route march, NVA commanders would have their troops prepare fighting holes, particularly for the crew-served weapons.

Each of the three regiments had normal regimental attachments of company size providing medical, engineer, transportation, and signal capabilities, as well as a 75-mm recoilless rifle company, an 82-mm mortar company, and a 12.7-mm antiaircraft company. The rigors of the infiltration trail had reduced the strengths of the regiments by an estimated 20 percent when the campaign kicked off. Replacement packets of platoon-sized units were, of course, in the pipeline and arriving on a regular basis.

The Field Front was commanded by Brigadier General Chu Huy Man. His principal assistants were Colonel Quan, assistant to the commanding general, and Senior Colonel Ha Vi Tung, the chief of staff. The Tay Nguyen Campaign was to commence in September 1965 and be completed by the beginning of the wet season in the spring of 1966. The Field Front leadership picked as an initial target the Special Forces camp at Plei Me and assigned missions to both the 32nd and 33rd regiments. It was the first time in South Vietnam that a North Vietnamese Army force would operate as a multiregimental divisional unit.

The Plei Me camp was targeted instead of Duc Co for several sound strategic and tactical reasons. Although the Special Forces camps in the highlands had been bothersome to the National Liberation Front, occasionally acting as interdiction forces for the infiltration of men and supplies into South Vietnam from Cambodia and Laos, in the overall scheme of things they were rather small fish. The real target was Pleiku City, the provincial capital and the locus of the headquarters of the II Corps Tactical Zone, commanded by

Major General Vinh Loc. Pleiku also was key in that it was the junction of two of the only all-weather roads in the highlands, National Highways 19 and 14. Highway 14, running north and south, linked the northern reaches of Kontum Province with Kontum City, Pleiku City, Ban Me Thout (in Darlac Province, 160 miles south of Pleiku City), and the more densely populated provinces to the south. South of Pleiku City, Highway 14 followed a high ridge line that served as a mini-continental divide. Streams and rivers east of the highway flowed eastward into the Song Ba drainage, which emptied into the South China Sea near Tuy Hoa in southern Phu Yen Province. To the west of the highway, numerous streams and rivers, bearing names like Tae, Drang, Meur, and Glae, flowed in a southwesterly direction, crossing the Cambodian border and emptying into the Mekong River.

Over the centuries, these streams had carved literally hundreds of cross-compartments in the terrain, making movement extremely difficult by foot and nearly impossible by wheeled or even tracked vehicles. The Plei Me camp was about forty-three kilometers due south of Pleiku City, but about twenty kilometers west of Highway 14. Provincial Route 5, a one-lane dirt road, linked the camp with Highway 14, both northward (a distance of twenty-three kilometers) and westward (about twenty kilometers). While movement of supplies by heavily armed convoy on the national highways was possible, traveling the side roads was hazardous under the best of conditions. The recent buildup of NVA strength in the western plateau had emboldened local-force guerrillas, who made resupplying by the provincial roads impossible. So, as with every other Special Forces Civilian Irregular Defense Group (CIDG) camp in the country, a dirt airstrip was bulldozed out of the red laterite soil just outside the camp's defenses and the Army's Caribou transport and the Air Force's C-123 Provider and C-130 Hercules became the logistic links to the outside world.

The Plei Me camp was a small chunk of Vietnamese real estate that was shaped like an equilateral triangle and enclosed with double entanglements of barbed wire, antipersonnel mines, claymore mines, and ditches. Inside the wire were fighting bunkers, linked by zig-zag communications trenches, and a dozen tin-roofed buildings that housed the command post, ammo bunker, mess areas for the Americans and native defenders, and sleeping areas. A helipad was also inside the compound. The only gate that could admit vehicles into the compound—looking for all the world like the main gate to a western ranch—was in the center of the northeast base of the triangle, adjacent to the airstrip. The camp's fighting force consisted of about 350 Montagnard CIDG troops recruited and trained by the Americans from the predominant Jarai tribe. The Montagnards were organized into what the Special Forces called a "strike force" and were commanded by a Vietnamese LLDB captain. In theory, he also commanded the camp. His American counterpart was the commander of the Special Forces Detachment A-217. In October 1965, that was Captain Harold Moore.

In the propaganda war, which often was more important than the shooting war, the Special Forces camps were disproportionately significant. While occasionally the strike forces would interdict an enemy force or successfully engage a local-force VC unit and occasionally (improperly) be committed to a regular army mission, the camp's inhabitants spent the bulk of their time preparing for attack. The forces in many of the camps became involved in their own defense—and the care of their own families, which lived just outside the wire—and, understandably, almost all of their energy was siphoned off to building up their own security rather than to the border surveillance, intelligence network building, offensive patrols, and ambushes that were part of their primary mission. The camps' tactical value was nil. Moreover, the South Vietnamese were not overly thrilled with the arming of the Montagnards. Just a year earlier, at a Special Forces camp in Darlac Province, the Montagnards of the Rhade tribe mutinied as part of the FULRO (Front Unifié de Lutte de la Race Opprimeé) separatist movement that had been going on among the Montagnards since before the French left Vietnam. The mutiny was settled peacefully, but rumors abounded throughout the western highlands that FULRO was planning a major offensive against key provincial towns, including Pleiku City. This paranoia about the Montagnards was one of the reasons why the II Corps commander always kept a large force in Pleiku City, a sort of Praetorian Guard, regardless of the tactical needs for the forces elsewhere in the zone. But, despite these factors, the psychological value of being able to point to these camps deep in "Indian Country" made it important to the government of Vietnam (with abundant American pressure) to defend the camps when they were threatened.

For the communist side, the camps had an equally important psychological value. The propaganda effect of overrunning one of these camps had an impact on American and South Vietnamese public opinion that was far out of proportion to the tactical value. And, because the NVA and VC knew the GVN was committed to reinforcement of the camps, a protracted siege could be counted on to bring a relief column which could then be ambushed and destroyed. This knowledge led to the development of the lure-and-ambush technique used early-on by VC and NVA forces alike throughout South Vietnam. It should be pointed out that the term *ambush* in this instance refers to the tactic of an NVA or VC force waiting along a route of march of a relief column that, as it approaches its objective, knows with a certainty that it will be struck. The unknowns are the exact location and the size of the enemy force. A true ambush occurs when total surprise is achieved by the ambushing force.

The 32nd Regiment's actions at the Duc Co camp had revealed that the terrain around Highway 19 in the area chosen for the ambush permitted tracked vehicles to range a considerable distance off the road and bring armored protection and superior firepower to bear against the regiment's light infantry. The NVA planners liked the rugged terrain on Provincial Route 5 much better, as it served to channel the armored vehicles and render them better targets for the antitank weapons in the ambushing force. Moreover, the Duc Co camp was literally at the end of the line. The purpose of staging an attack on a Special Forces camp was to lure out a relief column. The Plei Me camp, being located only twenty kilometers from the vital Highway 14, provided a much juicier plum for the NVA.

Once the target was chosen, there was the painstaking work of preparing the battlefield, a series of actions and techniques perfected over the years by the Chinese Communist route armies, then by the Vietminh in their battles against the French, and finally by the Vietcong. From the caches in the Pong Mountains, transportation units began carrying extra ammunition, weapons, and rice to forward caches in the battle area. Scout parties located trails from the targeted camp to first aid stations, a field hospital, and various rendezvous and rallying points. The trails usually were clearly marked by blazes on trees and thus were easily followed. The aid stations were set up about two to three kilometers from the battle area. Casualties were brought there, either on litters or under their own power. The ones too seriously wounded for much hope were simply laid aside to die and then placed in graves that had thoughtfully been predug by the men of the transportation battalion. Those able to be sent back to the fight were patched up and returned. And those with hope of recovery who were able to walk or to be evacuated were given emergency treatment and sent down the blazed trail to the field hospital, usually about ten kilometers back toward the base area. The hospital usually was located in an area providing cover from aerial observation, with creeks running through it for water supply, and with some kind of major terrain feature nearby to aid stragglers and wounded to locate it if they lost the trail. The NVA sometimes positioned one or more company-size reserve units close to the hospital to provide security and help collect stragglers from the battle areas.

For the first of the two regiments tabbed for the Plei Me battle, the preparation of the battlefield began as early as

September 19, when the ambush site was reconnoitered for approaches to and around it. A preliminary operations order was issued by 32nd Regimental headquarters (the final, written order was issued October 12 and is reproduced in appendix II), the site and the surrounding areas were reconstructed on sandtables, and numerous exercises and rehearsals were conducted by each unit. Meanwhile, the regiment's transportation company, assisted by local VC laborers, was rushing to prestock food and ammunition.

Even before its last element had closed into the regimental assembly area near ANTA Village, the 33rd Regiment found itself deeply involved in its preparations. Ten days of tactical exercises in rehearsal for the attack was all the time it had—not nearly enough, had its mission been more complex, but sufficient for the job of staging the siege on Plei Me camp.

For the 1st Cavalry Division at An Khe, blissfully unaware of the frenzied activities of the NVA to the west, the balance of the month of September was devoted to finishing the job started by the advance party of creating a base. Even as the division was closing into the base, Vietcong sniper fire and light-probing attacks began. The first fire mission by artillery in support of the division base came not from an organic 1st Cav artillery unit but from a 105-mm howitzer battalion, the 2nd of the 17th, which had been attached to the Cav and had arrived in the base area shortly after the advance party began working on the helipad. The 1st Brigade of the 101st Airborne Division was responsible for the security of the road from Qui Nhon as well as the entire An Khe Valley, but the division was responsible for its own perimeter defense. On September 18, the 2nd Battalion, 12th Cavalry (2/12) was placed under the operational control of the 101st for the purpose of relieving the 1st Battalion, 327th Infantry, of its An Khe Valley security mission. This permitted the 101st to mount Operation GIBRALTAR, an offensive operation in the adjoining valley to the east of An Khe, the Vinh Thanh Valley. When the main force VC battalion that ringed the landing zone chosen by the Screaming Eagle task force chose to stand and fight rather than melt away into the jungles, the Cav got the mission of providing artillery reinforcement. The 11th Aviation Group assembled mission-ready aircraft and lifted Battery B, 1st Battalion, 77th Artillery, into a position where it could support Gibraltar. On September 28th, the division assumed full responsibility not only for its base defense, but also for a tactical area of operations (TAOR) consisting of 15,625 square miles in central Vietnam. On that date, General Kinnard noted:

> This was 104 days from the date Secretary McNamara announced the formation of the 1st Air Cavalry Division, and 90 days after General Orders activated the unit on 1 July, 1965. Somewhere in the annals of military organization there may have been outfits activated, organized and moved 12,000 miles to combat, all within the space of 90 days, but none comes immediately to mind. That the 1st Cavalry Division (Airmobile) did just that not only is a remarkable achievement, but a tribute to the men of the division who devoted an unbelievable amount of time and effort to accomplish the task.

The TAOR assigned the 1st Cav was the largest ever assigned a single divisional-size unit. Generally, it conformed to the boundaries of the II Corps Tactical Zone. Although the TAOR theoretically extended over twelve GVN provinces, Kinnard—after consultation with his boss, Major General Stanley (Swede) Larsen, the commander of Task Force Alpha at Nha Trang—recognized that the primary NVA and VC threat was in Binh Dinh, Pleiku, and Kontum provinces. Rather than having the full division force trying to become familiar with the entire area, Kinnard gave responsibility for a province to each brigade headquarters. The 1st Brigade was given cognizance of Pleiku Province, the 2nd Brigade had Kontum, and the 3rd Brigade Binh Dinh. Each brigade headquarters was charged with conducting extensive reconnaissance in the assigned province, getting to know all of the players on the friendly side. Then, all things being equal, if the division got in a fight in one of those three provinces, the assigned brigade would get the mission. Kinnard gave John Stockton and his 9th Cavalry squadron responsibility for developing intelligence over the entire front, while still asking the squadron to provide direct support with troops for each brigade. Kinnard organized his division to fight with two brigade headquarters and six battalions operating outside the base area, with one brigade and two battalions responsible for base defense and ground lines of communication (LOC) security. Under normal circumstances, each brigade headquarters maintained constant ownership of certain battalions. The 1st Brigade had assigned to it both the 1st and 2nd Battalions, 8th Cavalry, and the 1st Battalion, 12th Cavalry. The direct support artillery battalion habitually assigned to 1st brigade missions was the 2nd Battalion, 19th Artillery. The entire brigade was parachute qualified, as was a proportionate slice of the division supporting cast. The 2nd Brigade was assigned the 1st and 2nd Battalions, 5th Cavalry and the 2nd Battalion, 12th Cavalry. Its direct support artillery battalion was the 1st Battalion, 77th Artillery. The 3rd Brigade had only two battalions, the 1st and 2nd Battalions, 7th Cavalry, although this shortcoming was remedied in late 1966 with the addition of the 5th Battalion, 7th Cavalry. The 3rd Brigade's direct support artillery was the 1st Battalion, 21st Artillery. *

On October 3 the 3rd Brigade kicked off Operation HAPPY VALLEY, designed to complete the job of clearing

---

* When the U.S. Army abandoned the regimental system in the mid-1950s, it touched off a never-ending, utterly confusing, and continually changing method of identifying combat units. The media never got the designations correct, nearly always referring to battalions as regiments. In the 1st Cavalry, the battalions were given the numerical designations of the old line regiments—Fifth, Seventh, Eighth, and Twelfth. Since there could only be one "First Battalion" of any one regimental designation, and the Army apparently had a limit to the number of regimental designations it wanted in active service, it followed that subsequent battalions were designated "Second Bat-

and pacifying the Vinh Thanh Valley that had been started by the 101st Airborne with Operation GIBRALTAR. Later, the 3rd Brigade began preparing for the division's first real offensive operation for the division, Operation SHINY BAYONET, in the enemy-saturated Suoi Ca Valley about twenty kilometers northwest of the port city of Qui Nhon. The operation was slated to kick off on October 10 and involved the two battalions of the 7th Cavalry plus a battalion from the 1st Brigade, Bob Shoemaker's 1st of the 12th. Intelligence reports indicated that the bases for two battalions of the 2nd Vietcong Main Force Regiment were located in the foothills. The scheme of maneuver called for the cavalry battalions to be inserted by air assault into blocking positions at the head of several small valleys, and to wait for units of the 22nd ARVN Division to drive the enemy into the vise. It was a good plan, except that most of the chickens had flown the coop. For most of the platoon of newsmen who had eagerly awaited the Cav's first combat action, the operation was anticlimactic and disappointing. In fact, Mal Browne of ABC was so disparaging about the capabilities of the division that Harry Kinnard actually had to answer a query from McNamara about the televised report.

Not all of the VC melted away; one battalion well dug in at the head of the Suoi La Tinh River valley chose to stay and fight. On October 12, both A and B Companies, 1/12, became heavily engaged. Two of the 15th Medical Battalion's medevac Hueys were shot down, and lift birds were needed to ferry out wounded as well as bring in reinforcements. That wasn't the way the maneuvers were played out in the Carolinas during AIR ASSAULT II; but this was a new ball game,

---

talion" or "Third Battalion." The artillery and the true cavalry were similarly designated. In this narrative, in order to relieve the monotony, battalions may be referred to in several ways, for example: Second Battalion, Twelfth Cavalry; 2nd Battalion, 12th Cavalry; Second of the Twelfth; 2/12 Cav; or, by the name of the battalion commander.

and increasingly, the lift birds, the "slicks," played a heavy role in medical evacuation, particularly in LZ's under fire. Major Joe Belochi, the battalion's executive officer (XO), made five trips into the battle area under withering small-arms fire in his OH-13 scout helicopter and ferried a total of eight wounded to safety. The battle lasted until dark, then the VC broke contact and retreated from the area.

The combat action also resulted in Morley Safer and CBS receiving the Peabody Award for the best television combat story of the year. Safer, who came in with his film crew on one of the medevac birds that was clipped by ground fire just as it flared for landing, was concurrently being photographed by a CBS team, led by John Laurence, who had been with the battalion from the start. Safer, as a "correspondent," out-ranked Laurence, who, at the time, was only a "reporter," so Safer got to do the all-important "stand-up" and got credit for the whole piece.

After the operation terminated, one veteran of the air assault testing days at Fort Benning quipped, "Just call it AIR ASSAULT III . . . with bullets." It was, of course, no laughing matter to the six dead and eighteen wounded.

Throughout the operations, the stay-behind brigades worked to improve their living areas, the base perimeter, and the base camp in general. More and more of the men were moved out of poncho and shelter half-hootches into tenting. The mainstay was the GP (General Purpose) Medium tent, approximately fourteen by twenty-six feet, made of heavy canvas. It was pitched over locally procured lumber frames and flooring. Bamboo matting made it possible to extend the side walls of the tent and increase its capacity. Smaller, hexagon-shaped tents, called aerofabs, which were introduced when the division was tested in the Carolinas, were used for orderly rooms and company officer quarters. The appearance of electric generators made jungle life somewhat more tolerable. Fans, coffee pots, and refrigerators were at a premium and somehow, they usually were found first in the aviation units. Similarly, it was the aviation units that first were able to alleviate the steady diet of individual C-rations or mess-hall-prepared dry rations with greens from the rich grocery growing area of Dalat, two hundred miles south of the An Khe base, which now was named Camp Radcliff, after Major Donald Radcliff, the first man from the division to die in Vietnam.

Concurrently, the defense barrier was taking shape with four rows of triple concertina separated from the jungle by seventy-five to one hundred yards of clearing. From the sky, the An Khe base—the Golf Course—looked like a gigantic, irregularly shaped pizza pie. The outer barrier and clearing was, of course, the crust. Just inside the barrier were fighting positions, towers and bunkers, linked by an outer loop-road. Inside the loop, ringing the entire perimeter, like rows of anchovies, were the troop quarters. Then there was an inner-loop road which was connected with the outer loop by dozens of radial spurs, as well as connecting to the giant cheese interior . . . the helipad containing 435 aircraft. Kinnard had been warned that conventional wisdom dictated against stationing all of the aircraft in one landing zone. But his assistant commander, Brigadier General Jack Wright, had a defensive scheme that virtually eliminated the most serious threat to the aircraft—mortar and rocket attacks. By having the infantry battalion responsible for base security—it was called "green line" duty—patrol aggressively outside the wire to a depth of mortar range, that piece of real estate was kept sanitized. Then, just before last light each day, the Cav squadron would conduct an aerial sweep of the jungle trails leading into the mortar zone to interdict VC mortar squads making their way into fighting positions.

This surveillance was supplemented with preplanned H & I (harassing and interdiction) artillery fires directed at trails, stream beds, and other likely collection points for VC attackers. The roar of the howitzers coming at irregular intervals all night long made sleeping difficult at first, but eventually the regular inhabitant would become accustomed to the noise. The press corps found the nightly H & I fires irritating; one reporter actually wrote a story for his paper saying that the 1st Cav's Information Officer, Major Chuck Siler, had deliberately put the reporter next to the muzzle of the guns. This wasn't exactly true, but it was a fact that the press tent was located close to one of the firing batteries. But then, so were the sleeping quarters of everyone in the Information section.

The international press corps covered the Cav like a blanket. At least forty reporters were on hand to greet the division when it landed at Qui Nhon, and the daily press load during the balance of September averaged eight to ten reporters. In a report rendered on October 4, Major Siler listed sixty-one reporters representing thirty-one different media groups who had visited the division at An Khe. When the Information section pitched the GP tent at the press site on September 16, in a driving monsoon rain, three reporters were present to help ditch the tent. The crush of the media made Siler and Kinnard realize that there was no way the Cav could afford to handle the press in the standard Army way—one reporter, one escort. So Kinnard sent a message out to the division saying that every commander and leader was responsible for handling the media in his area. The ground rules were simple: you could talk about *your* job and what *you* had done, but not about someone else's job, and you couldn't talk about what was going to happen. And then the division turned the reporters loose, allowing them to make their own way anywhere they could hitch a ride on a chopper. It was high-risk, high-gain public relations, and it paid rich dividends for the Cav, making it the most publicized division in the American Army. But the policy also incurred the ire of public information officers up the chain of command who still believed that every reporter should be escorted by a press relations officer.

One of the most unique as well as difficult construction jobs was the leveling of the top of Hon Cong, the mountain that rose sharply some nine hundred feet above the floor of the valley on the western edge of the preliminary perimeter. The mountain was troublesome in that it provided a location for the VC's duty sniper to pop a few rounds into the base area. Initially the Green Line excluded the mountain, but as time went on, the entire mountain was included as the barrier perimeter was expanded. A platoon of the 8th Engineers was airlifted to the top to begin construction of a combined communications and observation station. By late October, ten feet had been shorn off the top of the mountain and communications and radar equipment installed. This allowed the division to communicate directly to Pleiku and Qui Nhon over the two dominating mountain ranges without resorting to an airborne radio relay unit.

As a sidelight to Hon Cong, it became the training area for new replacements. Since the division had been deployed with troopers having less than sixty days to do in the Army, some of those folks already were lining up to go home even as the division settled into its base area. The replacement stream started by the end of September, and part of the training the new people received was a chance to run a patrol up on Hon Cong. The chance that there still might be some VC hiding out on its jungled slopes provided sufficient realism to capture the full attention of the new sky troopers. In the offing, though, was a series of events that would capture the attention not only of the full division, but of the entire world. A North Vietnamese Army division was about to open the Tay Nguyen Campaign with an attack on the Plei Me Special Forces camp. For the first time in the Vietnam conflict, an NVA multiregimental force under divisional control would take the field in South Vietnam.

4

THE LURE AND
THE AMBUSH

At secret jungle headquarters, located halfway between the Cambodian border and Plei Me, Brigadier General Chu Huy Man, the commander of the Field Front (division) controlling the NVA units in the western plateau, and his two principal assistants, Colonel Quan, the assistant to the commanding general, and Senior Colonel Tung, the chief of staff, made a last minute review of the battle plan. It was Tuesday, October 19, and the two regiments designated for the opening of the Tay Nguyen Campaign were in place. The attack on Plei Me was to be many things. But more than anything else it was to be a test case, a sort of shake down of the ability of the NVA regiments to operate under the control of a field front. It was the beginning of division-controlled, multiregimental operations in the South, and the eyes of the NVA and VC already committed in the South as well as those of the high command in Hanoi would be watching and awaiting the outcome. It was no sure shot, by any means. Heretofore, all of the actions in the South had been small-unit engagements, with a regiment being the largest force involved. North Vietnam's senior commanders had had no real experience with division-level operations since the Vietminh had defeated the French in 1954.

The plan for the attack of Plei Me consisted of three phases. First, the 33rd Regiment would surround Plei Me and harass the defenders, exerting enough pressure to force the ARVN to send a reaction force. In the second phase, the 32nd Regiment would ambush and destroy the relief column. Finally, in the third phase, both regiments would combine forces to overrun and destroy the camp itself. The time estimated by the NVA to accomplish this final task was just one hour.

At 11:00 P.M. on October 19, 82-mm mortar shells began landing inside the compound at Plei Me. This was followed by heavy machine gun and small-arms fire, with the heaviest concentration of fire coming from the southwest side of the camp. The 2nd Battalion of the 33rd Regiment had deployed three companies in well-prepared positions less than three hundred meters from the protective wire of the camp. The camp was defended by two CIDG companies of about one hundred men each, armed with outmoded American weapons—the M-1 rifle, the M-2 Carbine, and the Browning Automatic Rifle (BAR). The third company was on a combat patrol about seven kilometers to the northwest, but was in radio contact with the camp. Two outposts and five squad pickets were situated outside the wire. The southern outpost and two of the pickets were quickly overrun by the NVA assault force. At thirty minutes after midnight, the NVA began its assault on the southwestern leg of the triangular camp. The attack was led by NVA sappers carrying satchel charges and bangalore torpedoes, followed by infantry wearing pith helmets and khaki uniforms and firing assault rifles.

The sappers, racing forward under the covering fire of the infantry, slid the explosive-laden pipe sections under the concertina wire barriers, blasting gaps in the wire with ear-shattering detonations. Red tracers from the camp's defenders, interlaced with the distinctive green tracers of the NVA, provided brilliant pyrotechnics for the battle. The NVA 57-mm recoilless rifles and B-40 rocket launchers were targeting the

corner bunkers, and within half an hour, the blockhouse on
the northwestern corner of the compound had been reduced to
rubble and shredded sandbags. Also knocked out in the first
barrages were the communications bunker, aid station, and
ammo storage bunker. The Special Forces sergeants and their
Jarai tribesmen fired their weapons so fiercely that the barrels
glowed a dull red in the darkness. Dozens of NVA infantrymen from the two companies of the second battalion
were piled up like cordwood in the protective wire and
minefields of the compound.

The 33rd Regiment's commander, in a cynical and ruthless
expenditure of human life, was sending just enough soldiers
in the assault to lead the camp's defenders into believing they
were in danger of being overrun, but never committing
enough forces to actually do so. The NVA riflemen and sappers went to their doom believing they were supposed to penetrate the outer barrier and overwhelm the camp, never
knowing that they were the unwitting pawns in the bigger
game of lure and ambush.

By 2:00 A.M., the first flare ship was overhead, a C-123
flown by Major Howard Pierson of the 309th Air Commando
Squadron out of Bien Hoa. It took a bit longer to get the flare
ship on station because it detoured by New Pleiku Air Base,
just north of Pleiku City, to pick up Captain Dick Shortridge,
a Forward Air Controller (FAC). Shortridge flew in the right-
hand seat and directed the first air strikes in defense of the
camp. Pierson remembers the weather as being particularly
lousy, forcing the flare ship to make lower than usual passes.
The magnesium flares, suspended under tiny parachutes,
soon flooded the camp with a flickering white light, illuminat-
ing the boundaries so that the first flight of A-1E prop-driven
fighter-bombers could make passes on suspected enemy positions at the south and southwest corners of the camp. Shortridge recalls it as having been a very hairy operation. The
flare ship had to fly a tight pattern over the camp, and neither
the fighters nor the flare ship could see one another. While he

couldn't put the strikes in as close to the camp perimeter as he could have in daylight, he said, "We still got pretty darn close; everybody was down in their bunkers and we laid some ordnance in on the perimeter fence." By virtue of being so close to the wire, the NVA assault forces managed to escape much of the effects of the napalm fireballs or the bomb blasts. The reserve battalions of the 33rd Regiment took some casualties from the air strikes on the first night, a precursor of the terrible beating they would take over the next eight days.

With the pressure thus far coming from the south and southwest, the families of the CIDG "strikers" were able to get inside the main gate on the northeast leg of the camp's triangular layout and spend the remainder of the night huddled in bunkers and trenches inside the compound. At 6:00 A.M. on the 20th, direct hits from 57-mm recoilless rifles blew away the anchor bunker on the northeastern corner of the camp. Now two of the three legs of the triangle had lost their vital corner bunkers. At 8:00 A.M., sappers, carrying satchel charges, tried to penetrate the wire defenses at the main gate, but were repulsed by small-arms and machine-gun fire from the defenders. At daylight, Shortridge, the Air Force FAC, was back on station in an O-1 Bird Dog, an aircraft that resembled a Piper Cub. Bird Dog spotter planes carried four rocket pods, two under each wing, that fired 2.75-inch rockets. Shortridge said that if they were lucky, the rockets would have white phosphorus (WP) heads. Generally, though, the FACs would scrounge HE (high explosive) warheads from the army. Additionally, most FACs went out on missions with a dozen or so WP smoke grenades that could be dropped out of the side window of the Bird Dog—a throwback to World War I aviators who dropped hand grenades on German positions.

Daylight brought the first medical evacuation helicopter into the compound. It was from the 498th Air Ambulance Company at Camp Holloway, the major Army base and airstrip just outside Pleiku City. Major Louis Mizell, over the objections of a superior officer, had volunteered to fly a dustoff chopper into Plei Me. With his copilot keeping his hands on the controls on the way in, Mizell brought the Huey ambulance in at one hundred knots, flaring radically at the last moment and dropping in rapidly on the north side of the compound between two buildings. The aircraft carried a passenger, Dr. (Captain) Lanny Hunter, the Detachment C-3 surgeon in Pleiku, who had been working in Plei Me the previous week. He returned to treat scores of critically burned and wounded men and, in the course of the battle, was wounded three times himself. Mizell remembers that his ship was rigged for three litters, but they took more wounded on board, putting them on the floor. Getting out of Plei Me was even more hazardous than coming in. Mizell said he picked the bird up, pulling red lines all the way, and zipped over the buildings in the compound, heading east, until his speed reached one hundred knots, then he clawed for altitude. He said they were at several hundred feet when they reached the tree line beyond the camp perimeter.

Although the medevac Huey was fired at coming in and going out, it wasn't hit. But the B-model Huey gunship "hog" that ran escort for Mizell wasn't as lucky. It was hit by antiaircraft machine-gun fire on takeoff and crashed, killing all four crewmen. Shortridge said he had warned the chopper pilot, "Don't go south, whatever you do." The pilot had disregarded this advice and broke south once he lifted off from the compound. A rescue team was dispatched from the camp to the helicopter wreckage, but the team had barely cleared the wire when it was heavily engaged by a NVA machine gun. The team leader, Sergeant First Class Joseph Bailey, was mortally wounded. The vicious firefight prevented the team from getting back inside the gate, and another Special Forces trooper was hit before suppressive fires from inside the compound extricated the team from its vulnerable position.

During the day, the Air Force really began punishing the North Vietnamese, pounding their positions with napalm, 250- and 500-pound bombs, rockets, and .50-caliber machine-gun fire. But it was not without cost. That morning, a B-57 Canberra bomber, on a low pass, was hit by a hail of 12.5-mm (equivalent to .50-caliber) machine-gun fire. The bomber crashed before it could reach the Holloway strip, but the two-man crew punched out and were rescued without incident. A second B-57 also was hit, but was able to make it back to its base at Cam Ranh Bay before crash landing. Its crew also was unhurt.

The third CIDG "striker" company had, of course, been notified of the attack by radio and had been making its way slowly back to the camp, arriving at a point just outside the NVA encirclement in the early evening of the 20th. Then, to the accompaniment of scattered small-arms and rocket-launcher fire, the one hundred-man company made a dash for the main gate and the dubious safety of the compound. The arrival of the third company back to Plei Me camp led the authorities up the chain of command to report that the camp had been reinforced. At the highest command level, MACV, the official communique reported that the reinforcement had taken place by helicopter. This was duly picked up by the news media and reported to the world. In fact, other than Mizell's medevac mission and another Huey slick that brought in some ammunition and a relief radio operator, Staff Sergeant James Bussard, there hadn't been a chopper on the ground within thirty miles of Plei Me.

Meanwhile, at allied headquarters in Pleiku and Nha Trang, the wheels were turning. Major General Vinh Loc, the II Corps commander in Pleiku City, conferred with his senior advisor, Colonel Ted Mataxis, about the appropriate action to be taken. Intelligence officers at II Corps had determined that the force attacking the Plei Me camp was a new NVA regiment, initially identified as the 101-B Regiment. (The NVA used multiple unit identifications, particularly with elements moving down the infiltration trail. Later, when everything was sorted out, it became clear that the 101-B was, in fact, the NVA 33rd Regiment.) That meant that the 32nd Regiment, which had attacked Duc Co in August, was lurking some-where between Pleiku and Plei Me and looking for a target. Closely monitoring the situation was Major General Larsen, commander of Task Force Alpha at Nha Trang, a coastal city about 150 miles to the east and south of Pleiku. Task Force Alpha, which had become operational only a month earlier, was the equivalent of an American corps command and was responsible for the American conduct of the war in the II Corps Tactical Zone. Another headquarters involved in the planning of reinforcement and reaction was the Fifth Special Forces Group, also located in Nha Trang.

The Special Forces headquarters ordered Major Charlie Beckwith, who commanded the SF's Project DELTA, a semi-secret, long-range patrol activity, to gather a reinforcing and reaction force. Beckwith spent a good part of October 20 ex-tracting some of his four-man reconnaissance teams from a forward base in Binh Dinh Province. He gathered fifteen American Special Forces types and two South Vietnamese ranger companies, a total of 150 men, and loaded onto a C-123 and C-130 at Nha Trang for the thirty-minute flight to Pleiku. They arrived late in the afternoon on the 20th, too late for any kind of movement to the Plei Me area, so the operation was slipped to the 21st.

Concurrent to the assembly and movement of the DELTA force, a ground-relief force was alerted for movement to Plei Me by road. It was essentially the same force that had been put together for the relief of Duc Co in August. Commanded by Lieutenant Colonel Nguyen Luat, it consisted of elements of his 3rd Armored Cavalry Squadron—an M-41 company of six tanks, an M-113 armored personnel carrier company, two towed 105-mm howitzers, an engineer platoon, Luat's squad-ron headquarters, and the squadron trains (the thin-skinned vehicles that carried rations, ammunition, and fuel). The Ar-mored Task Force (ATF) moved south out of Pleiku City and provided security for a work party repairing the only two-span bridge on the route. The bridge had been blown earlier by local-force Vietcong. This effectively kept the ATF out of harm's way for another full twenty-four hours.

The only infantry reinforcement to the ATF was to be provided by the 21st Ranger Battalion. The American advisors to General Loc argued strenuously that this force was not enough to carry the day against what was sure to be at least an NVA regiment in prepared positions. General Loc already had agreed reluctantly to send the only armored force in the highlands, so, despite the arguments of Mataxis, the II Corps commander remained adamantly opposed to stripping away the remainder of his palace guard, the 22nd Ranger Battalion, or bringing in an infantry battalion from the 24th Tactical Zone headquarters in Kontum. General Larsen flew to Pleiku on the 22nd, and put pressure on Vinh Loc to commit enough strength to the reinforcing element to assure it a chance of survival. Loc was still concerned that the entire operation might be a clever NVA ruse to lure the ARVN forces out of the provincial headquarters at Pleiku City and then send the 32nd Regiment against the defenseless city. To counter this threat, Larsen promised that he would commit enough American forces in Pleiku to guarantee its safety. With Pleiku's defense now underwritten, Loc decided to send two more battalions with the relief column. Larsen, in turn, passed the mission for Pleiku security on to the only American force available, the 1st Air Cavalry Division at An Khe.

Meanwhile, to the north of the beleaguered camp, the 32nd Regiment awaited a relief column from Pleiku. All units had prepared ambush-assault sites and now were resting in readiness positions that were well concealed from aerial observation; all that remained was to see whether the ARVN would take the bait. In planning the operation, Field Front was confident that the lure of the attack on Plei Me would bring a reaction force from Pleiku City. In the 32nd's operations order (which was captured later in the campaign), the Field Front and regimental planners were chillingly accurate in their estimate of the forces that the ARVN II Corps commander would commit to relieve the pressure on Plei Me. The estimate was almost precisely what General Loc would have sent down the road had not the American command and advisory structure intervened. The NVA also had an estimate of how the ARVN forces would react when struck by the ambushing elements.

The ambush site was a stretch of about four kilometers of Provincial Route 5, about ten kilometers north of Plei Me and thirty kilometers south of Pleiku City. Here, the road, a hard-packed dirt trace, ran in a generally southerly direction along a broad ridge line broken up by small stream beds, with rolling, densely forested terrain on either side of the road. The underbrush and heavily foliated hardwoods grew to within a few feet of the roadbed, affording superb concealment to the ambushing force. After a straight stretch of nearly seven kilometers, the road made a sharp reverse S curve, and this was where the NVA planned to trigger the ambush. The curve in the road permitted assault forces to place fields of fire directly down an approaching column. The operations order placed the 635th Battalion on two small hills just south of the first curve in the road, positioned to bring maximum firepower on the roadbed. The regimental 75-mm recoilless rifle company was attached to the battalion with the mission of destroying ARVN tanks.

A second battalion, the 344th, was deployed along nearly two thousand meters of the western edge of the road, occupying three small hills that afforded fields of fire on the road. On the east side of the road was extremely rugged terrain into which the NVA hoped to drive the ARVN, dividing them into small packets that could be leisurely picked apart later. A third battalion, the 966th, was placed in a reserve position about two thousand meters due west of the ambush area. It was to be prepared to support either of the two engaged battalions or to attack any ARVN heliborne forces that might be airlanded to support the relief column. Accordingly, the regimental order had attached to the 966th the antiaircraft gun company, which was armed with 12.7-mm machine guns.

At first light on the morning of the 21st, Major Beckwith and Colonel William A. "Bulldog" McKean, commander of the Fifth Special Forces Group, climbed aboard a Huey from the 52nd Aviation Battalion at Camp Holloway and headed south to look for a landing zone for Beckwith's DELTA forces. They needed an LZ far enough away from the camp that it couldn't be taken under fire by the NVA, but not so far that the troops would be exhausted before they reached the action. They picked an area about five kilometers north of the camp. Enroute back to Holloway, an escorting gunship threw a rotor blade and crashed with all four crewmen. Back at Holloway, Beckwith mounted up his force in a mixed bag of helicopters—some slicks from the 52nd Aviation Battalion and H-34s from the Marine Corp's 363rd Medium Helicopter Squadron.

The airlift occurred without incident, and by 10:00 A.M., the fifteen Americans and one hundred fifty Vietnamese rangers were edging their way southward. The journey would take all day, and by nightfall the DELTA force was within earshot of the shooting. Believing that the risks of getting shot accidentally by the defenders outweighed the advantage of concealment from the enemy offered by the darkness, Beckwith decided to wait until daylight to make a dash for the gate.

Early on the morning of the 22nd, Beckwith radioed the camp that his force was coming in. From the cover of the jungle, they sprinted across the three hundred yards of open ground to the main gate. The NVA were either surprised or didn't care; the small-arms fire was desultory and relatively ineffective. One round smashed into the head of a radio newsman, Charles Burnett, of KTLA-TV in Los Angeles. A South Vietnamese lieutenant also was killed and five others lightly wounded during the dash. Now, truly, the Plei Me camp had been reinforced—a mere two days and three nights after the initial attack. Once inside the compound, Beckwith took charge and began reorganizing defenses.

That afternoon, on orders from Colonel McKean, who was high overhead in a command-and-control helicopter, the two ranger companies staged an assault on the northern slope which, by now, was the sector from which the heaviest fire was coming. The two companies barely cleared the gate when a battalion of the 33rd opened up from well-dug-in positions. Additionally, a heavy machine gun, with its crew chained to it, opened up from the flanks of the attacking rangers. The result was chaos. The rangers quickly became a disorganized mob and retreated in disorder through the gate back into camp, but not before fourteen men had been killed, including the American ranger advisor, Captain Thomas W. Pusser.

Despite the antiaircraft fires, several medevac choppers made their way into Plei Me to take out the seriously wounded. The wounded newsman was taken out and sent to the 8th Field Hospital in Nha Trang, where he later died. There were, incidentally, two other newsmen in the compound: Eddie Adams, an Associated Press photographer, who had been at Plei Me when the shooting started and was stuck there, and Joe Galloway, a reporter for United Press International, who sweet-talked a helicopter pilot buddy of his to give him a lift into the camp after the battle was underway. Beckwith claims he made both of them into corner bunker machine gunners.

Had the North Vietnamese intended to take out Plei Me, they could have accomplished it with relative ease, given the agonizingly slow response by the South Vietnamese authorities at Pleiku and the American advisory effort. By nightfall, October 22, the ATF finally had been reinforced and was ready at last to move south toward Plei Me. It was the Air Force that carried the load during those first four days. Running air support operations day and night, the fighter-bombers pounded NVA positions mercilessly, with over three hundred sorties. Most of the casualties sustained by the 33rd Regiment at Plei Me came from air-delivered ordnance. The NVA didn't take the pounding without resistance. Every sortie flew into a hailstorm of machine-gun and small-arms fire; two sky raiders were shot down. One pilot, Captain Mel Elliot, punched out just southwest of the camp and spent an uneasy two days holed up in the brush awaiting rescue. The other pilot, bailing out farther north, was rescued immediately. Despite the continuing bad weather, the camp received excellent airdrop support from the Air Force's 310th Air Commando Squadron (C-123) and the Army's 92nd Aviation Company (CV-2 Caribou). More than 333,000 pounds of badly needed ammunition, food, first aid supplies, and water were dropped by parachute, with only 9,000 pounds landing outside the wire. The cargo birds had to run the same gauntlet of antiaircraft fire that the fighter-bombers did, but they had to fly it a lot lower and slower. As a result, nineteen C-123s were hit by ground fire, seven so badly that they were scrapped. Two Caribous were similarly shot up.

At An Khe, Friday the 22nd was a day of frantic preparations. The order by General Larsen gave the 1st Cavalry an extremely limited mission: to move to Camp Holloway and assume the security role for Pleiku City and the ARVN II Corps headquarters. It took an extraordinary amount of lobbying on the part of Kinnard to get his forces leeway to even provide a reinforcing role to the ATF. Although Larsen's mission order asked only for a battalion, Kinnard was prepared to do far more. He ordered a battalion task force to move by air to Camp Holloway at first light on the 23rd. Kinnard and his staff smelled more than just a routine reinforcement in this operation. So concurrently he began extracting his 1st Brigade from its operations near Binh Khe, just east of An Khe across the Deo Mang Pass. Pleiku Province was, after all, the area assigned to the 1st Brigade; therefore, to Kinnard, it made sense to get the brigade, as a controlling headquarters, into a spring-loaded position in Pleiku City. The brigade was being commanded then by its deputy commander, Lieutenant Colonel Harlow Clark, whose boss, Colonel Elvy Roberts, had been evacuated for treatment of an injured leg. Preparations also were made to send a division Tactical Operations Center (TOC) to Pleiku, with Brigadier General Knowles to run the show.

The first element into Camp Holloway on Friday morning, the 21st, was Task Force INGRAM, composed of the 2nd Battalion, 12th Cavalry (2/12 Cav), commanded by Lieutanant Colonel Earl Ingram, a battery of the 2nd Battalion, 17th Artillery (2/17 Arty), an aerial gun section from the 1st Squadron, 9th Cavalry (1/9 Air Cav), two lift platoons from the 229th Assault Helicopter Battalion (229 AHB), and assorted supporting forces. The task force closed at Holloway at 1:00 P.M. on Friday. While that move was going on, Kinnard finally obtained permission from General Larsen to send the 1st Brigade to Pleiku. The Brigade, with its headquarters element, the 2nd Battalion, 8th Cavalry (2/8), and two firing batteries of the 2nd Battalion, 19th Artillery (2/19 Arty) extracted from Binh Khe by 3:00 P.M. Friday and closed by air at Camp Holloway by midnight, where it assumed operational control of Task Force INGRAM.

After setting up his field headquarters just outside the II Corps command in Pleiku City, Knowles was chomping at the bit. His instructions were extremely confining. Everything was predicated on the relief of Plei Me being entirely an ARVN show, so Knowles was told he was only to assist the ARVN if called on to do so, and then only after he received specific permission, first from Kinnard back in An Khe, then from Larsen in Nha Trang. Knowles called Kinnard and said, "Hey boss, communications being what they are, we have potential for problems with the setup the way it is. If you and Swede [General Larsen] don't have enough faith in me, then get someone up here who does." Knowles didn't have to work hard to convince Kinnard, who was a strong believer in delegating to subordinates. But Kinnard had to convince Larsen that Knowles needed to have the flexibility to operate. This was still very early in the active American involvement in the war, and senior commanders were generally tiptoeing their way into positions of dominance. So Knowles's orders were amended to read: "Assist the ARVN if called upon to do so, and seek permission if time and communications permit." Essentially, it was a carte blanche for Knowles.

On the morning of the 23rd, the ARVN relief force started down the road to Plei Me, albeit slowly and cautiously. At 2:00 P.M. the 22nd Ranger Battalion was helilifted to a landing zone about two and a half kilometers from the road at a point where the ARVN and American planners believed was the most likely spot for the ambush. The mission of the battalion was to attack to the east toward the Phu Me–Plei Me road, destroy any enemy forces found in the vicinity, and serve as a blocking force so that any enemy along the road would be caught between them and the attacking ATF. The LZ was less than two thousand meters from the ambush positions prepared by 635th Battalion. The NVA kept a wary eye on the rangers, but since they seemed indisposed to move off the LZ, Colonel Khan, the 32nd Regimental commander, decided to let them alone for the time being. He had bigger fish to fry. The official after-action report filed by Colonel Archie Hyle, the senior advisor for the 24th Tactical Zone, is strangely silent on the role the rangers played in the subsequent action.

The ATF moved without incident down the road until about 5:00 P.M., when it halted about two kilometers north of the S curve in the road. Bob Poos, a reporter for the Associated Press who was riding along on the lead tank with Lieutenant Colonel Luat, remembers that Luat was able to point to the exact point on the map where an ambush would take place. Preplanned air strikes were put in on suspected ambush positions and then the task force moved slowly forward. The trains portion of the column, protected by two companies of rangers, had been trailing the column by about two kilometers. For some reason, the transportation commander at the trains decided to start preparing the evening meal, apparently believing that the 5:00 P.M. halt concluded the day's march.

But at 5:50 P.M. the tanks and infantry support began moving again. The two NVA battalions, which had weathered the air strikes by staying in their ready positions, rushed forward to their ambush positions and within minutes were delivering a heavy volume of fire on the head of the column.

The NVA had every reason to expect the ARVN forces to panic when confronted with punishing fire; that had been the unfortunate pattern in so many similar cases throughout Vietnam. But this time they were in for a shock. The light tanks, mounting 76-mm cannons, wheeling left and right to face the attacking forces, fired canister and .50-caliber machine guns at the NVA positions, inflicting heavy casualties. The M-113 armored personnel carriers, rolled into fighting positions along the tanks, also delivered a heavy volume of machine-gun fire. Accompanying infantry maintained positions and provided suppressive small arms from the protection of the tanks and APCs. Overhead, F-100 jets delivered withering concentrations of rocket and cannon fire, along with napalm, while Army gunships placed rocket and machine-gun fire on mortar and recoilless rifle positions. Lieutenant Brady Thompson, an armor advisor, was in the lead tank talking by radio to the FACs and to the Army gunships. It was his accurate fire direction that enhanced the lethality of the supporting fires. For two hours the ferocious firefight raged, then it gradually began to slacken. And it was the NVA that first broke contact. Once again, the 32nd Regiment had been confronted with a superiority in numbers and in firepower; a single battalion, regardless of how well-disciplined and well-positioned, simply cannot carry the battlefield against a tough armored element. With a clear failure to achieve victory on the first assault, the 635th Battalion was pulled back to positions where it could deliver harassing fire on the column while Regiment made some decisions.

About five kilometers to the north, the trains were not as lucky. The advisor to the 21st Rangers, Captain Paul Leckinger, and his assistants had gone back to get the trains moving. While he was arguing with the ARVN transportation commander, the 344th opened up with recoilless rifles, 90-mm rockets, mortars, and a high volume of small-arms fire. Without the massive firepower of the tanks to deter the assault by the NVA, the thin-skinned vehicles of the trains were easy prey for the 344th's marksmen. Thunderous explosions rocked the area as the gasoline and ammo trucks detonated and columns of black smoke billowed up into the rapidly darkening sky. Many of the ARVN rangers, better known for their brawling in the Pleiku City bars and brothels than for a determined fight against a tough enemy, simply disappeared. Leckinger, whose radio had been knocked out, gathered enough of the ARVN warriors to put in a perimeter defense, using what was left of the vehicles as a part of a circle-the-wagons operation. Great concern for the safety of the trains was felt at the head of the column by Luat and his advisors, who now had coiled his force into a tight perimeter about a kilometer north of the original ambush site. The towering smoke columns were visible just before dark, and, without radio contact, advisors in the main column feared the worst.

Once again, the Air Force played a key role. It was dark now, but Captain Hank Lang, who was Leckinger's roommate at the II Corps compound, was one forward air controller who wouldn't give up. After putting in air strikes in support of the main column, Lang flew back up the road and spotted the twinkling of gun flashes in the darkness. He knew that there still was resistance and called in a strike by F-100s, who laid napalm on the NVA positions. The fighter-bombers used Lang's Bird Dog as a guide in the darkness as Lang flew with his landing lights on just over the NVA positions, drawing heavy antiaircraft fire as he did so. The air strikes broke the back of the assault by the 344th Battalion, even though some elements had briefly captured the two 105-mm howitzers, and it drew back south along the road.

That night, Colonel Khan tried once more to crack the relief column. He ordered the 966th Battalion, which had been in reserve during the firefights in the evening, to assault the armored column from the north. After making an approach march, the battalion split into three company-size columns and launched an attack at three o'clock in the morning on the 24th. Once again, the tankers in Luat's squadron poured canister at the attacking North Vietnamese, and again the casualties were heavy. With the concurrence of Field Front, Khan ordered the withdrawal of the 32nd Regiment, leaving only harassing parties to cover the withdrawal. By daylight, what was left of the three battalions had covered enough distance to be safe in the unlikely event the ARVN would probe toward the west. It was common knowledge that, following a violent firefight, the ARVN preferred to stay put and lick their wounds rather than aggressively follow up and exploit the situation. So the 32nd's commander felt quite secure.

As dawn broke over the split column, it was very clear that the ATF was going nowhere very soon. Although the main force had taken casualties, it had not lost any armored vehicles. The luckless trains had sustained the heavy damage. Destroyed by recoilless rifle and rocket fires were two M-8 armored cars, two five-ton ammo trucks, and two gas tankers. Heavily damaged were two more five-ton trucks, one M-8 armored car, one bulldozer, one lowboy carrier, two three-quarter-ton trucks, and two 105-mm howitzers. Astonishingly, none of the American advisors were hurt, and even the ARVN forces sustained only moderate casualties. Having lost most of the ammunition and fuel supplies, Luat elected to remain at the site until resupplied from Pleiku. Even then he and his subordinate officers really wanted to go back to Pleiku. The NVA had broken contact, but it was still ten kilometers to Plei Me, and the camp still was getting pressure. So, as far as the ARVN was concerned, there still were two NVA regiments between the relief column and Plei Me. The 22nd Ranger Battalion, which had been lying doggo on its LZ during the entire action, finally rejoined the column during the 24th. While the resupply column was making its way south to the relief column, senior American advisors were trying to persuade Luat to get the column moving as soon as possible. He was adamant that he would not move without adequate artillery support. This was the cue the Cav had been waiting for.

General Knowles was informed by Colonel Mataxis that the ARVN now desired direct American assistance—artillery support for the ATF. Knowles gave the mission to the 1st Brigade and by 8:30 A.M., B Company, 2/12 Cav, led an air assault into Objective FIELD GOAL, an open field just off the road, about nine kilometers north of ATF perimeter. The rest of the battalion followed, securing a perimeter for B Battery, 2/17 Arty. Knowles took care of getting artillery forward fire direction to the task force by putting an artillery liaison officer from the 1st Battalion, 77th Artillery, Captain John B. Avera, and his party, aboard a medevac chopper that was going in to the ATF perimeter to pull out casualties. The colonel in charge of the air ambulance company objected, claiming it was a violation of the Geneva Convention to use ambulances to haul combatants. Knowles dismissed the argument as irrelevant; too many Dust-Off birds had been shot at by the Vietcong and the NVA to worry about the niceties of international law. Avera and his party went in by medevac.

When it became apparent that Luat wasn't going to move his column on the 24th, Clark, the acting commander of the 1st Brigade, decided to move the artillery closer to the ARVN element, thus providing increased range down the road. At 4:00 P.M. the 2/12 Cav moved by road to FIELD GOAL SOUTH, which was only about three kilometers north of where the ATF was coiled. Concurrently, the A and C Companies of 2/8 Cav made an airmobile assault, seizing LZ SOUTH, and securing the position for B Battery, 2/19 Arty. This position was roughly halfway between Plei Me and the ATF, and from here, artillery could be used to support both.

This was the Cavalry's first real operation in the campaign, and on the surface it seemed to have gone off like clockwork.

Behind the scenes it was a different story. Virtually none of the participants had been exposed previously to combat operations in Vietnam. The brief activity of the Cav in early October had involved only three infantry battalions and a small part of the helicopter lift capability. General Knowles recalls that there were some tense moments about the selection of LZ SOUTH. First the battalion commander got spooked about landing out in the middle of nowhere. He kept telling Clark and Knowles that he needed more ammo, more water, more support, more this, more that. Finally, Knowles turned to Clark and said, "I don't care if we go in with only bayonets, we're going in on time. Can you handle this, or do you want me to?" Clark assured the general that he could handle it, and the battalion did okay once it got going. At the same meeting, the lift battalion commander said that the LZ was grossly inadequate. He recommended an alternate landing zone, but it would have taken the better part of a day for the troops to get to a position where the artillery could provide support. So Knowles took the commander in his own chopper, flew to the LZ, landed, and then turned to the lieutenant colonel and said, "Well, Colonel, do you think you can land in here?" It wasn't easy—the ground was all broken up—but the landing went off on schedule. Once the early jitters were calmed, the units began doing what they knew they could from the air assault days, and the NVA was about to face a foe for which they were completely unprepared.

With two batteries of artillery in position to support the ATF, senior advisors were confident that Luat would be moving early on October 25. Not so. The task force didn't start rolling until nearly 1:00 P.M., and then not until Captain Avera, the artillery forward observer, got in the lead tank and literally walked the artillery fire down the road in front of the advancing column. At around 3:00 P.M., the column received small-arms fire from the front. This was about five kilometers south of the original battle site. The Cavalry artillery and air strikes quickly suppressed the fire and the column moved on.

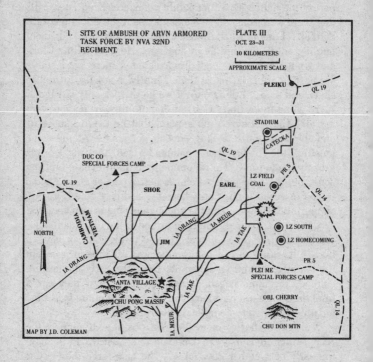

1. SITE OF AMBUSH OF ARVN ARMORED TASK FORCE BY NVA 32ND REGIMENT.

PLATE III

OCT. 23–31

10 KILOMETERS

APPROXIMATE SCALE

PLEIKU

QL 19

STADIUM

CATECKA

QL 19

DUC CO SPECIAL FORCES CAMP

LZ FIELD GOAL

PR 5

QL 14

SHOE

EARL

IA DRANG

IA MEUR

IA TAE

1

LZ SOUTH

LZ HOMECOMING

NORTH

CAMBODIA

VIETNAM

JIM

IA TAE

PLEI ME SPECIAL FORCES CAMP

PR 5

IA DRANG

IA TAE

IA MEUR

ANTA VILLAGE

CHU PONG MASSIF

OBJ. CHERRY

CHU DON MTN

QL 14

MAP BY J.D. COLEMAN

It was never learned whether the fire came from a stay-behind force from the 32nd Regiment or from local-force Vietcong from the villages that lay just to the west of the road. The task force reached Plei Me around dusk and coiled into a perimeter on the north side of the camp. It had taken the relief column six full days to travel thirty miles.

Meanwhile, to better support the advancing column and to provide close-in support of the camp itself, the First Brigade moved two batteries of the Second Battalion, Nineteenth Artillery, to Position HOMECOMING during the day. The new position was only seven klicks (kilometers) from the camp, and the artillery was soon delivering a heavy volume of fire in support of both the advancing task force and the Plei Me camp.

By October 25, it became evident to the 33rd's Regimental commander that his unit had taken more punishment than it could stand. Of the three battalion commanders, two had been killed and the other seriously wounded. Within the 2nd Battalion, the initial assault unit, nearly two hundred fifty men—just about half of the Battalion's strength—had been killed. The 1st and 3rd Battalions also had considerable losses, and the regimental mortar company was wrecked, with half of its personnel killed and five out of nine tubes smashed. Nearly all of the heavy antiaircraft machine guns had been blasted into scrap by the bombs, rockets, and, now, artillery fire. The meticulously prepared, carefully rehearsed plan of Field Front had crumbled. The NVA division ordered the regiment to withdraw to its Chu Pong base area. At 10:00 P.M. on the 25th, regimental headquarters ordered the withdrawal, leaving the 3rd Battalion as a rear guard.

Early on the 26th Lieutenant Colonel Luat was given the mission of conducting a sweep around the Plei Me camp. The task force moved out from its night position just north of the main gate and, hugging the wire, swept around the northwestern corner of the camp, heading toward the southern side of the triangle. Initially, the task force advanced in a two-column formation, with the tank company and the 22nd Rangers on the left and the APC troop, the 1st Battalion, 42nd Infantry, and the 21st Ranger battalion on the right. The columns moved without incident until the tracked vehicles hit some terrain that could not be negotiated. The columns then tried to turn around and retrace their path, but during the confusion of the turning movement, the 3rd Battalion of the 33rd Regiment pounced, opening up with machine guns, assault rifles, recoilless rifles, and B-40 rockets. For the better part of an hour, the NVA laced the hapless ARVN column with violent fires until the combined weight of artillery concentrations and air strikes broke the back of the attack. The ATF attacked back across the terrain and, when contact was broken by the NVA, limped back around the northwestern corner of the compound to set up a defensive perimeter where it had been the night before. The foray cost the task force twenty-seven killed and eighty wounded. On the NVA side the 3rd Battalion of the 33rd lost one hundred forty-eight killed and had five soldiers captured.

The smell of putrefying flesh permeated the very pores of the men who defended Plei Me. The ghastly odor hung over the camp like a pall and could be smelled in helicopters flying into the area. Even grizzled, battle-toughened sergeants in the Plei Me compound were retching as they loaded body bags on outbound helicopters. The constant bombardment had made a moonscape of the outside of the camp. It was on the scarred northern slope that the 2nd Battalion, Eighth Cavalry, made an airmobile assault at 10:00 A.M. on the 27th. The effect of the smell was immediate; the troopers were soon vomiting their guts out. Staff Sergeant Steve Coulson, a squad leader with the First Platoon of Bravo Company, the lead assault unit, remembers diving into a crater made by a five-hundred-pound bomb: "There were six or seven NVA bodies all tore up in there; it was god-awful." The battalion quickly moved on foot around both the eastern and western ends of the camp and toward what was known as Objective CHERRY, a 400-meter hill mass that lay two kilometers south of the Plei Me camp. The battalion faced only sporadic sniper fire in its movement, and the objective was secured with only one man killed and another wounded. The first casualty of the young campaign was Staff Sergeant Charles W. Rose of Company B, who was killed by a sniper after leading his squad up the hill and onto the objective. Rose and Captain Avera share the honor of having been the first cavalrymen to be honored with valor awards, both of them receiving Bronze Stars with "V" devices; Rose's, of course, being awarded posthumously.

It was clear now that the NVA forces that had staged the lure and the ambush, having failed in both aspects of their maneuver, had fled the battlefield. What was not known by American intelligence was where they had gone and what they would do next.

5

BEGINNING THE SEARCH

Two regiments of North Vietnamese had vanished from the battlefield and intelligence officers and commanders on every level of command from the 1st Brigade up to MACV were agonizing over several questions: What are the enemy's capabilities? Where is he located? What are his intentions? It was clear that the old policy of reaction was not going to work in this new ball game. On the afternoon of October 26, General Westmoreland made a momentous command decision, couching it in a phrase that made it one of the most unique mission orders in history.

When the First Cavalry Division entered the fray on the 23rd, it was strictly in support of the ARVN. Its overall mission still was reinforcement and reaction, nothing more. The artillery bases were given very small areas of operations (AO). For example, when Ingram's battalion (2/12 Cav) secured Objective FIELD GOAL, the AO was only three kilometers on either side of the base, just enough to provide local security. On the 26th, the area of operation was expanded slightly into an elongated slash covering the route the ARVN column was traveling to Plei Me and the terrain just south of the camp. This provided for artillery support and a cavalry screen in the immediate area of Plei Me. The importance of a formal AO cannot be overstated. Within the boundaries of a defined area of operations, a commander could do just about anything he wanted to accomplish his basic mission. But to go outside the boundaries required prior coordination with adjacent or higher command levels. And if the area outside the AO boundaries belonged to the ARVN, the coordination patterns got complicated and time-consuming.

That same morning, the 1st Brigade headquarters moved its forward command post (CP) location from Camp Holloway to LZ HOMECOMING to better coordinate the final actions around Plei Me. On the afternoon of the 26th, Generals Westmoreland, Larsen, Kinnard, and Knowles met for a conference at the 1st Brigade's command post, at LZ HOMECOMING. The meeting marked the turning point in the division's operation at Plei Me. Even with the limited intelligence available to allied officers at the time, it was apparent that the NVA effort at Plei Me had been something more than a routine baptism-of-fire operation for a newly infiltrated unit. In the conference between Westmoreland and the division officers, Kinnard hammered on the theme that U.S. forces must now do more than merely contain the enemy or simply reinforce the ARVN. The NVA, he felt, must be sought out aggressively and destroyed. Of course, as far as Westy was concerned, Kinnard was singing to the choir; Westmoreland long had yearned for the opportunity to go on the offensive. Kinnard and Knowles also spent considerable time at the conference explaining to Westmoreland and Larsen exactly what the division could do and how well it could do it. Westmoreland eventually turned to Larsen and said: "Give Kinnard his head."

It was the opening Kinnard had been waiting for. In a twinkling, the division's scope of operations changed from one of reinforcement and reaction to one of unlimited offense. It was released from a small, confining zone of operations and provided a tactical area of operations that covered nearly twenty-five hundred square kilometers: the entire vast sweep of terrain from Route 14 on the east to the Cambodian border on the west, and from Highway 19 on the north to the province boundary on the south—nearly one-half of Pleiku Province. The division was given the mission of searching out, fixing, and destroying enemy forces that provided a threat to Plei Me, Pleiku, and the entire central highlands. The 1st Brigade was given the divisional mission.

Its concept was to conduct an intensive search for the enemy, looking everywhere—in the villages, in the jungles, and along stream beds. By widespread dispersion, made possible by excellent communications and helicopter lift, the brigade was to sweep large areas systematically. Each battalion was to be deployed with supporting artillery and then was to further disperse its companies. Vigorous and intensive patrolling from company bases was to be conducted. When contact was established, a rapid reaction force was to be assembled swiftly and lifted by helicopters to close with the enemy. The immediate artillery strike capability would be provided by the unique aerial rocket artillery batteries, along with prepositioned tube artillery. If fire support reinforcement was needed, it could be provided by additional batteries of tube artillery, moved rapidly into position by medium-lift helicopters. The tactical fire support plan included extensive use of Air Force tactical air strikes.

This concept now seems so elemental and commonplace; but in October 1965 it was revolutionary. No one had tried it before. This was to be airmobility's acid test. The next month would reveal whether three years of planning and testing would bear the fruits of victory—for a concept and for a division.

To better understand just how revolutionary this methodology was, it is necessary first to recall that all previous wars fought by the United States had been so-called "conventional" wars. In conventional warfare, there is a clearly delineated front line, held by infantry and accompanied by forward observers from the artillery. In theory, everything behind those front lines was friendly territory. Artillery was based where it could mass fires in support of the infantry, and security of the artillery was of minimal concern. Behind the artillery was a layering of support elements, as well as a layering of various higher headquarters—regiment, division, corps, and army. Finding the enemy was generally no problem. Somewhere in front of the forward edge of the battle area he could be found, usually in force. Advances were measured in yards and miles and in point objectives—Hill 519, the town of Avranches, Bloody Ridge, and so on.

The situation in Vietnam, though, differed from the conventional in almost every respect. There was no constant front line; the enemy was elusive and mobile and rarely presented himself in sufficient force where massed fires of artillery and air would be effective; success was measured not in terrain objectives but in the mathematics of attrition. Thus, the infamous "body counts" along with weapons counts and calculations of meters of trench line destroyed, bunkers busted, supplies captured, and any other means of conventional measuring of military success in an unconventional war. The French had had a very conventional war background. Their response to the Vietminh threat was to place a lot of little *beau geste* forts on a string along roadways and man them with a small detachment of infantry and two artillery pieces. This then set up the oft-repeated and highly successful Vietminh tactic of lure and ambush. Despite the obvious bankruptcy of the French tactics, the South Vietnamese Army had tended to copy them, with predictable results. Even the presence of American advisors and the infusion of American arms and equipment had not done a great deal to alter the French mindset of the South Vietnamese Army.

So for the North Vietnamese, nothing that had happened thus far was much out of the ordinary, although they had not anticipated the fury of the air strikes at Plei Me. The NVA had no way of knowing that Westmoreland had thrown down the gauntlet at Plei Me—that he had told his Air Division commander at Tan Son Nhut not to spare any airplanes in making sure that Plei Me remained in friendly hands. The NVA planners also were startled that the ARVN would beef up the armored relief column, and certainly they were surprised that it fought as well as it did at the point of ambush. But the ARVN reacted just as anticipated once the attack was broken off. The presence of American artillery that close to the road was not much out of the ordinary, either. So, once contact was broken and the movement of the regiments started west across the roadless jungle and savannah toward Cambodia, the NVA were confident that there was nothing more to fear.

On the 28th, the 1st Brigade was given another infantry battalion, the 1st of the 12th, commanded by Lieutenant Colonel Robert Shoemaker. This gave the brigade three infantry battalions, reinforced by an artillery battalion with three firing batteries, as well as a battery of the 2nd Battalion, 20th Artillery (the aerial rocket artillery battalion). Although the Pleiku Campaign was considered a division operation for the 1st Cavalry, at no time during the thirty-five days of the campaign were more than one brigade or four infantry battalions deployed into the western plateau. Any deployed brigade also had a proportionate slice of the division support—a company of the engineer battalion, a piece of the division signal battalion, and a composite group from the division's support command, consisting of supply, ground, and aviation maintenance and medical support. The brigade also might have attached to it a part of the aviation support. At the outset, the 1st Brigade was allocated two lift companies from the 227th Assault Helicopter Battalion, each company consisting of four D-model Huey platoons of four birds each and an attached B-model gunship company for lift escort. The gunships, or "hogs," were armed with the XM-16 system, which consisted of four 7.62-mm M-60-type machine guns and two 2.75-inch, 7-tube rocket launchers mounted on each side of the ship. The brigade also was given one company of the medium lift Chinook battalion.

Later, as the command and control procedures were smoothed out, many of the division assets such as aviation units and the cavalry squadron were controlled by the division's forward tactical operations center and parceled out to the committed brigade on a mission-by-mission basis. This had the effect of relieving the brigade commander of the chore of trying to provide administrative support for these attached units and gave the division better control of precious assets. This particularly became important later in the campaign, when the amount of flying time of aviators and blade time of aircraft had to be monitored very carefully. The same concept was generally true for the air cavalry squadron. At the outset of the campaign, its troops were attached to the 1st Brigade, but eventually it worked under divisional control.

The 227th Assault Helicopter Battalion (AHB) deployed forward from the An Khe golf course pads to a newly created laager area located in a broad, open field about halfway between Camp Holloway and New Pleiku Air Base. The purpose of creating the base area was to relieve the pressure on Camp Holloway, which rapidly was becoming the division's forward logistical base in addition to housing the II Corps advisory aviation assets, and simply had no room for an extra hundred helicopters of all shapes and descriptions. Some wag in the battalion, a veteran of the Air Assault II days in the Carolinas, nicknamed the place the "turkey farm" and the name stuck. At its center, wallowing in earthen revetments like fat, contented sows, were the five thousand gallon bladders that contained the lifeblood of the Cav, the fluids (JP-4 and Avgas) that fueled its helicopters. The refueling area surrounded the bladders, and around those were arranged the landing pads for the helicopters. From the air it did indeed resemble a poultry farm. The big bladders were supplied by tankers, when convoys were able to get through from the coast. Otherwise, they were filled by emptying the five hundred gallon blivets that were air-transported in. The blivet, which resembled a very fat, wide truck tire with a narrow hub, was a development of the air assault test days. The hub had clevises on both sides to permit sling-loading. The hub also served the same purpose as a truck tire hub, allowing the blivet to be towed around the ground for limited distances. And when the containers were empty, they collapsed under their own weight, so half a dozen of them could be hooked together in one Chinook sling load. The blivets also were airlifted to forward refueling sites, thus keeping the cavalry's birds from flying their blades off just to tank up.

During the early stages of the operation, General Knowles had operated out of his command-and-control chopper, carrying with him a skeleton staff of operations and intelligence officers. With the new mission, the division placed a complete forward tactical operations center (TOC) adjacent to the II Corps headquarters in Pleiku City. This TOC consisted of a specially outfitted "people pod" that the CH-54 Flying Crane could lift and detach at designated locations. The pod was about eight feet high, ten feet wide, and thirty feet long—an air-portable mobile home. It had desks, radios, map table, and even a mini-conference room where the tactical commander could confer with key staff officers or subordinate commanders. Power to light, heat, or air condition the pod was provided by a diesel generator placed in an earth revetment some distance from the pod.

Forward elements of other divisional organizations also deployed forward, co-locating either at II Corps with the divisional TOC Forward or at Camp Holloway, which was to be the division's forward logistical base. To handle the expected press load, a public information officer captain with two enlisted information specialists and a three-quarter-ton truck, set up a small press center tent a few yards from the DTOC, and used the vehicle to transport correspondents from Camp Holloway or New Pleiku to the press center, or vice-versa.

The division also had been given control of the 17th Aviation Company, a Caribou company, to provide logistical lift from either the An Khe base or from Quin Nhon, where the Army's logistics command had a supply, maintenance, and medical operation. A couple of the 17th's birds had been rigged as aerial radio relay stations and had been boring holes in the sky, relaying radio traffic between Plei Me and Pleiku City from about the second day of the battle. The same radio relay also worked for communications between An Khe and the operational area. The one thousand-meter-high mountain range between the Cav's divisional headquarters and the western plateau effectively blocked normal FM traffic.

The people manning the division's forward control element moved into the MACV advisory compound at II Corps headquarters, causing a doubling-up in the dormitory rooms to accommodate the newcomers. This was not always done with good grace; many of the First Teamers tended to take the attitude that the Cavalry had come to the rescue of the advisors, while the advisors felt that a quiet little war had been unnecessarily heated up because of the 1st Cavalry. A lot of the American advisory people didn't have a clue about the size of the NVA elements operating out in the valley, and they were convinced that the whole operation had been staged to give the 1st Cavalry an introductory showcase. One advisor was heard to grumble to another at the bar that "it was a nice war until the Americans came in."

Colonel Clark, now armed with a new mission but still only sketchy intelligence, immediately deployed the 1/12 Cav into four locations about twenty-five kilometers due west of the original ambush site. Clark hoped that remnants of the NVA force that had ambushed the armored task force would still be located east of the area where he inserted three rifle companies and the headquarters and fire support elements of the battalion. There was no contact at any of the landing zones and the companies settled in for the night of October 28 without incident.

That same day, Clark realized that he could not set up a permanent brigade command post at HOMECOMING, and moved to a location he called STADIUM. It was located adjacent to the sprawling Catecka tea plantation, which lay astride Route 19, just five kilometers west of its junction with Route 14. The highway was surfaced all the way to Pleiku City, a distance of some fifteen kilometers, and fairly easily secured by aggressive patrolling action along the roadway. This allowed logistical support of the brigade base by road and eased the requirements for aerial resupply. Additionally, the supporting engineers began carving out a dirt strip that would accommodate the Caribous and the Air Force C-123 Provider.

During the same day, there was a shuffling of the two battalions around the Plei Me camp, as the fragmented command lines that had occurred during the past three days got sorted out. The 2/12 Cav got all its units back under its control and, along with B Battery, 2/17 Arty, set up at an LZ named PUNT about seven kilometers north of the Plei Me camp. The 2/8 Cav did the same thing at HOMECOMING with two batteries of the 2/19 Arty.

All three air troops of the 1st Squadron, 9th Cavalry began conducting aggressive aerial reconnaissance and surveillance west, south, and east of the Plei Me camp; allied intelligence had no way of knowing which way the NVA forces went after they broke contact at the camp. Flying H-13 helicopters, the glass-bubbled helicopter that really looked like a dragon fly, the scouts began making sporadic contacts late in the day west of the camp. The scout pilots (the White team), flying right on the deck and nosing their choppers into the edges of clearings to check on trails and possible camouflaged positions, were protected by the troop's B-model gunships (the Red team), which flew low orbits over the scouts. It was the beginning of what the scout pilots, a swashbuckling lot, called "recon by decoy." If the NVA nibbled at the bait and opened fire at the scout, immediately the enemy would be hit by machine-gun and rocket fire from the overwatching gunships. Then, if the contact appeared promising—something more than an isolated NVA straggler—then the troop's aerial rifle platoon (the Blue team) would be inserted to develop the situation. The high degree of mobility of the squadron's troops meant that broad sweeps of terrain could be scouted rapidly for signs of enemy movement. At night, the rifle platoons would establish a patrol base and set up night ambushes.

On October 29, Clark and his operations people established battalion areas of operations within that of the division's AO. These were fairly large chunks of real estate, averaging 120 square kilometers. Each area was given a code name—SHOE, JIM, and EARL, after the commanders of the three battalions. Two of the areas, SHOE and EARL, contained a number of small villages, most of which were connected by road or trail to Route 19, which lay just to the north of the areas of operation. This early in the operation, the division and brigade intelligence officers just didn't have much of a feel for the nature of the enemy. Although it was becoming clear that the enemy included regular army forces from the north, commanded by a divisional-type headquarters, there was still a feeling that the enemy would behave more like the Vietcong would in a similar situation. Since so many of the VC main force units were manned by NVA regulars who had been sent south in company-size packets, it was entirely within the parameters of the commanders' knowledge to anticipate similar behavior. This is why the small villages to the north and west of the ambush site and Plei Me looked promising. There was an assumption that the enemy would seek support and sanctuary in an area that could provide those services. Not until later in the campaign would allied intelligence realize that the NVA units were totally self-contained organizations supplied from well-stocked bases in Cambodia. The two regiments of the Field Front neither needed nor desired any contact with indigenous populations.

So October 29 passes uneventfully for the infantry units; they were operating too far north to concern the NVA 33rd Regiment, which withdrew from Plei Me in a generally southwesterly direction toward its forward assembly area, about fifteen kilometers west and south of the camp. At least two battalions of the 32nd Regiment had already passed through the area where the American infantry now was conducting searches and were safely back in sanctuary on the northern bank of the Ia Drang just east of the Cambodian border. The exact location of the third battalion, which had the stay-behind mission at the ambush site, remains a mystery to this day. From available evidence, it appears that, following some brief but sharp clashes with infantry units about fourteen kilometers west of the ambush area, it was given a mission of moving north and west to link up with local-force Vietcong and work on the interdiction of Route 19 between the Duc Co Special Forces camp and Pleiku City.

In one of those clashes, Captain Eugene Fox's Alpha Company, 2nd Battalion, 12th Cavalry, landed right in the middle of a small-weapons and food cache, and was immediately engaged by an estimated reinforced platoon of NVA that had been guarding the site. The firefight lasted less than thirty minutes, then the surprised survivors of the platoon took to their heels and disappeared into the jungles to the west. The NVA left sixteen dead on the battlefield and sustained another dozen or so wounded. Moreover, eight soldiers were captured along with fifteen hundred pounds of rice, individual clothing and equipment, nine AK-47s, and a supply of hand grenades and ammunition. The Cav rifle company sustained only one man wounded, who was medevaced back to Camp Holloway. It was the division's first significant contact. Interrogation of the prisoners later revealed that the cache was located near the site of the forward battle headquarters of Field Front.

But while most of the infantry was flailing fruitlessly about in the jungle, the Cavalry squadron was finding juicier targets along the 33rd Regiment's route of withdrawal. Lieutenant Colonel John Stockton had moved the three air troops of his squadron to the 1st Brigade base at STADIUM. Basing his helicopters out of STADIUM rather than Camp Holloway or the Turkey Farm cut down on blade time; the choppers were in an operational area virtually from the moment they cleared the brigade base. The squadron's ground troop, using jeeps mounted with M-60 machine guns and 106-mm recoilless rifles, conducted roadrunner activities to keep the ground lines of communication open on Highway 19 near An Khe. Several Red and White teams from the squadron remained in An Khe to provide support for the division base as well as support the division forces keeping the two main passes on Highway 19—Deo Mang and Mang Yang—clear of insurgent threats. The division also needed support for the one battalion it had conducting pacification operations in the neighboring Vinh Than Valley.

All during the day of October 30, Cavalry scouts spotted enemy elements, many of whom seemed to think their camouflage was sufficient. The scout birds or their gunship backups fired into positions, often causing individuals to break and run or to return fire, which was generally ineffective and usually fatal for the man on the ground. The NVA was beginning to learn a fact that would become so apparent during the course of the war—that the armed helicopter was an incredibly lethal weapon against an infantryman in the open. When the gunship rolled in hot, it fired bursts from its machine guns on its first firing run. Pulling up sharply in a steep bank in a sort of sideways skidding motion, it then presented one or the other of its door gunners a clear shot at the target, until the chopper rolled back in on another firing run. The two door gunners (one was the crew chief) fired M-60 machine guns slung by heavy elastic cords from the roof of the Huey. If there were more than two or three men on the ground, the gunship would fire off a couple of rockets. The survivability of the men on the ground was almost nil. And attempts to fire effectively on the attacking aircraft resulted in surprisingly few hits; the helicopter is a lot harder to hit than its size and bulk might seem to indicate. There was no way that the Cav pilots and gunners could accurately assess casualties; no one landed to count bodies. But it was obvious that the enemy was being kept stirred up and was forced to stay on the move.

Each night, the Blues would be placed in ambush positions at likely avenues of retreat. All but one of the ambush positions were dry holes. And that one misfired simply because the patrol leader was worried about the size of the enemy force that was moving down the trail and never pulled the trigger. The next morning, at the squadron's base, Stockton was relaying the information to Knowles and Kinnard and was nearly handed his head. Stockton reportedly defended his patrol leader by saying, "It was scary out there." Knowles responded, "Of course it was scary, Colonel. We're fighting a war here." Knowles says Kinnard was ready to fire Stockton on the spot. Despite his gentle demeanor, Kinnard was a tiger in combat and believed that contact must be aggressively sought and, once gained, maintained at all costs. He felt that Stockton had been too timid and that somehow this had been communicated to his troops. Knowles remembers that he intervened on Stockton's behalf, an action he says he later regretted. A visibly shaken Stockton got the word to his troop commanders: aggressively seek, obtain, and maintain contact.

Contact. A simple word, but its meaning speaks volumes. In a war with an elusive enemy, where success was measured by sheer attrition, contact, to paraphrase a famous coach, not only was everything, it was the only thing. It was of vital importance to the commander. It also scared hell out of the man on the ground. A good indication of how the trooper felt about it was the graffiti seen on a helmet cover, the billboard upon which each soldier proclaimed his individuality. On this particular helmet was inscribed: "War is hell, but contact is a mother fucker."

The techniques for gaining contact by an infantry unit were different from those employed by the Cavalry squadron. Generally, it involved moving an infantry company by air into a target location. The planners for the operation tried to select a landing zone as close to a suspected enemy location as possible, to keep the troops from having to expend excess energy threshing through the bush on foot. If the location of the enemy was unknown, then the infantry companies would be inserted and given a search route to maximize the coverage of a given area. Every company commander was keenly aware that his unit could become a division reserve unit on a moment's notice. Kinnard disliked putting a large unit on reserve status, feeling it was a waste of personnel assets. Instead, because of the enormous mobility of the division, his concept was that every unit not in actual contact could be pulled from its position by helicopter and thrown into battle wherever the massing of force would be decisive. Accordingly, every day, each company commander was required to file with his battalion operations officer a "thunderbolt" plan, providing information on the number of Hueys it would require to lift each of the platoons and the locations from which each platoon could best be extracted. Every leader, from squad to battalion, constantly had to think about the air movement phase of operations; spotting landing and pickup zone locations was paramount with every map and aerial reconnaissance.

To further simplify the operation, Kinnard suspended the usual changing of radio call signs. Signal Corps types strongly recommended that the division's SOI (Signal Operating Instructions), which assigned call signals and frequencies, be changed once a week. This would preclude the enemy's monitoring radios and obtaining valuable intelligence. Knowing that he ran a risk of intercepts, Kinnard nevertheless kept the old air assault call signs and frequencies in operation because it would enable every tactical unit to be completely familiar with all others in the AO. Aviation units could check into the infantry and artillery nets without confusion. Overall, the divisional reaction time was enhanced.

The importance of being able to check into the artillery

nets was extremely important to the aviators. On a linear battlefield, there were well-established air corridors for aircraft flying to and from the front lines. In the Cav's AO, where artillery bases were scattered around, the fires could come from any direction, and with helicopters bouncing around the landscape like clouds of grasshoppers, close and continuous coordination between fire support and aviation units was mandatory.

Nor was the helicopter's use limited to tactical work. Kinnard believed that the morale of the troops and, hence, their fighting potential would be enhanced by keeping them well supplied. Accordingly, whenever possible, infantry companies would set up night positions at around 4:30 P.M. and await the arrival of the "log bird," the logistics helicopter that would carry in the hot evening meal, ammunition, changes of clothing, and that all-important morale booster, mail. In retrospect, it may seem that the practice was hideously wasteful of helicopter assets, but Kinnard justified it on the basis of morale and the efficiency of the infantry unit.

The 1st Cavalry was deployed with the heavy twill fatigue uniforms of stateside duty; no lightweight jungle fatigues would be available in quantity until December. Yet the profile of the infantry soldier most familiar in the United States from the Vietnam era is the man bent over under a bulky rucksack. The term grunt, widely used to describe the infantryman in Vietnam, is said to have originated by the sound the man made when he swung the sixty-pound ruck onto his back. But the rucksack hadn't been introduced into the army inventory in 1965. Instead, the infantryman wore the web gear and loadbearing equipment designed for another kind of war— one in which he would shed everything but a weapon and ammunition before a fight. Obviously, in the jungle, that course of action was impractical. Without a method of comfortably carrying a two- or three-day resupply of food and ammunition, the daily logging flights were the best alternative.

The 1st Cavalry pioneered the concept of the artillery fire base. The assault battalion would first seize an area that could be used as an artillery fire base so that the tube artillery could, in turn, give the infantry artillery support during its phase of the operations. Later in the war, the fire base became so institutionalized that they almost became little *beau geste* forts, with all of their vulnerabilities. But under Kinnard, the artillery bases moved regularly. His philosophy was that if they never stayed in one place for more than forty-eight hours, then a foot-mobile enemy would be hard-put to even locate one, much less mass a significant force against it. Therefore, the security requirements were minimal—never more than an infantry company, sometimes less. Usually, the maneuver battalion headquarters would be co-located with the artillery battery, and the headquarters personnel would be used for base security. It was the beginning of a symbiotic relationship between infantry and artillery, each depending on the other for support.

All three of the 1st Cavalry's organic artillery battalions were armed with the new M-102 howitzer, while the attached battalion, 2/17 Arty, had the M-101A1. The M-101 fired a 105-mm, thirty-five pound shell 13,478 meters, while the M-102, with a slightly longer barrel, fired the same shell 13,752 meters. The M-102 was the ideal weapon for airmobile operations. Despite being low-set, which made loading more difficult than with the M-101, the M-102 weighed a ton less than the older model, making it easier to manhandle, to tow, and to airlift. It had a closed trail firing platform which easily permitted it to be swung into firing positions in a full circle. The old model could only be traversed twenty-three degrees right or left before it was necessary to manhandle the trail spades out of the ground and swing the tube around to the new direction. Additionally, the M-102 could fire at a higher angle, a decided advantage when shooting out of jungle clearings. A six-tube battery usually set up with five guns in a star pattern, with the sixth in the center, to act as the base howitzer for registration as well as to be able to fire illumination rounds during night fire missions.

When Kinnard first began using the artillery fire base, he was apprehensive that the installation of the base might tend to telegraph the main punch, but very soon he appreciated the value of the feint. In fact, Kinnard also started using helicopters to make false insertions of troops to keep the enemy off balance. Later in the campaign, as the NVA became more familiar with the air assault methodology, these false insertions did, in fact, cause the enemy to beat its way through a lot of jungle in a fruitless search for American infantry. But on October 31, the NVA was more intent on getting back to base areas than on batting at the cavalry hornets. The second real contact by the infantry occurred at 7:10 A.M. on the 31st, when a platoon of A 2/12 Cav, out at a platoon ambush site about two kilometers southwest of where the company had fought its way into a cache the previous day, engaged a North Vietnamese force of about platoon size. A brief but sharp firefight ensued, and the American platoon, aided by two 9th Cavalry gunships, killed a half dozen NVA soldiers before the enemy broke contact and faded away into the jungle. The platoon captured a couple of NVA weapons and some hand grenades. One sky trooper died in the fight.

Further to the south, the 9th Cavalry squadron scout and gun teams were making life miserable for the retreating 33rd Regiment. There were numerous contacts throughout the day, and on several occasions the Blues were inserted, but ground contact was never made. The effect on the 33rd was to continue the fragmentation of an already badly fragmented unit. Companies got split into platoons, platoons into squads, and squads into individuals who tried to evade the helicopters. Contributing to the problems of the 33rd was the acute shortage of food and medicine caused by the inability of units to reach their prestocked supply caches.

Meanwhile, the infantry units were making a number of air assaults throughout the search area. In Search Area JIM, which was the responsibility of the 2/8 Cav, two batteries of artillery were lifted into LZ CON, a position from which they could provide support to both the 2/8 and 1/12 Cav infantry elements, which now were operating totally within their search areas. LZ's PUNT and HOMECOMING were closed, and with them went the last vestiges of Cav support to the Plei Me camp.

The unprecedented use of helicopters as part of the ground scheme of a maneuver began taking its toll on available aviation fuel at Camp Holloway. Under the 1st Cavalry's concept of operations, its helicopters and attached fixed-wing aircraft would be used in "retailing" supplies to front-line units. "Wholesaling" would be the responsibility of the Army's logistical command, using either the ground line of communication and supply, Route 19 from Qui Nhon to Pleiku, or air lines of communication, Air Force C-123 and C-130 aircraft from several logistics bases in Vietnam. The Cav was at the end of the longest logistical pipeline the Army had ever maintained, and it broke down quickly under the strain of the division's operations.

Brigadier General Jack Wright, the assistant division commander for support, who had the responsibility of keeping logistical monkeys off the backs of tactical commanders, ran into a problem not far into the 1st Brigade's operations. The logistics people still were not confident enough in the security of Highway 19 to risk putting fuel tankers in a convoy from Qui Nhon to Pleiku. The memory of the fate of the French Groupement Mobile 100 on Highway 19 just west of An Khe in 1954 still haunted many commanders. So it remained for the Air Force to fly in the blivets of JP-4 and Avgas, as well as the beans and the bullets and the mail. And the Air Force flew only when it was asked to do so by MACV in Saigon. As the battle developed and the supply of fuel dwindled, Wright and Knowles tried to compensate by having the attached Caribous of the 17th Aviation Battalion fly supply missions to Qui Nhon, and even by having the Chinooks sling-load JP-4 blivets and haul them down to the brigade base from Camp Holloway. The division was literally flying the wings and rotors off its aircraft in its attempt to do both the wholesaling and the retailing. Resupplies of fuel and artillery rounds, both high-weight, high-volume items, particularly took their toll. And the division was steadily losing ground.

Finally it got to the point where the stockage levels were such that there was just enough fuel to bring all of the troops back from their deployed positions. So Knowles called Kinnard in An Khe and Swede Larsen in Nha Trang and gave them the situation. He asked for and got permission to make a strong case with the head of the Army's Support Command in Saigon, Brigadier General John Norton. Knowles said that everybody seemed to be working on the problem, but no one seemed to have a handle on the criticality of the Cav's supply situation. Apparently, Norton was sympathetic but told Knowles there was nothing he could do. So Knowles came right to the point: "Sometime tonight, probably about 12 o'clock, I'm going to get to the point where I ain't got any more JP-4. What I am going to do then is shut down this operation." Knowles went on to tell Norton that he would lift out all of the troops he could with the fuel available, abandon the equipment they could not carry, and walk back to Pleiku with those that couldn't be lifted. Norton was aghast. "You're joking," he said. "You can't do that." "I'm dead serious," Knowles replied. "American lives are at stake." And he hung up.

Knowles said he doesn't know who Norton talked to after that—maybe it was Westmoreland—but he got things rolling. Within hours, the first of a stream of C-130s arrived at New Pleiku and the JP-4 blivets rolled off. Thereafter, the Air Force maintained a steady flow of birds into New Pleiku. There still were some problems to be ironed out, however. At the logistics bases in Saigon, Cam Ranh Bay, and Qui Nhon, Air Force personnel initially loaded supplies onto 463L pallets, which were too big for the division's load-handling equipment. This required a double handling of supplies, a problem compounded by the need to transport everything by ground from New Pleiku to Camp Holloway, a distance of seven miles. Since the 1st Cavalry had very few ground vehicles, Knowles negotiated the use of the ARVN and Navy leased trucks to handle the logistical flow. Later in the campaign, the Air Force began loading smaller, four-by-four pallets on top of the larger pallets, which eased the unloading problems in the operational area. This was particularly true of flights that went in directly to the 1st Brigade's forward base at the Cateka tea plantation. The further forward the fixed-wing aircraft could fly, the fewer the hours the rotary-wing aircraft would have to expend to keep the logistics pipeline open.

Everything was in readiness. The logistical base was set; the infantry was spoiling for a fight, and the cavalry squadron was buzzing around the area of operation like a swarm of bees. But on the night of October 31, the big question in brigade and division headquarters was: where were the North Vietnamese—not the stragglers and poor lost souls that ran afoul of the Cav's gunships, but the company- and battalion-strength units?

6

CAPTURING
THE HOSPITAL

Strangely enough, at that same time, the commander and political cadre of the 33rd Regiment had the same question as the Cavalry commanders: where are the units? By November 1, the headquarters elements of the 33rd Regiment had closed in on ANTA Village, the NVA code word for the regimental base area, located in a copse of hardwoods and waist-high plateau grass at the foot of the easternmost projection of the Chu Pong Massif. The regimental headquarters, which had left the Plei Me area first, had a relatively uneventful route march, even though it had to dodge Cavalry scout helicopters from time to time and part of its trip was made under cover of darkness. The rest of the regiment was scattered across twenty-five kilometers of jungle between Chu Pong and the Plei Me camp, and the journey of the surviving members of the three battalions that had assaulted the Plei Me camp was anything but uneventful. And none of the North Vietnamese elements had any problem recognizing where their enemy was located.

The 2nd Battalion, the one that had been the most badly mauled at Plei Me, was a short day's march behind regimental headquarters. But, as with the regimental mortar and anti-aircraft companies, it had been scattered badly by the constant threat of air attacks. Not only were the cavalry helicopters a danger in themselves, but they also seemed to be bringing in heavier attacks by Air Force fighter-bombers.

Actually, the success of the air strikes on the retreating NVA forces was the result of a closely coordinated targeting system directed out of the division's forward tactical operations center in Pleiku. The forward DTOC received direct reports from the aerial surveillance and target acquisition platoon, flying OV-1 Mohawks fitted with either infrared detectors or side-looking airborne radar. All additional available intelligence, including radio intercept reports, special agent reports filtered up through the ARVN and Special Forces channels, and spot reports from the air cavalry squadron, were evaluated, and information on any confirmed target in the vicinity of the maneuver elements was passed on to the controlling brigade headquarters. The brigade then reacted by maneuvering forces to engage the target, firing artillery, or directing supporting tactical air strikes, or by any combination of these actions.

If a target was not an immediate threat to the maneuver elements, the forward DTOC recorded the target for strike by already airborne close air-support aircraft that were about to run out of stay-time over the maneuver area. If within range, the target was also scheduled for harassing and interdiction artillery fires. Working together within the forward DTOC on secondary targeting were the division's G-3 air and G-2 air, the division artillery fire coordination officer, and the U.S. Air Force Air Liaison Officer (ALO). The ALO, Lieutenant Colonel John B. Stoner, headed the USAF Forward Air Controller team of forty-three officers and men, the largest then assigned to any Army division.

The accuracy of the strikes was unnerving to regimental cadres; the doctrine they had assimilated in schools and training in the north did not include the potential of incessant air bombardment in areas that ostensibly were safe and secure. So accurate were the strikes that soon after arrival at

ANTA Village, the regimental cadres called a meeting to determine how the Americans could make such repeated, accurate air strikes. It was concluded that the only explanation was that there were spies within the ranks that were furnishing the Americans the locations and movements of the regiment's elements.

But if the tactical air and Army gunship strikes were vexing to the cadres, they were nightmarish to the rank and file soldier. The soldiers being encountered by the 1st Cavalry were, by and large, young enlistees who had been in the Army less than two years. They were superbly trained in straight infantry tactics, and in the refresher courses they took before heading down the infiltration trail they learned guerrilla survival techniques. They also were conversant with air power, and were better than average in the art of camouflage and concealment from air spotters. But nothing in their background and training had prepared them for the type of punishment they already had taken at the hands of the fighter-bombers and for the hourly terror they were experiencing on the long trek back to the supposedly safe base area. Neither did they, or their commanders for that matter, have any experience with real airmobility. True, helicopters had been used in South Vietnam for air assaults since 1963, but the ARVN, which controlled the tactics of assault, were conservative and utterly predictable. The ARVN favored large landing zones that permitted them to insert at least a company-size force simultaneously. The concept of using only a single-ship LZ to assault and reinforce was unheard of.

On the evening of October 31, the remnants of the 1st Battalion, 33rd Regiment, reached the vicinity of the regimental aid station, about twelve kilometers west and slightly south of the Plei Me camp. The battalion had sustained nearly 40 percent casualties at Plei Me camp and probably had no more than 250 effective fighters by the time it reached the hospital. The hospital area was located on a small stream, a tributary of the larger Tae River which flowed lazily south and west toward Cambodia. The battalion occupied fighting positions that had been prepared much earlier, when the units were moving forward to attack the Plei Me camp. The main defensive positions were located about fifteen hundred meters almost due east of the hospital site. The position resembled a large V, with the open end facing east, the direction of Plei Me, from which the NVA planners believed pursuit, if any, would come. More than 150 well-concealed fighting positions had been dug just inside the tree line along this V-shaped line of resistance. At the center of the V was a large open field, large enough to accommodate a dozen or so helicopters at one time. At the apex of the V were the bulk of the automatic weapons, sited to bring grazing fire across the clearing. The battalion commander deployed two companies into the lines of the V, and placed one platoon of the third company in a position where it could swing the door shut on the open end of the V, driving the attacking enemy force deeper into the trap. Two other platoons were placed in reserve and for local security for the hospital. The fourth company, the weapons company, armed with four 82-mm mortar tubes and five recoilless rifles, two 76-mm and three 57-mm, was positioned where it could bring fire upon the clearing. All fighting positions were, of course, well dug in and superbly camouflaged.

The regimental surgical hospital itself was located in a heavily wooded area along the stream bed. The hospital was about five hundred meters up the small tributary from its juncture with the Tae River. The embankment on the southern side of the dry stream was about three to four feet high and served as a backdrop for the shelters built into its earthen walls. Smoke from cooking fires was carefully diffused by a series of small tunnels up through the embankment and out onto the jungle floor. Orderlies had built bamboo operating tables, and several hand-cranked generators were used so that surgery could take place at night in the carefully thatched lean-to's along the embankment. The hospital had thirty-four patients on the morning of November 1.

At 7:20 A.M., a scout/gun team from B Troop, 1/9 Cav spotted a dozen or so NVA soldiers through a break in the jungle, about five hundred meters southwest of the hospital site. It is unknown whether or not they were part of the 1st Battalion's security for the hospital or a group of stragglers making their way back to the regimental area at the ANTA Village. The soldiers were immediately taken under fire by the gunship and retreated to the northeast, disappearing into the woods. A scout team from C Troop, which had heard the initial contact report on the radio, was flying into the area from the north and spotted about thirty enemy troops on the ground near a small clearing that was about two hundred to three hundred meters northeast of where the first contact was made. The gunship rolled in hot, but again the NVA soldiers chose to avoid contact and did not return fire, instead disappearing to the northeast under the heavy forest cover.

The B Troop rifle platoon, which had been on strip alert at Catecka, was cranked and airborne within minutes, and at 8:08, all five lift ships with the B Troop Blues were inserted on a fairly large LZ about fifteen hundred meters southwest of the stream bed. Within minutes, the nineteen-man platoon had formed a long skirmish line, shaped in a shallow V, with about ten to twelve meters between each soldier. The terrain was typical of the western plateau jungle: a single canopy of hardwoods, each tree with an average trunk of between eight to twelve inches, spaced about five feet apart and with an average height of forty feet. This was the dry season on the plateau, so the foliage was relatively spare except in the stream beds, where there was ample moisture. There the canopy was much more dense. The ground was covered with various highland grasses, looking very much like the prairie grasses in the American west. These ranged in height from one to three feet. Interspersed among the trees were giant anthills, some rising to heights of fifteen feet, covered with brush and saplings. They were hard as concrete and stopped bullets quite nicely, thus serving both sides as fighting positions.

The platoon leader, Captain John H. "Jack" Oliver, was at the point of the V, heading in a northeasterly direction, eagerly seeking contact. Four scout aircraft acted as a screen and as guides to the direction of the enemy. The choppers were hovering right over the stream bed and the hospital and still the NVA did not fire, apparently unwilling to give away their positions. But the sound of the aircraft drowned out any sound of the approaching rifle platoon.

The platoon hit the hospital dead center. As the men slid over the embankment, they confronted an astounding sight. Oliver said they had caught the NVA totally by surprise. "When I stepped through a little patch of cane, there was this guy lying in a hammock, just three feet in front of me. Just as I saw him, there was a shot to my right, then firing broke out all along the line." Because of the surprise and because his skirmish line covered some two hundred meters of ground, Oliver reckoned that the NVA thought the force that hit them was much larger. In the brief firefight that ensued, Oliver's platoon killed fifteen and captured forty-three more, including the hospitalized patients and staff. The fight was over in thirty minutes, with a force that Oliver estimated to be around one hundred men breaking and running to the northeast. Incredibly, not a single American was hit. It was the baptism of fire for the Bravo Blues, the precursor of hundreds of nasty little battles over the next two years that would gain the rifle platoons of the 9th Cavalry Squadron worldwide notoriety as the devastatingly lethal "Headhunters." Despite their greenness in this, their first firefight, they responded splendidly, laying down a ferocious rate of fire from the M-16s. Leaders credited the tough eighteen months of training that had preceded the Cav's deployment as the reason the troopers fought so well. The attack carried the platoon on through the stream bed and onto the north bank, where a hasty defense perimeter was set up while the situation was being sorted out. Oliver immediately notified the troop commander, Major Robert Zion, of the magnitude of the find. Zion radioed the information to John Stockton, who by this time was overhead in his aircraft. Squadron headquarters relayed the news of the hospital's capture to brigade and division headquarters. Stockton immediately alerted the squadron's two additional rifle platoons, the A and C Troop Blues, to be prepared to move to the hospital site at a moment's notice. In the meantime, a scout helicopter flew back to Catecka to load up with surrender leaflets and came back and dropped these into the jungle to the east and northeast of the hospital site. In the light of what was to ensue, this may have been the most wasted effort of the day.

Stockton also decided to immediately evacuate the medical supplies and what eventually became a couple of duffel bags full of documents. It was, as Oliver noted, "a G-2 dream come true." Between the ground element and air reconnaissance, a tiny clearing was located only a few meters from the edge of the stream on the southern bank. It was so small that it could accommodate only one aircraft at a time, and then only precariously. Oliver remembers that the first ships to land there clipped off a lot of foliage from the trees on the way in and out. Stockton also decided to land and take charge of the situation himself; mostly he acted as the head of a greeting committee and visitors' bureau. From the time the hospital area was secured, around 9:00 A.M., until nearly 2:00 P.M., there was a constant stream of VIP visitors. Kinnard flew in and looked at the site. Of course, the brigade commander, Harlow Clark, came in to have a look. Then there was a chopper with a couple of Vietnamese generals, including Vinh Loc. And the senior advisor from Pleiku. It was, after all, a feat of great importance. Never before in the conflict had a regimental-size aid station been overrun. And never with the booty this one held. There were dozens of square cans of morphine, each about a cubic foot in size. In each can there would be a layer of morphine ampules, then a layer of cotton, then another layer of morphine. The squadron hauled out hundreds of pounds of medical supplies, five hundred pounds of rice, the documents, and assorted arms and ammunition. There was also the captured NVA medical staff, including a larger-than-average man who Oliver still believes was a Chinese surgeon.

Stockton directed Oliver to have most of his men work on the backhauling of the captured materiel, leaving just a reinforced squad on the north bank as security. According to Oliver, Stockton had been promised a rifle company by brigade headquarters. It was scheduled to arrive by 2:00 P.M. and take over the operation, allowing the Bravo Blues to extract. This apparently was the reason why Stockton did not immediately commit the A and C Troop rifles. However, an examination of the First Brigade's operations journal reveals no commitment by Quarterback (Harlow Clark's 1st Brigade headquarters) to Scout (Stockton's 1st of the 9th Cavalry Squadron) of any reinforcement. The only help Stockton asked for was additional lift ships from the 227th Huey battalion, plus slings and nets to lift the loot out of the hospital site. Brigade headquarters seemed to have vague plans to exploit the contact by sending in a full battalion to the area— not necessarily directly to the hospital, but somewhere in the vicinity. This was evidenced by a log entry at 9:45 A.M. to the commander of the 2/12 Cav, Lieutenant Colonel Earl Ingram, to have one company ready to move by air on order. Ten minutes later, the journal shows, the order was rescinded and the battalion ordered to continue with its search missions in its present area of operations. Captain Gene Fox's Alpha Company had been designated initially, and even after the standdown, still was in a greater state of readiness for a move than it might have been otherwise. Fox had two platoons and his command group fairly close to a pickup zone, but two other platoons, which had been involved in the contact the previous day, were a fair distance from any pickup area.

Most of the equipment and prisoners, both wounded and nonwounded, had been evacuated from the battle area, all by means of that tiny landing zone, when aerial scouts reported that a large enemy force was approaching from the east and

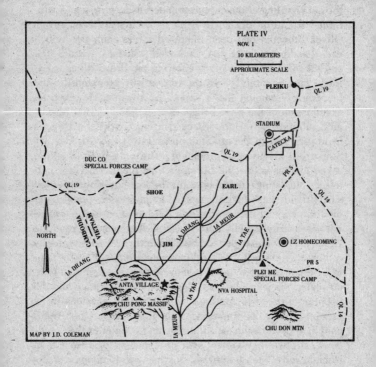

PLATE IV

NOV. 1

10 KILOMETERS
APPROXIMATE SCALE

PLEIKU QL 19

STADIUM

CATECKA

QL 19

DUC CO
SPECIAL FORCES CAMP

PR 5

QL 19

SHOE EARL

QL 14

NORTH

IA DRANG

IA MEUR

IA TAE

IA DRANG

JIM

LZ HOMECOMING

CAMBODIA
VIETNAM

IA DRANG

PLEI ME
SPECIAL FORCES CAMP

PR 5

ANTA VILLAGE

IA TAE

IA MEUR

NVA HOSPITAL

QL 14

CHU PONG MASSIF

CHU DON MTN

MAP BY J.D. COLEMAN

northeast. This was about ten minutes past two o'clock in the afternoon. Almost simultaneously, Oliver's squad leader on the northern bank called him by radio and asked, "Are there any friendlies to the north of us?" Oliver told him there were none and the sergeant reported that he had just spotted about six troops dashing across the crest of a gently sloped ridge that lay to the north of the stream. Oliver gathered what men he had left from the evacuation and prisoner security details—about eleven—and headed out of the stream bed up the finger, intent on getting as far up as possible to be able to hold the position. The small skirmish line got about three-fourths of the way up when the NVA opened fire, pinning it down.

On the LZ several things were happening. One of the visitors at that moment was General Knowles, who had brought with him Swede Larsen, the Task Force Alpha commander. In order not to impede the backhauling operations, the general had sent his bird back out, so when the firing broke out, there was a major general and a brigadier general on the ground, with only nineteen infantrymen and a lieutenant colonel squadron commander as security. Knowles realized the danger, called for his aircraft, piloted by Lieutenant Wayne Knudson, and told Larsen, "We better get the hell out of here, General."

At the same time, Stockton, who realized after a quick yell for help to brigade headquarters that it was going to take some time to get a reaction force in, called in his two other rifle platoons. He brought in the A Troop Blues, commanded by Captain Donald A. Valley, feeding in one ship at a time on the small LZ, and sent Captain Charles M. "Chuck" Knowlen's C Troop Blues in to the large LZ, some fifteen hundred meters to the southwest. As each element of Valley's platoon got in, they were directed to report to Oliver across the stream bed.

The NVA battalion, which had been waiting for the Regimental Medical Company to clear up the hospital's patient load and begin moving the aid station back to Chu Pong, had been poised in fighting positions for a potential attack from the east. Now it found its position threatened from the rear. Not only was its escape route to the west blocked by a helicopter-borne force, but the Americans had overrun the regimental hospital. The constant buzz of helicopters coming and going initially misled the NVA about the size of the force in the hospital area. But it really didn't matter; the battalion's original mission was to get back to the ANTA Village with the aid station and to avoid heavy enemy contact if possible. Now that the hospital was irretrievably lost, the battalion commander's obligation was to get most of his men back to the sanctuary as quickly as possible. The only way now open to the North Vietnamese would be to slip to the north and then to the west, leaving a small force to stage a diversionary attack. So the battalion commander ordered his troops out of their holes with possibly as much as one company sent directly west to attack the Americans in the stream bed. The remainder were to skulk out of harm's way to the north. It is possible that the Cav scouts saw the entire battalion moving and deduced that the entire force was going to attack the hospital; but in fact, only a small element of the battalion actually made contact with the Cavalrymen. The line of attack itself was down a long ridge line that ran from a small hill about four hundred fifty meters northeast of the hospital. The ridge line paralleled the stream bed about two hundred meters north of the stream line, rising to a height of about twenty meters from the elevation of the northern embankment of the stream. The remainder of the two NVA platoons were still positioned on or behind the hill when Oliver's squad leader spotted the khaki-clad soldiers on the ridge line.

Stockton's situation report to brigade said he was being attacked by a battalion, and that news galvanized Clark and his staff. All of the brigade's deployed battalions were queried about the availability of reinforcements and told to be ready to execute their "Thunderbolt" plans on order. Specifically, Clark ordered A 2/12 to move by air to the hospital area, and he sent five Hueys to start the movement. But while he was waiting for Alpha Company to get moving, Clark was scrambling to get any other available forces into the fight.

One unit that was immediately available was the 1st Platoon of B 2/8 Cav, which was on guard duty at an artillery base about seventeen kilometers northwest of the fight. The platoon was ordered to saddle up and move by air to the battle area. Five more lift birds from the 227th Assault Helicopter Battalion, which had been laagered at Catecka, were assigned the mission. The platoon was airborne by 3:00 P.M. The next unit available was the reconnaissance platoon from the 1/12 Cav, located on command post security at LZ CHARGER CITY some twenty-five kilometers to the northwest. The battalion commander, Lieutenant Colonel Robert M. Shoemaker, was working some Eagle Flight operations in the extreme northwestern section of his AO when he heard the warning order from the brigade. He had five Hueys at his disposal and he sent these back to the battalion base with orders to pick up his reconnaissance platoon and fly them to the battle area. Shoemaker flew down to the hospital in his command chopper and watched as the platoon, led by Lieutenant Art West, was landed one ship at a time. He called Stockton, Bullwhip-6, and told him that he was giving him the platoon, wished him luck, and flew back to his AO. Meanwhile, the 3rd Platoon of A 2/12 was landing at the larger LZ some fifteen hundred meters south of the hospital. This was the same LZ that Oliver and his Blues had landed on earlier that morning. Captain Fox and a radio operator, who had flown into the LZ on Ingram's command chopper, formed up his platoon and met the guide from the Cav squadron. Captain Richard S. Sundt, the artillery liaison officer, had volunteered to go by himself through the 1,500 meters of unsecured jungle to meet the reinforcements. As he led the platoon back toward the fight, Ingram and a radio operator remained on the LZ to meet the remainder of Alpha's platoons as they were shuttled in.

In the fight itself, the advancing NVA platoons were taken under rocket and machine-gun fire by the squadron's gunships, but after an initial volley, its lead elements on the ridge had closed to a point so close to Oliver's platoon that the gunship fire could not safely be employed. Oliver remembers that the rocket attacks when the enemy first crested the hill were effective and probably bought his platoon a little time. The gunship fire on the remainder of the enemy forces helped keep them pinned and semi-immobile. In fact, based on the relative strengths of the two combatants in the hospital area early on, the Cavalry units could have been overrun in short order without the fire support provided by the squadron's gunships, the Aerial Rocket Artillery Battalion, and tactical air. These strikes kept the NVA behind the immediate line of contact unable to maneuver freely. The NVA commander could only reinforce his elements in contact piecemeal. The evidence indicates that probably there were no more than one hundred NVA soldiers in actual contact with the cavalry platoons, while the balance was being ripped apart by the fire support.

When his lead elements made contact with the Americans and were finally halted in their advance by the Bravo Blues' determined resistance, the assault commander attempted flanking movements to both his left and right. To his right, the movement was to reinforce the stalled attack down the ridge to the hospital. To his left, the objective was to move down off the hill, through the stream bed to the south side and on to the helicopter landing zone. Unchecked, this would have put his forces in a position to threaten and even overrun the tiny LZ. To counter this threat, Stockton first had devastating firepower placed on the forward slope of the hill and then ordered Knowlen's platoon, the Charlie Troop Blues, which had just arrived, to move to the east of Oliver's positions and hold against the threat moving down off the hill. The crescendo of fire increased and bullets crackled through the American positions, cutting off tree limbs, denuding branches of leaves, and smashing through tree trunks, leaving them with white, splintered scars. Plunging fire scythed the grass and brush on the tiny landing zone.

At about the same time, Valley's Alpha Blues were fed into Oliver's sector to reinforce the line. A limited counter-attack by Valley's forces, combined with the pressure now being exerted by Knowlen's platoon to the east, made it possible for Oliver to withdraw down the open slope to the relative safety of the northern embankment of the stream bed, bringing his wounded with him. The NVA, clad in their mustard-brown uniforms and camouflaged pith helmets, darted from tree to tree, using overwhelming fire from AK's and RPD's to move within one hundred meters of the stream bank. One of Oliver's men, Sergeant Kilcrease, had been badly wounded in the leg, and Oliver tugged him back into the protective cover of the stream bed. As he lay there, panting for breath, an AK slug buried itself within an inch of his nose. Because there was no way the bullet could have come in from the ridge to the north, Oliver realized that there was someone directly overhead in the tree. A trooper named Mitchell was on his belly firing up the hill when Oliver whispered to him: "Mitch, there's somebody in the tree over us. On the count of three roll over." They rolled over and sprayed the tree branches overhead. An NVA sniper soon was hanging lifeless in his rope. Oliver ordered everyone to spray the trees overhead, and soon three more snipers were dead in their positions. Incredibly, all four had been there since the position had been overrun that morning! Not one man had thought to look up into the trees during the brief fight or after. Needless to say, checking trees for snipers became de rigueur in the division thereafter.

Just before 3:00 P.M., the platoon from 2/8 Cav arrived and began landing one ship at a time. Two of the lift ships were hit by fire. They were flyable and got out, but had to make precautionary landings at the large LZ to the south. Stockton fed the platoon into positions adjacent to those held by Knowlen's platoon at the eastern flank of the battle area.

The LZ was about as hot as it could get without being

closed down, and it was impractical to continue using it as a reinforcing LZ, so Stockton directed that all further inbound birds use the original landing zone. The only exception was the occasional slick that would hover in to kick out ammunition and water and to carry out wounded. The squadron and the reinforcing platoons were beginning to suffer casualties. Four riflemen were dead and a dozen more wounded on the ground, plus some air crewmen from the squadron who were hit by small-arms fire. Typical of the bravery and skill of the aviators who flew into that postage stamp LZ under fire that day was Chief Warrant Officer (W-2) David L. Ankerberg, flying one of the B Troop slicks. His citation for a Distinguished Flying Cross said, in part:

> Without regard for his personal safety, Chief Warrant Officer Ankerberg maneuvered his helicopter into the difficult landing zone under intense enemy fire and delivered the badly needed ammunition before he was forced to leave due to the fire he was receiving. His helicopter had received 11 hits from enemy small arms and automatic weapons fire during the landing and take off."

Temporarily thwarted in his attempt to flank the Americans to the east, the NVA commander attempted to shift forces to reinforce the eastern wing of his attack, bringing that element of the cavalry's hasty defensive position under heavier small-arms and machine-gun fire. But it was too late. The reconnaissance platoon of the 1st Battalion, 12th Cavalry had arrived and was committed to reinforcing Knowlen's position. The added volume of fire from the reinforcements stalemated the NVA move, but the pressure remained. The NVA recoilless rifles were never committed to the battle, but the mortar tubes were uprooted from their carefully prepared, but now useless, positions to the east of the battlefield and repositioned just a few hundred meters northeast of the firefight.

Then the lead platoon of A 2/12 arrived, double-timing up the trail from the south LZ. When Gene Fox and his platoon arrived, Fox found Stockton, his shaven head gleaming in the afternoon sun, standing by the edge of the little clearing, surrounded by crouching radio operators snatching first one handset and then another. Fox said that there was a civilian with Stockton, some guy with a white shirt and a .38 revolver. There was no time for introductions. Stockton immediately had Fox send his platoon into the stream bed to beef up his eastern flank. The platoon arrived just in time to beat back a determined NVA assault. The hail of gunfire killed one man and wounded the platoon leader, Lieutenant Gary Hoebeke, along with half a dozen others. That assault was the highwater mark of the NVA counterattack on the hospital site, but the fight was far from over.

Stockton initially made Jack Oliver the overall commander of the ground elements, but found the communications problems nearly insurmountable, with six platoon-size elements plus the squadron support using the same radio frequency. So Stockton told Fox to take command of the two infantry battalion platoons, along with his own platoon, and counterattack up the hill to the northeast. Fox said he had a "hell of a time" coordinating the attack, but finally got all three platoons on line and began an assault up the hill. The brunt of the NVA defensive fires apparently fell on the recon platoon of 1/12. The platoon had three men killed and another seven wounded. One of the wounded was Staff Sergeant Oscar Rubio, a squad leader of the recon platoon. Grenade fragments had peppered his body, but he refused medical treatment and continued to expose himself to NVA fire while leading his squad up the slopes of the hill. Lieutenant Colonel Shoemaker said later that the actions of Rubio and Staff Sergeant Harvey E. McLaurin, the platoon sergeant, were instrumental in helping carry the day. When the platoon leader, Lieutenant West, was wounded early on, McLaurin helped move him and another wounded trooper to a sheltered position, then took command of the platoon and led it on to the objective.

As the assault of the hybrid American company kicked off,

the balance of the Alpha Company, 2/12 was being shuttled in the direction of the fight, landing at the south LZ. Even as A 2/12 was landing, the brigade commander was alerting his own brigade command post security element, B 1/8 Cav, which had just arrived at Catecka from An Khe, to saddle back up and prepare for movement to the battle. The balance of Fox's company landed without incident at the larger LZ and set out at a trot for the fight to the northeast. The crescendo of fire could be heard even over the roar of the helicopters at the landing zone.

By now, the NVA had their 82-mm mortars unlimbered and delivering fire throughout the battle area, including the small LZ. The mortars were being walked back and forth through the stream bed and on both sides of the banks. One explosion in the stream bed killed a medic from the 2/12 as well as the North Vietnamese soldier he was treating. Infantrymen hate mortars. In a firefight with rifles and machine guns, the art of staying healthy is just plain poker-playing sense: maintaining a good, low, running profile, finding strong, healthy hard-woods to duck behind or ditches to jump into. But with mortars, it's like betting in a dice game: there isn't much a soldier can do except hope he's lucky. For the troops on the ground, the mortar barrage went on for what must have seemed like hours. In fact, within minutes, one of the Cav scouts spotted the mortar firing position and called in the gunships. Two of the Huey gunships made rocket and machine-gun firing runs and silenced the mortars. A close pass by the scout revealed four tubes smashed and the gun crews dead or scattered. There were no more mortars that afternoon, although an occasional RPD round lobbed in from the NVA positions kept people nervous.

There was another lull in the fighting as B 1/8 arrived at the south LZ. Clark decided to leave the company on the LZ to secure the two aircraft that had made precautionary landings there. At the same time, Lieutenant Colonel Earl Ingram, commander of the 2/12, who had remained at the landing zone to direct traffic, was directed by Clark to assume command of the battle so that Stockton and his men could be extracted. The Blues, after all, had done all that could have been expected of them, fighting against overwhelming odds to save the hospital site from recapture.

Before leaving the scene, Oliver wanted to go back up the hill and retrieve his dead. The successful attack by Fox's hybrid company to the east had rendered untenable the NVA position directly to the north of Oliver's forces, and the enemy began pulling back, leaving only a few snipers in the trees to make life miserable for the cavalrymen. When the American force finally made it back up the slope to the point where Oliver's platoon had first been hit with a hail of bullets earlier that afternoon, they found the body of Specialist Four Thomas Duncan, surrounded by thirteen dead NVA soldiers. Oliver said that as his men started toward Duncan's body, he suddenly yelled, "Be careful when you start to move him." Oliver said he still doesn't know what made him think the body might be booby trapped. It was, but nobody got hurt. Oliver recalls that Duncan was an outlaw as a soldier, always in trouble, but a hell of a warrior. He put him in for the Medal of Honor. (The 1st Cavalry awards board in 1965 was a conservative lot, with a soon-to-be-gained reputation for downgrading and disapproving, and there is no record of Duncan ever having received a valor medal of any kind.)

Even as the situation was stabilizing in the hospital area, Clark was setting things in motion to orient the pursuit farther to the south of the original search areas. He also needed to get tube artillery within range of the hospital area, so Alpha Battery of 2/19 Arty was moved to a new location, LZ CAVALAIR, about eight kilometers due west of the battle area. The landing zone had been secured by an unopposed air assault by A 2/8 Cav and followed up by Lieutenant Colonel James H. Nix's battalion headquarters. The remainder of the battalion continued search operations in the southern part of area JIM. By 6:00 P.M., just as the cavalry squadron rifle platoons were being extracted and sent back to Catecka for rest and refit, the tube artillery was being employed by Ingram to help Fox's reinforced rifle company, now in control of the hospital area, beat back a desultory counterattack by the NVA and to consolidate positions on the high ground to the north and northeast of the stream bed. Ingram was anxious to get the high ground secured and to be able to put a thin defensive screen around the south and west portions of the battle area before nightfall. Ingram, directing operations from his command-and-control chopper, had Fox pull in the two attached platoons and use them for security screens to the south and west, keeping his company intact along the north and northeast sectors of the hospital site. Ingram also was eager to get the two downed aircraft out of the south LZ; they presented too attractive a target for NVA rocket gunners. Chinooks from the 228th Assault Support Helicopter Battalion lifted the wounded birds out and took them back to forward maintenance at Camp Holloway, and Bravo 1/8 settled down to an uneventful night securing the landing zone.

By darkness, an uneasy quiet had fallen over the battle area. The NVA had broken contact and fled to the north and west, but no one knew how far they had gone or whether there would be another attempt in force to take the hospital site. But the presence of an artillery battery just eight klicks to the west did a great deal to ease the men's anxieties.

Meanwhile, both commanders and intelligence types were having a field day with the materials taken from the hospital site. Some of the documents had first been dispatched to brigade headquarters at Catecka, where Clark, Knowles, and Kinnard pored over a map taken from a medical book. It was a beautifully preserved sketch map that showed the major infiltration trails leading from Cambodia through the Ia Drang Valley into the Chu Pong Massif and, from there, the attack positions at Plei Me. Besides showing the principal routes of approach used by the 33rd and 32nd Regiments, it pinpointed many important unit locations and other valuable data. Based on this map, the solid indications from the fighting that was ensuing at the hospital site, and the dry holes being worked by his other units, Kinnard decided he had placed too large a portion of the search effort too far to the north and northwest of Plei Me. Accordingly, he directed that a tighter search pattern be established in and around the hospital site and in areas just to the west of the Tae River. Accordingly, Clark ordered the Second of the Twelfth to concentrate on the area immediately north of the hospital, while the Second of the Eighth was to search the area west of the hospital. The First of the Twelfth was left in place. It had been flailing about fruitlessly in search of the NVA, but had been doing some good things with civic action and pacification among the Montagnards in its sector just south of Highway 19. Two days later, Shoemaker's battalion would be moved into the search area abandoned by Ingram's Second of the Twelfth when it was shunted to the hospital area.

At II Corps headquarters in Pleiku City, the division's G-2, Lieutenant Colonel Bobby Lang, and a couple of his analysts worked with the II Corps G-2 advisor, Major William P. Boyle, plus the G-2 people at II Corps. Also involved was Major Wilmer Hall, the 1st Brigade intelligence officer. They worked long into the night and through the next day. Although the total intelligence find—the documents and the prisoner interrogation reports—was a mother lode that would be mined for months, the first twenty-four hours of study gave some solid clues to the allied intelligence officers about who the enemy really was and where he had come from. With this intelligence coup, the Communists were put in a unique position in the Vietnam War. They knew less about the opposition than the opposition knew about them.

The other booty from the hospital, including some $40,000 worth of medical supplies, was delivered to the ARVN. The rice was used to help feed refugees in camps outside Pleiku City and at Le Thanh District Headquarters; the weapons, mostly AK-47s, soon found their way into souvenir channels;

and the ammunition that could not be used by the ARVN was earmarked for destruction.

When dawn came at the hospital, Ingram ordered out a platoon-size reconnaissance in force to see what had become of the NVA. The night had been quiet with the close-in ambush positions and listening posts undisturbed, although Captain Fox had agreed to have some Aerial Rocket Artillery fire harassing and interdiction (H & I) missions some 500 meters north of the company's position. Fox chose Lieutenant Bill Schiebler's platoon for the recon mission. When his platoon left the northern perimeter at first light, it was accompanied by a civilian newsman, Columbus (Georgia) *Ledger-Enquirer* reporter Charlie Black, who had come in from An Khe with B 1/8 Cavalry late the preceding afternoon. It was the first time in this young campaign that a reporter had accompanied the cavalry line units in combat; it would not be the last. As soon as the Saigon press corps realized that they could come to the 1st Cav and find a fight almost any day, they began flocking to the scene.

The platoon first swept the reverse slope of the hogback due north of the hospital site. They found abandoned packs, some uniform items, and blood stains, but no bodies. The patrol then cautiously approached the reverse slope of the hill to the northeast, the place from which the NVA battalion had kicked off the attack the previous afternoon. Again, nothing was found but the usual battlefield debris. There was plenty of evidence that the NVA had taken a pasting from the rocket runs and air strikes, and a couple dozen bodies were found in shallow graves on the reverse slope of the hill. The patrol continued on to the northeast for a couple more kilometers and found the useless positions that had been so carefully prepared by the NVA battalion. A number of them were now serving a more macabre purpose; during the night they had been converted to graves for the NVA soldiers killed by the American gunships. Finding no enemy, the patrol returned to the hospital site just in time to help the rest of the company gather up more material from the hospital for either backhauling or destruction.

While this was going on, the remainder of the Bravo and Charlie Companies of the 2/12 airlanded peacefully at the clearing east of the hospital, the one the NVA had so patiently ringed with positions. Back at the hospital site, the platoons that had been "borrowed" for the fight were airlifted back to their units. The first platoon of B 2/8 Cav rejoined its parent unit at a location twelve kilometers southwest of the hospital, B Company having made an air assault into the new search position earlier that morning. The recon platoon of 1/12 Cav flew back to the battalion base at CHARGER CITY and resumed its mission of providing intelligence and reconnaissance patrols for the battalion. Bravo Company 1/8 Cav was returned to STADIUM, the brigade base at Catecka. Before the units left the hospital site, a full-scale police call was made of the battlefield, resulting in a substantial amount of arms and ammunition being recovered. The captured ammunition—twenty 75-mm recoilless rifle rounds, thirty-five 82-mm mortar rounds, six thousand 12.7-mm machine-gun rounds, and sixty thousand 7.62-mm rifle rounds—were placed in a pit and blown up with about ten pounds of Composition C-4. The members of the human supply train stretching from North Vietnam through Laos to Cambodia likely would have wept in frustration at the sight.

Even as the other units were outbound, the 2/12 command post element and B Battery, 2/19 Arty were being lifted from their old positions in the center of Search Area EARL south to the main LZ that had been used throughout the hospital fight.

The fight had been extremely costly to the NVA. The official after-action report lists ninety-nine killed by actual count plus an estimated 183 more. Commanders on the ground estimated that there were more than two hundred wounded in the battle. The so-called body count also may have been estimates; Fox simply doesn't recall that many bodies on the bat-

tlefield, and the estimates are anybody's guess. But one concrete figure was the forty-four NVA soldiers captured, about
half being the wounded and disabled in the hospital. The
figures on captives astounded the members of the press corps,
who were already accustomed to sneering at body-count figures posted by American units. Other units in other parts of
Vietnam had captured a few VC and a few NVA, but nobody
had pulled in this many North Vietnamese regulars in a single battle. The cost to the 1st Cavalry in this, its first real fight
of the campaign, was light in contrast. A total of eleven were
killed, all on November 1, and fifty-one wounded, all but four
on the first day. A total of eight aircraft took hits, but all were
flyable, although two took precautionary landings at the south
LZ.

Altogether, it had been a highly successful operation. With
the exception of the usual glitches that could be expected
with any new unit, everything had gone pretty much according to direction. The cavalry scouts had found the enemy; the
Blues had fixed them; airmobility had made it possible to
reinforce the battle area with units from all over the area of
operations as well as provided immediate fire support. Now
the challenge was to maintain the momentum by regaining
contact with the NVA and continuing the battle of attrition.

7

THE DRANG
RIVER AMBUSH

The 1st Cavalry's brain trust, after careful study of the captured map, realized that if the North Vietnamese were in fact retreating westward from the battlefields around Plei Me, they quite likely would be using the same trails to go back to Cambodia that they had used to come in. General Knowles was particularly intrigued by a trail that seemed to be located between the northern slopes of the Chu Pong Massif and the Ia Drang (River). He wanted to take a closer look at it and the whole valley of the Drang River where it flowed into Cambodia. To take this look would require a giant leap of men and equipment far from any fixed base. It was twenty kilometers south of Duc Co and thirty kilometers due west of Plei Me, and the roads to both camps were far from secure. An adventure of this kind would have been unthinkable with a conventional force. But this was the airmobile division, and, as Harry Kinnard had often said, the helicopter had freed the soldier from the tyranny of terrain.

The logical unit—in fact, the only unit—to conduct a reconnaissance-in-force that far from the remainder of the division's troops was the cavalry squadron. John Stockton's cavalry unit was fast becoming as valuable to the division as Jeb Stuart's cavalry had been to Robert E. Lee: it was the eyes and ears of the commander, and it had the capability to create a lot of nastiness when the enemy was found and fixed.

But first there was the matter of threshing out who would provide immediate reinforcement for the squadron's rifle platoons. According to Oliver's recollection, as soon as Stockton got out of the hospital fight, he went immediately to Kinnard and told him that he would not again put his Blues on the ground unless there was a rifle company in reserve and he, Stockton, held the string on it. Kinnard recalls no such conversation; neither does Knowles. But the orders for attachment and detachment do show that the cavalry squadron was detached from 1st Brigade control on the morning of November 2 and placed under the operational control of division headquarters, even though the squadron maintained its base area adjacent to the brigade base at Catecka. Because of the proximity to the target area, Stockton elected to use as a forward base area the Duc Co Special Forces camp, which was just a few kilometers inside the Vietnamese border from Cambodia.

Meanwhile, a fresh battalion was coming into the AO from An Khe. It was the 1st Battalion, 8th Cavalry, one of the three parachute-qualified battalions of the First Brigade. Captain Roy Martin's Bravo Company already had a slight taste of action at the hospital the day before and now was back guarding the brigade base at Catecka. The battalion headquarters remained at Camp Holloway under the command of Major Guy Eberhardt, filling in for Lieutenant Colonel Kenneth D. Mertel, who was in a hospital in Qui Nhon recuperating from one of those mysterious tropical diseases that prey on strangers to the tropics. The battalion's Charlie Company still was on a support mission with an artillery unit at Tuy Hoa on the coast (Task Force AMOS), but Alpha Company was at Holloway looking for something to do. It was tabbed as the division reserve. At first blush it would seem that putting a rifle company in reserve flew in the face of Kinnard's dictum of every unit in the division being a potential reserve, and that it was uneconomical for the troops of a company-size unit to be sitting around on their duffs waiting for something to happen. And while it was true that some of the staff officers at division headquarters were having serious second thoughts about the practicality of the theory, the designation of Alpha Company as the reserve was primarily to give the unit a mission. A one-company battalion is about as useful as a two-legged stool, so the mission made perfect sense.

Under normal circumstances, the company would have remained on alert at Camp Holloway. But Stockton somehow persuaded Knowles to let him put the company out in his area. Quite likely he used the argument that the company could provide security to his forward base while it was waiting for a call from someone in need of assistance.

There has been a world of controversy over the status of Alpha Company vis-à-vis the cavalry squadron. Captain Oliver and other members of the squadron believed that the company was attached to the squadron outright, with no strings attached. Thus the company was Stockton's to do with as he wished.

On the other hand, the forward G-3, Lieutenant Colonel John A. Hemphill, a tough-talking veteran of the Korean War, insists that the company was a division reserve with priority on commitment to the 1/9, but that division headquarters retained the right to approve the commitment or to send the company in relief of any other force in the divison that might need help. Hemphill said, "I wrote the operations order and I remember it very well. I put it [the string attached to the company] in twice, because with Stockton you had to put it in twice." Hemphill had the restriction in the body of the order and again in the coordinating instructions. Those instructions made it very clear that Stockton could not commit the reserve without General Knowles's permission. There never was any indication in the order that the company was attached to or put under Stockton's operational control. What muddied the waters somewhat was the attachment of Alpha Company's mortar platoon to Stockton's squadron. In Army doctrine, the term "attachment" meant that the mortar platoon was Stockton's to do with as he chose.

Alpha Company was under the command of Captain Theodore Danielsen, a handsome, dashing West Pointer from the class of 1960. In a divisional competition at Fort Benning earlier in the year, he had been chosen to be the company commander that the ABC television network's "Saga of the Western Man" series would follow once the cavalry got to Vietnam. Producer John Hughes and a camera crew followed Danielsen and his "Alphagaters" through a series of uneventful patrols just east of An Khe, and out of the exercise came a one-hour special entitled "I am a Soldier." Ironically, the filming, where there never was a shot fired in anger, was temporarily suspended just a few days before Danielsen's company was sent to Pleiku.

After getting the mission to conduct the reconnaissance-in-force, the cavalry squadron moved quickly to coordinate the use of the area around the Duc Co Special Forces camp as a forward operational base. The CIDG camp, which was located about eighteen kilometers north of the Chu Pongs, had a dirt strip that could be used by fixed-wing aircraft to resupply the operation. Stockton found an open field about a kilometer south of the camp and used that to laager the squadron's aircraft. This cut down the amount of dust that the rotor blades would stir up and in the process make life miserable for the unfortunates caught in the downdraft, and it smelled a little better than areas immediately adjacent to the camp. Alpha Company was lifted in from Holloway to assist in the security of the new base area. The afternoon of November 2 was spent making aerial recons of the objective area, a three- by six-kilometer rectangle, with the long axis running east and west, bounded by the Drang River on the north and the east, the steep slopes of the Chu Pongs on the south, and the Cambodian border on the west. This was the area where the Ia Drang funneled out of Vietnam into Cambodia. The Ia Drang, which is fed by scores of smaller streams and rivers in a seven-hundred-square-kilometer sweep of the western plateau, flows in a southwesterly direction until it butts against the northeastern escarpment of the Chu Pong Massif. There it is forced into a northwesterly direction, flowing almost northerly for about three kilometers before looping into a general westerly passage through the funnel and into Cambodia.

Roaring at treetop level, the scout ships and the command choppers spotted numerous small trails running east and west and at least two fairly well-traveled trails. The one running along the base of the hill mass was easy to spot: a bright red ribbon on the valley floor, cut into the hard, laterite soil by thousands of Ho Chi Minh sandals. Another trail, also quite distinct, ran east and west parallel to the southern bank of the Ia Drang, crossing it at a ford where the river line briefly ran north and south. Under the cavalry squadron's SOP (Standing Operating Procedures), when the rifle platoons of the squadron were grouped, they would habitually be under the control of Major Bob Zion, the commander of Bravo Troop. So it was that Zion was out scouting for a patrol base and ambush locations late on the afternoon of the 2nd. A passenger in his aircraft, which dashed and darted at treetop level, was Charlie Black, the reporter from Columbus, Georgia.

Further to the east, throughout the 1st Brigade's area of operations, there was furious activity as the units were shifted into new search areas south and east of the original zones. The 1st of the 12th made long leaps southeast to LZs TEXAS, OKLAHOMA, and MISSISSIPPI, generally in the same area that the 2/12 had vacated when it was moved to the hospital site. Ingram's battalion continued to search the area within six kilometers north and east of the hospital, while the 2nd of the 8th worked search patterns southwest of the hospital. The supporting artillery batteries also were moved, an action consistent with the belief in the cavalry that if you moved every twenty-four hours, no one could lay a glove on you. Then, too, as the infantry units shifted, so did the artillery batteries, moving so as to provide the best fire support for the searching units, as well as mutual support for each other. The only contact made during the day of November 3 was a brief flurry near Objective H, about five kilometers north of the hospital, when B Company 2/12 overran another medical supply and weapons cache guarded by an NVA platoon. In the brief firefight that ensued, one NVA soldier died and several were wounded. There were no friendly casualties.

For the NVA Field Front, the divisional headquarters controlling the Communist effort on the western plateau, most of the news it had been receiving from its units was bad. The headquarters was located in a bunker complex near the abandoned village of Plei Lao Tchin on the northern bank of the Ia Drang, a scant fifteen-hundred meters inside the Vietnamese border. The 32nd Regiment had two battalions in its staging area, about eighteen-hundred meters north and slightly east of the division headquarters. The latest word from the 33rd Regiment was that it had lost its regimental hospital and at least part of the battalion assigned to guard it. One of its battalions had closed on ANTA Village, and Field Front ordered the regiment to continue moving deeper into the Chu Pong sanctuary. By nightfall, November 2, the regimental headquarters was nestled along the northeastern slopes of Hill 732, one of the highest peaks of the massif. But in the midst of the bad news there was one bright spot for Field Front: the fresh 66th Regiment had just arrived off the infiltration trail, and a week behind it was a battalion of 120-mm mortars and a battalion of 14.5-mm twin-barreled antiaircraft guns. The 7th and 9th battalions of the 66th already had crossed the Cambodian border and were hidden in camouflaged positions just east of the Ia Drang where it flows in a north-south line. All of the racket from the helicopters making reconnaissance flights caused some nervousness on the part of Field Front. From their positions north of the river, the division staff could hear the aircraft making repeated passes across the valley. But there was no gunfire, and NVA patrols on the night of November 2 revealed no American positions.

So on November 3, when helicopters again were heard buzzing about the valley, it was not considered by the NVA to be a cause for great concern. Field Front ordered the 8th Battalion to cross over the border and join the remainder of the regiment east of the Ia Drang. It was scheduled to begin its movement at 5:00 P.M., with the most critical part, the crossing of the open plateau just north of the Chu Pongs, being made after dark.

Stockton's plan for the squadron was to place three platoon-size ambushes along the most used trails—two about eight hundred meters apart along the southern bank of the river and a third some sixteen hundred meters south, placed along the well-worn trail skirting the mountain. Equidistant between the ambush sites was a slight clearing that could be used as a landing zone and as the patrol base. Stockton named the landing zone LZ MARY, in honor of the wife of reporter Charlie Black, who had covered the squadron steadily during its formative days in the 11th Air Assault Division. As Charlie later pointed out, it was a dubious honor because "she damned near lost her husband there before it was all over." One other newsman was going in with the squadron, NBC cameraman Vo Huynh, who was carrying in a Bell and Howell to shoot silent footage that the network would use to illustrate a war story. Huynh was to stay at LZ MARY with Zion, while Black was to accompany Jack Oliver to an ambush site. The force to be used in the plan included all three aero-rifle platoons of the squadron plus a CIDG Eagle Flight platoon of Montagnards. Additionally, Stockton asked Lieutenant Stewart Tweedy's mortar platoon of A 1/8 to provide fire support at the patrol base. Since the mortar platoon was attached to the squadron, this was an authorized assignment for the mortars.

Major Zion was to set up a command post and perimeter on LZ MARY with Don Valley's A Troop Blues, the mortar platoon, plus some machine guns that were dismounted from the lift ships. The gunners manned the eastern and western portions of the perimeter, and the Alpha Blues spread out in a

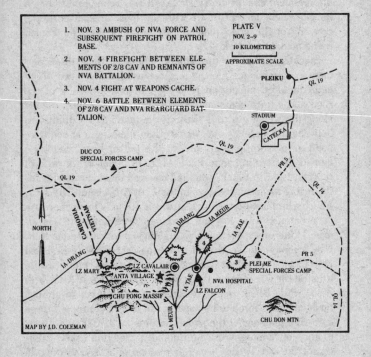

1. NOV. 3 AMBUSH OF NVA FORCE AND SUBSEQUENT FIREFIGHT ON PATROL BASE.

2. NOV. 4 FIREFIGHT BETWEEN ELEMENTS OF 2/8 CAV AND REMNANTS OF NVA BATTALION.

3. NOV. 4 FIGHT AT WEAPONS CACHE.

4. NOV. 6 BATTLE BETWEEN ELEMENTS OF 2/8 CAV AND NVA REARGUARD BATTALION.

PLATE V

NOV. 2–9

10 KILOMETERS
APPROXIMATE SCALE

PLEIKU

QL 19

STADIUM

CATECKA

QL 19

DUC CO
SPECIAL FORCES CAMP

QL 19

PR 5

QL 14

CAMBODIA

VIETNAM

IA DRANG

IA MEUR

IA TAE

NORTH

IA DRANG

1

LZ MARY

2

LZ CAVALAIR

ANTA VILLAGE

IA TAE

4

3

PLEI ME
SPECIAL FORCES CAMP

PR 5

NVA HOSPITAL

LZ FALCON

QL 14

CHU PONG MASSIF

IA MEUR

CHU DON MTN

MAP BY J.D. COLEMAN

thin screen around the LZ. The plan was to have the Charlie Troop Blues man the southern end of the perimeter when they came back from the ambush position, with the Bravo Blues handling the northern side. Valley's platoon would then shift to take the east, and the CIDG platoon would fill in at the western end.

The ambush position to the northwest was to be manned by the CIDG platoon. The ambush some eight hundred meters to the east of that position would be handled by Oliver's Bravo Blues. The Charlie Troop Blues under Chuck Knowlen would man the southern position by the mountain.

At 3:30 P.M., the squadron began feeding the men into LZ MARY, landing four ships at a time but spacing out the flights so that the activity would not be too conspicuous. Zion came in first, flying his Huey fast and low across the clearing and circling, coming back the other way. The idea was to draw any gunfire if there was opposition on the landing zone. The gunships would then blast the LZ and prep it for landing. But it was clean, and Zion landed along with four other slicks carrying Valley's platoon. As soon as the security element was in place, another four choppers dipped in and dropped off the Charlie Blues; then came the CIDG platoon, the mortar platoon, and, finally, the Bravo Blues. The LZ was part of an area that had been slashed clear by Montagnards a few years previously and was covered by brush, grass, and young hardwood saplings that had grown to a height of about five feet. The helicopters would hover about four feet off the ground and the cavalrymen would jump from the skids, landing on the run. Actually, the troopers would be standing on the skids while the bird was still flaring, twenty to thirty feet up. It was not operationally necessary to stand on the skids, but it didn't hurt, and it reinforced the swashbuckling image of the cavalryman.

Zion set up his command post in a little grove of trees that surrounded a ten-foot-high anthill on the southern end of the perimeter and held a last-minute leader's conference on the locations of the ambushes, the actions to be taken if they were sprung, the routes in and out of the perimeters, the radio frequencies to be used, and other such vital information. At 5:00 P.M., the ambush patrols moved out, leaving the perimeter at predetermined locations. At the northern end, where Oliver's platoon was departing, one of the troopers on picket duty had used his bayonet to carve into one of the black rocks that cropped out of the rusty soil a memorial to the Cav. It read: "Fuck Communism, Courtesy First Squadron Ninth Cav, Nov. 3, 1965."

The trek to the ambush positions was tense but uneventful. The terrain was much like it was along the Tae River, generally flat with plateau hardwoods five or six feet apart. It seemed open at first glance, but the troopers on point realized that the openness was deceptive. The gray-green canopy, even though thinned by the dry season, the anthills, the brush clumps, and the little folds of ground with gullies and ditches all cut up the plateau into a series of little compartments that concealed more than they revealed. It made walking point a sphincter-tightening, dicey affair. At the river's edge, the foliage changed to dense bamboo clumps, higher trees with thicker crowns. The floor of the jungle along the river was in perpetual twilight. Oliver's platoon eased into positions along the trail that led to the ford. His platoon was disposed laterally on the southern side of the trail. Oliver also placed a two-man listening post with a radio on the eastern side of the river. The object of the exercise, after all, was to ambush the retreating NVA forces; no one suspected that a new regiment was moving in from Cambodia.

Each platoon carried from eight to ten Claymore mines. The M-18A1 Claymore is one of the deadlier items in the infantryman's inventory of killing devices. At five inches high and ten inches wide, it looks like a little olive drab "keep off the grass" sign when it is staked into the ground. A shaped charge against a curved metal backing sends seven hundred steel ball bearings through a thin plastic front shield in a 60-

degree swath of death. Lethal out to fifty meters, the mine can be either command detonated or rigged with trip wires or other enemy-actuated devices. When used in an ambush, the detonator is a switch that generates a tiny charge of electricity and sends it coursing down twenty meters of wire to the mine. For these ambushes, when the leader fired the first Claymore it would serve as a signal for the detonation of the remainder of the mines.

The two aero-rifle platoons also carried special models of the M-79 grenade launcher. The regular infantry launcher looks much like a fat shotgun and is a single-shot, firing a 40-mm shell. This special, test model, which Stockton had somehow procured for his Blues, had a spring magazine that allowed three grenades to be fired as fast as the grenadier could pull the trigger. Its disadvantage was that it took a bit of time to reload. Nevertheless, it was a very nice weapon to have along in an ambush, where a high volume of fire at the moment of truth was essential.

Knowlen set up his ambush on the northern side of the trail that ran along the foot of the mountain. Like Oliver, he expected the NVA to be coming from the east, heading west to Cambodia, and he laid out his ambush with that in mind. His men placed eight Claymore mines in the brush, about ten meters off the trail, with a kill zone of about forty meters. The Claymore at the eastern end of the zone was pointed up the trail, the direction from which the enemy was expected to come. The troopers were assigned positions along the trail, where they could bring fire to bear on the trail with their M-16s or with the special model of the M-79 grenade launcher. An M-60 machine gun was sighted up the trail, also toward the east.

All three ambush positions were in and the men concealed well before darkness. All that remained was the tough part: the patient wait, hiding in the bushes, smokeless and motionless, using mental voodoo on ants and mosquitoes instead of moving a hand to slap at them. After dark, the swarms of mosquitoes, particularly at the positions close to the river, made the waiting painful. Unfortunately, as with many of the mosquitoes in Vietnam, these were carrying malaria. Several of the troopers were stricken and evacuated later in the campaign.

At the northern position, Black remembers hearing the gurgle of the water as it splashed along the banks. The sound of the water masked other sounds and made the ambush very dicey. An NVA patrol could be on top of the platoon before they would know it. Small animals moving down to the river for water also kept everyone in a state of tension much higher than a normal ambush position usually produces. Around 8:30 P.M., the men heard the unmistakable big cat sounds of a tiger just across the river. Then, within a few minutes, they heard the thin, high-pitched sound of a horn coming from somewhere in the east, also across the river. There were some answering horns and then the sound of men moving through the brush, heading south along the eastern river bank.

When the NVA troop movement started, the two men Oliver had placed on the eastern bank as a listening post whispered on the radio that the enemy was getting close, but appeared not to be headed west toward the ford. Then they couldn't even whisper. Oliver asked them to just key the transmitter if the enemy was too close to their position to permit talk. They did, and lay petrified as the NVA battalion moved by their position toward the south.

At the southernmost ambush site, the brilliant moon illuminated the trail as brightly as a flare. The men edged themselves against trees and rocks or nestled down in the grass, trying to become one of the shadows on the valley floor. Suddenly the troopers went rigid. From the west came the clear sound of troops on the move. Sergeant Eugene Pennington was stunned: "We were looking for them to come from the east, then we heard them coming toward us from the other direction." The lead element of the NVA column stopped just outside the kill zone of the ambush and took a break while other elements to the west apparently caught up. The point man for the NVA column came within fifteen feet of Pennington, where he was flattened out in the grass. "I'll never understand how they missed seeing me," he said.

The answer is simple. Soldiers see only that for which they are looking. This far from any government outpost and just inside Vietnam from the Cambodian sanctuary, the last thing the NVA soldiers expected to see were American soldiers lying in ambush. For what seemed to be hours to the men lying in wait, but in actuality about twenty-five minutes, the NVA column took their rest break. Finally, a few minutes after 9:00 P.M., the column started moving. Pennington counted forty-eight men carrying rifles and eight more carrying loads slung between them on bamboo poles, two to each bundle. Then came what obviously was a weapons platoon, a long line of NVA soldiers walking very close together, carrying mortars, recoilless rifles, and machine guns. Knowlen let the weapons carriers get well within the kill zone, then blew his Claymore. Within seconds, seven more Claymores scythed through the hapless North Vietnamese. The Charlie Blues blazed away with M-16s and M-79 grenades. The violence of the fire detonated grenades and ammunition on the bodies lying in the trail. Rifle and machine gun fire from the eastern flank security position blasted the trail edge of the enemy's lead element. As bright as it was in the moonlight, the sky was further lit up by the violent ambush fire. So complete was the surprise, so total the devastation, that not one single NVA weapon was fired in exchange.

Pennington, who, along with three others, had the right flank security mission, fired M-79s and M-16s at the trail to the west. There wasn't a North Vietnamese soldier left alive for fifty meters along that trail; those on either side of the trap had vanished. Knowlen, recognizing that he was probably in the middle of a much larger force, opted not to delay by having his men search the bodies on the trail. He signaled his force to break back for the prearranged rendezvous point.

There they formed up and prepared to head back to LZ MARY.

Now was when the presence of Alpha Company's mortars came in handy. Even as the NVA began regrouping their shattered forces and commenced probes toward the ambush positions, the mortar platoon began dropping preregistered concentrations along the trail. Although the registrations had been made only by map coordinates rather than by adjusted fire (in order to maintain secrecy and security during the afternoon), Tweedy's gunners were amazingly accurate with their fire. This delayed the pursuit by the NVA and permitted Knowlen's force to completely break contact and make its way back to the patrol base. The down side of the mortar fire was that it clearly told the North Vietnamese that there was an American patrol base close by and pretty much where the base was located.

After the southern ambush was sprung, Zion radioed Oliver and the advisor with the Montagnard patrol to stay put. He was hoping that the outfit across the river from Oliver would try to cross, or that survivors of Knowlen's ambush might drift far enough north, where they could be dispatched by the two unsprung ambushes. So the two remaining patrols maintained their positions. When Knowlen's people returned to the LZ, they hastily took up positions on the ground on the southern edge of the perimeter, permitting Valley's men to move on to other prearranged positions. No one had dug in, not even the mortar platoon, and the only cover available to the LZ defenders were small folds in the ground, anthills, and brush clumps.

At 10:00 P.M., a rifleman on the southern perimeter spotted some men with helmets skittering from tree to tree in the moonlight. He opened fire, and within seconds the landing zone was under NVA small-arms fire. Zion reported the contact to Stockton, who was at the squadron base at Duc Co. The thrust of the first probe was at the southern sector of the base perimeter. The fire from Knowlen's platoon repulsed the probe, but the NVA soon climbed into the trees surrounding the LZ and began sniping at any cavalryman who moved. The bright moonlight gave the NVA all the advantage.

At 11:15 P.M., the NVA threw another assault wave at the southern perimeter, supported by 60-mm mortars and RPG rockets. Although the NVA riflemen came within a few feet of the defending troopers, they still did not overrun the LZ. But it badly splintered a force that was never fully organized for defense. Knowlen radioed Zion that he had lost contact with most of his people. Up at the northeastern ambush site, Oliver monitored the radio conversations and was not surprised when Zion ordered him to abandon the position and work his way back to the perimeter. Oliver said that Knowlen had reported that he didn't know the whereabouts of but three of his people and assumed the rest had been wiped out. With that gloomy report from the most critical part of the perimeter, and with NVA sniper fire now coming in from all points of the compass, Zion radioed Stockton and yelled for help.

Stockton's personal after-action report to General Kinnard stated: "During the 2315 attack Maj. Zion informed me that if he was not immediately reinforced his force would be overrun. I ordered A Co, 1/8 Cav Bn to the patrol base immediately, a platoon at a time, which was the maximum capability of the LZ at night."

Stockton's ordering in of Alpha Company was not preceded with a request to division headquarters to commit the reserve. In fact, he did not initially communicate with division at all. He used the ARVN-advisory channels to send a message to the division's TOC at the II Corps compound. It said, "Unless you have some objection, I am committing the division reserve." By the time the II Corps duty officer trudged across the compound to the Cav's TOC, Hemphill already had a clue about what was happening. He was monitoring the 1/9 command frequency and picked up the conversation between Stockton and Zion to the effect that Alpha Company was slated for relief of the LZ. "It was very obvious that they were loading to go to war and that Stockton had committed the reserve without Knowles's permission," said Hemphill. He sent for Knowles, who was asleep in his room in the advisory compound.

The tall, lanky general rushed up the hill from his quarters, clad in pajamas, combat boots, and a field jacket. He immediately got on the radio and called Stockton. "Bull-whip-6 this is Longstreet. Don't you dare commit that company." There are as many variations of the ensuing conversation as there were participants and witnesses. One division staff officer who was present in the TOC remembers Stockton coming right back with a terse comment: "This is Bullwhip-6. Too late; they're already in. Out." But others remember there having been more conversation between Knowles and Stockton. Danielsen, with one platoon already en route to the landing zone, was standing next to Stockton at his command chopper. He recalls that Stockton said: "If I don't commit them [Alpha Company] I'm going to lose my force." And when Knowles insisted that the division reserve not be committed, Danielsen remembers Stockton responding, "I see no other course; I must." Declared Danielsen, "*That* took a lot of balls." Hemphill, on the other hand, recalls Stockton saying: "I'm the commander on the scene; I see what needs to be done. I can make the judgment and I'm doing it."

In any case, the clear implication at the division TOC was that the relief force was still at Duc Co at the time of the transmission. In point of fact, by the time Knowles contacted Stockton, Alpha's Third Platoon was already on the LZ and Danielsen was getting his next platoon and his command group saddled up.

The estimation of the size of the enemy force in contact also was controversial. Reports from Zion that were relayed by Stockton's operations officer to division headquarters indicated a reinforced battalion surrounding LZ MARY. Hemphill frankly doubted the enemy strength estimates, suggesting that lack of combat experience and the spooky situation led to greatly exaggerated figures. Hemphill believed that a full NVA battalion would have easily overrun the small LZ on the first assault and concludes that the NVA strength probably never exceeded that of a single rifle company. In light of subsequent battles in the Ia Drang and elsewhere, Hemphill probably was correct. The number of casualties taken by American forces on the LZ simply did not add up to a battalion-size enemy force.

Nevertheless, for the troopers climbing aboard the choppers for a wild night ride into a landing zone that they knew was under fire, the discussion of enemy strength estimates is academic. Most of the men of the 3rd Platoon, the lead element committed by Danielsen in response to Stockton's relief order, knew only that they would be assaulting to the south or to the left of the line of flight when they hit the ground. Danielsen briefed the platoon leader, Lieutenant John Hanlon, about the situation and the fact that there were friendlies along the south end of the perimeter. He instructed him to make sure his men kept their fire up when they dismounted from the aircraft.

The ride from Duc Co to LZ MARY took only minutes, and the four choppers on the lift roared in at treetop level, flared, and dropped into the LZ. The moon bathed the landing zone in a cold white light. Adding to the illumination was a flare dropped from an Air Force C-47 that had been called on station when the ambush was sprung. Zion felt that maximum illumination was necessary; this, after all, was the first night helicopter assault into a hot LZ ever attempted by American forces. The lighting served the purpose; the pilots could see the ground clearly as they made their approach. But the NVA gunners also made the most of the illumination, blazing away at the choppers. Several of the 3rd Platoon's men were hit when they left the birds, and all of the four lift ships were hit, but they were still flyable.

The ships headed back to Duc Co and the rest of

Danielsen's company. In a paper written for the Infantry Officer Advance Course at Fort Benning late in 1966, Danielsen recalls getting into LZ MARY at about half an hour after midnight. Danielsen's 2nd Platoon was the next unit to go in, although the Company command group took up three slots on the lead ship. Danielsen didn't know the name of the landing zone and remembered having dubbed it "LZ Spiderweb" as his flight neared the site. This was because the various colored tracers spun an intricate web around and across the entire LZ—the bluish-green NVA tracers, starting on one side and continuing across the LZ and out the other side, and the red tracers of the American weapons flashing a counterpoint to those of the North Vietnamese.

When his lift touched down, Danielsen deployed the 2nd Platoon to the right of the 3rd Platoon and immediately gained the tree line and began assignment of sectors of fire. He left a gap between the two platoons; it was filled on an interim basis by some of the Charlie Troop Blues and Danielsen's command group. This gap was for the company's last platoon—the 1st Platoon, which had been handling picket-line duty at Duc Co—to arrive. When the last platoon arrived, Danielsen began sending out his wounded on the empty birds, all of which had taken multiple hits but were still flying.

It took some extraordinary flying, requiring both skill and courage, to pull off the night air assault and the continual reinforcement of the landing zone under fire. The aviation part of the engagement was led by Lieutenant James W. Rosebrough, Bravo Troop's flight platoon leader. Captain Oliver's Blue birds sustained multiple hits, some worse than others, but all were able to fly out of the LZ. On the second lift, one of the pilots had left his FM transmitter on, and those who were monitoring that frequency heard the pilot tell the copilot: "We've lost our hydraulics." The copilot came back with: "So what. Let's get this fucker out of here." And they proceeded to do just that, flying back to Duc Co and landing without incident.

Two U.S. Air Force A1E Skyraiders make runs at North Vietnamese Army soldiers who had laid siege to the Plei Me Special Forces camp in what became the opening battle in the Pleiku Campaign. The long buildings just outside the compound are where the families of the Montagnard Strike Force live. The smooth surface of the dirt airstrip is on the near side of the compound.

Master Sergeant James A. Bussard operates radios linking the besieged Special Forces camp with reinforcements on the way from Pleiku as well as U.S. Air Force fighter bombers that flew almost constant top cover over the camp.

(Associated Press photo by John Wheeler)

Elements of the 2nd Battalion, 8th Cavalry, of the 1st Air Cavalry Division struggle up Ho Mountain (Chu Ho) just south of the Plei Me Special Forces camp in an attack on OBJECTIVE CHERRY. It was the first offensive action by the Cav in the young campaign and was where the division sustained its first man killed in action.

(Photo by J. D. Coleman)

As the Cav geared up to chase NVA forces retreating westward from the Plei Me camp, the long-range eyes of the division were provided by these H-13 scout helicopters of the 1st Squadron, 9th Cavalry. Here, an Alpha Troop A bird lifts off.

(Photo by J. D. Coleman)

Much of the punch of the 1st Cavalry was provided by its armed helicopters. A crewman from the 227th Assault Helicopter Battalion arms the weapons system on the "B" Model Huey prior to an escort mission.

(U.S. Army photo)

A typical air landing in the highlands near the Plei Me Special Forces camp. The nearer the Cav got to the Chu Pong Massif, the more difficult the terrain became. This waist-high plateau grass, which was yellow-green in color, provided excellent concealment to crawling North Vietnamese soldiers. The grasslands of the western plateau had very little of the better known elephant grass, which was higher than a man's head and had blades that cut like rapiers.

(Photo by J. D. Coleman)

An Air Force O-1 Birddog spotter aircraft circles the area where it just fired a white phosphorus rocket marking an NVA position near the Meur River. A flight of fighter bombers were already into their bomb run when this picture was made.

(Photo by J. D. Coleman)

Lift ships of the 229th Assault Helicopter Battalion carry sky troopers of the 1st Air Cavalry Division into another of the scores of landing zones assaulted by the division during the Pleiku Campaign.

This was the way casualties from the isolated 7th Cavalry platoon at LZ XRAY were carried down off the mountain. It was also the way most casualties during the entire campaign were evacuated from forward positions. Long pieces of bamboo were tied into a poncho to create a crude litter. Sometimes these field-expedient litters stayed with the patient all the way back to the aid stations at Catecka or Camp Holloway. The strain of battle clearly shows on the faces of these young troopers.

(Photograph by J. D. Coleman)

Smoke billows upward from the south edge of LZ XRAY as fighter bombers pound NVA positions during the three-day battle. Napalm and five-hundred-pound bombs delivered by the Air Force were instrumental in shattering the NVA attacks.

(Photograph by J. D. Coleman)

Artillery support for the battles in the campaign was provided from fire bases like this. Here, the new M-102 howitzers support Cavalry troopers maneuvering against the NVA in the Ia Drang Valley. Note the high angle of fire possible with the new howitzer.

(Associated Press photo by Rick Merron)

Part of the toll paid by the 1st Cavalry Division are these poncho-covered bodies of the young men who died in the brutal battles in the Ia Drang. Lieutenant Colonel Harold Moore, the Cavalry commander on LZ XRAY, said, "There are men with less than a week to go in the Army lying there. They never quit. They gave everything they had." The sorrowful task of carrying them to their final helicopter ride falls to their exhausted comrades.

(Associated Press photo by Rick Merron)

Wounded and dead Americans are gathered along the edge of LZ ALBANY waiting evacuation by helicopter. Those still alive were among the survivors of the 2nd Battalion, 7th Cavalry that collided with a North Vietnamese battalion on November 17.

Secretary of Defense Robert McNamara (center in khakis) looks at a display of weapons captured by the 1st Air Cavalry Division in the Pleiku Campaign. Describing the booty at the An Khe base is the division's commander, Major General Harry W.O. Kinnard, at right. At left is General Earl K. Wheeler, Chairman of the Joint Chiefs of Staff, and John McNaughton, Assistant Secretary of Defense.

The air crew promptly went out and "borrowed" another Huey. They made the next flight in right on schedule.

Once Alpha Company was on the ground, organized, and returning volumes of fire, the crisis was all but over. But for the thirty or forty minutes that Hanlon's platoon was defending the southern side of the perimeter, the situation was pretty scary. Hanlon was severely wounded shortly after the platoon assaulted out toward the tree line. The bullet coursed through his chest and lodged against his spine, causing not only the classic sucking chest wound but also paralysis from the waist down. Hanlon remembers vividly:

> I found myself passing out from loss of blood. But the Lord's hand was on my shoulder and I was able to place a first aid packet and a poncho jacket over the chest wound and seal off the air leak with the belt from my trousers. I yelled for Ortiz, the platoon medic, who crawled over and gave me a shot of morphine. I knew I was paralyzed and I tried to pull myself into a position where I could lead the platoon, but I kept passing out.

Realizing that he was becoming a liability to his platoon, Hanlon summoned his platoon sergeant, Sergeant First Class Kenneth Riveer, and told him to take over the platoon. Riveer remembers that Specialist Four Raymond Ortiz, although badly wounded, kept moving about the perimeter, tending to other wounded. In fact, Ortiz had received a severe shoulder wound almost immediately after leaving the helicopter, rendering his left arm useless. During that initial half-hour on the LZ, he was hit at least three more times. He received the Distinguished Service Cross for his heroism. The citation for his medal is a testament to his gallantry:

> Ignoring [his wound and] the intense small arms and mortar fire striking all around him, he began to treat and evacuate the wounded personnel from their exposed locations. With

one arm hanging useless at his side, Specialist Ortiz personally carried six wounded soldiers to evacuation helicopters some 50 meters across an open area. Disregarding the shouts of his comrades to take cover, he proceeded to aid a wounded platoon leader. After advancing several yards, Specialist Ortiz was knocked to the ground by hostile fire. Although now bleeding from a chest wound, he rose to his feet and continued toward the platoon leader. Again he was struck in the chest by hostile small arms fire and fell to his knees. Specialist Ortiz refused medical treatment and evacuation until all other wounded had been treated. His display of gallantry under intense hostile fire saved the lives of several men and provided an inspiring example of courage to the platoon.

Riveer, in moving about to control his platoon, came across a captain behind a tree stump. Riveer said that he asked the captain where all of his people were, and he responded, "They're all dead. We're all going to die here." Riveer said, "Well, I ain't going to die tonight," and crawled off. Hanlon had also run across this captain in about the same location just before Hanlon was shot, and had had a similar conversation with him.

Danielsen credits the determined defense by his 3rd Platoon and the spectacular shooting by Lieutenant Tweedy's mortars in saving the landing zone in the period before Alpha Company was on line in full strength. The mortars, operating in the open and subject to grazing fire, were firing without a plotting board or firing tables. All fire was adjusted by direct sight, and corrections were made by turns on the traversing or elevating screws. During the course of the firefight, the platoon fired two basic loads in extremely close proximity to the front-line trace of the LZ without inflicting a single friendly casualty. It was the payoff of months of exhaustive training at Fort Benning and in the Carolinas.

At 1:15 A.M., the North Vietnamese again began moving toward the southern end of the perimeter, while stepping up their fires from the forces that had the LZ surrounded. This time, Danielsen's company had no problem in repulsing the limited attack. Once more, the firing dwindled to sniper fire that targeted anything on the landing zone that moved. The bright moonlight still gave the NVA all the advantage. Zion, after pleas from the leaders on the perimeter that the additional illumination was hurting more than helping, had sent the flare birds back to bed.

As Hanlon's platoon struggled to hold the southern edge of the perimeter, Oliver's ambush force started back toward LZ MARY. The big problem for Oliver was that the LZ was surrounded and, even though the NVA did not have a big force on the northern side of the perimeter, the defenders were laying down a heavy volume of fire. A three-man point party led the way, but every time the scout group got close enough to the LZ where recognition signals could be exchanged, NVA skirmishers opened fire. For the better part of three hours Oliver's thirty-man patrol played cat and mouse with the NVA, dodging both their bullets and the fire from the LZ. During one nasty little firefight, Charlie Black, the correspondent, felt a tug at his camera strap and found that an AK slug had neatly pierced the leather film-carrying case. Finally, at 3:00 A.M., the patrol, slithering along like reptiles through little ditches and gullies, made it safely back into the perimeter. Oliver immediately took over responsibility for the northern end of the perimeter, releasing the Blues from Alpha Troop to handle both the eastern and western sectors, since Zion wisely had kept the Montagnard platoon at its original ambush position. By 3:00 A.M., Danielsen had his entire company in on the southern side of the landing zone.

At 3:30 A.M. the NVA tried once more to crack the barrier. By this time the North Vietnamese had an 82-mm mortar battery in position to aid in the assault. When the mortars started falling, Major Zion called for help from an AI-E flight that was orbiting overhead. One pilot quickly spotted the muzzle flashes of the mortars and in a twinkling sent a ripple of rockets at the battery. Charlie Black reported that only thirteen mortar rounds had fallen before the Skyraider silenced the guns. No sooner had the mortars been taken care of than four aerial rocket artillery gunships from Catecka came on station. Lining up right over the center of the landing zone, they ripped off a volley of more than 120 of the 2.75-inch aerial rockets. There was a thunderous roar, and the NVA guns fell silent. As soon as the ARA birds touched off the volley, they broke away from the LZ, clearing the air space for a resupply mission by the squadron's lift ships. For the first time since the fight started, the aircraft landed, discharged cargo, loaded wounded, and took off without a single shot being fired at them.

From 4:00 A.M. until dawn, the battle consisted of sniper fire from NVA soldiers in the trees. The bright moonlight and the lack of entrenchments in the LZ made the defenders easy targets. But the NVA didn't have an easy task; every muzzle flash in a tree brought prompt answering fire from the perimeter. The M-79 grenade launcher was particularly effective in blowing snipers out of their perches. The sniper fire did serve to cover the breaking of contact of the main NVA force and helped mask the pulling of their dead and wounded away from the battle lines.

At first light, Danielsen, with the concurrence of Zion, ordered an assault to the south. The assault proceeded without incident a distance of some one hundred meters from the trace of the perimeter. The company left outposts at the outer limits of advance and then moved back to the perimeter to consolidate their positions. Danielsen said he was asked for a body count, but, while seeing ample evidence that a lot of men bled and died on the ground over which his company walked, he never actually saw a body. Danielsen is pretty matter of fact about his conduct of the battle during the night, but others are not shy about extolling his leadership and heroism.

Charlie Black, who had just returned to the LZ with

Oliver's group, had headed to Zion's anthill command post when the 3:30 NVA assault came. As the intensity of the fire increased, Zion shouted to Black, pointing toward the southern end of the landing zone. Black says he looked and saw Danielsen, easily recognized by his cigar (also, he was an old acquaintance of Black's), with an M-60 machine gun in his hand, firing steadily into the tree line. "I saw three snipers fall from his fire out of the trees about twenty-five meters high at a close range right on the edge of the clearing," recalls Black.

About half an hour after daylight, Bravo Company, which had been relieved of duty as palace guards at Catecka, arrived on the LZ, along with Delta Company and Major Eberhardt, the acting commander of the battalion. Once the 1/8 Cavalry was on the ground and in control, Stockton turned the landing zone over to the infantry and extracted his squadron troops. The results of the night's activities are difficult to evaluate, given the degree of controversy that surrounded the battle. Stockton's after-action report lists seventy-two NVA confirmed as killed, with an estimated additional twenty-four dead as a result of American fire. This included the enemy soldiers in the ambush area as well as those attacking the patrol base. A wounded enemy soldier also was captured (eventually, intelligence would learn from this soldier that a new NVA regiment had arrived in South Vietnam). The squadron had two dead and ten wounded, while Alpha Company lost two men and had fifteen wounded. Six Hueys were hit by enemy fire, but all were back flying after repairs.

Three significant events occurred during the engagement: (1) For the first time in the division, and perhaps anywhere in Vietnam, an American-mounted night ambush was successfully carried out in an area remote from any government outpost. (2) For the first time anywhere, a perimeter under attack was reinforced by heliborne infantry platoons at night. And while all lift helicopters were hit by enemy fire, none were damaged beyond repair. (3) For the first time anywhere, final protective fires were delivered at night within fifty meters of the patrol-base perimeter by rocket-firing helicopters. There were no friendly casualties as a result of this fire; its volume and accuracy probably turned the tide of battle.

Despite the apparent success of the mission, Knowles wanted to court-martial Stockton for disobedience of orders and other actions. Kinnard, however, was against it, arguing that, in effect, Stockton was a lucky Custer and that nothing positive could be gained from a high-profile court-martial. Knowles said he told Kinnard, "Look, I'm not worried about my own reputation; I'm looking for what's best for the division. So if that's your decision, I can live with it. But I do request one thing. Get him out of the division by any means you can." Kinnard had the last word, though, gently jabbing Knowles by saying, "You should have let me throw him out before." But the entire action was vintage Stockton; all the episodes of evading both the spirit and the letter of orders during training had finally come home to roost in combat. The affair did substantially subdue Stockton's flamboyance, and within hours after the end of the campaign in late November, he was transferred to a staff job in Saigon.

Acting on the recommendation of the 1st Brigade commander, division headquarters chose not to exploit the obvious presence of North Vietnamese troops in that part of the Ia Drang drainage, giving the 1/8 only limited search missions in the vicinity of LZ MARY. The search operations were supported by a battery of tube artillery (B 2/19 Arty) which was lifted into an LZ about three kilometers north and slightly to the east of LZ MARY. At 4:00 P.M., the two-company battalion was ordered to extract from LZ MARY and return to the brigade base at Catecka to provide a command post security and to serve as a brigade reaction force. Simultaneously, the artillery battery moved by Chinook helicopters back to the artillery base it had been sharing with another battery of the 2/19 Arty.

By 5:00 P.M., the North Vietnamese had the Chu Pongs and the Ia Drang to themselves again—not that the cavalry had any lack of targets further east. Both the 2/12 and the 2/8 Cav battalions had begun stirring up something of interest, and Knowles reluctantly concurred with Harlow Clark that it would be wisest to avoid spreading the brigade across the landscape and risk defeat in detail. With two full NVA regiments and a divisional headquarters in assembly areas within five kilometers of LZ MARY, Knowles and other senior commanders have always wondered what might have been had the division thrown in another brigade and a couple more battalions to follow up that night ambush on the Ia Drang.

8

THE FIRST
BRIGADE'S
FINAL
BATTLES

On November 4, the First Brigade had only been committed to the battle for some ten days, but to Lieutenant Colonel Harlow Clark, the acting commander, it must have seemed like months. He was a tough, highly capable commander; an aviator and a master parachutist who had commanded an airborne rifle company in Korea. But he had never before commanded any kind of an outfit with the span of control of a deployed brigade, and, normally, combat is not the place for on-the-job training for the senior commander. It was a mark of the confidence Kinnard and Knowles had in the man to leave him in the command slot during such a critical time. Colonel George Beatty, the chief of staff, who had led the 1st Brigade through the entire 11th Air Assault Division days, was readily available for the brief period that Colonel Elvy Roberts was absent from the division. But Clark had mastered the complexities of the job with amazing rapidity and, by November 3, was managing the airmobile field operations of four battalions like a seasoned pro.

From an airmobility standpoint alone, the activities of November 3 resulted in the equivalent of seven company and two battery moves, for a one-way distance of 250 kilometers. The next day, there were twelve company and two battery moves, for a total distance of 325 kilometers. Additionally, there were numerous ground movements of company- and platoon-size elements. And the logistical requirements were staggering.

The logistical situation never became a problem because of the efforts of the Third Forward Support Element (FSE) of the division's Support Command. Division headquarters sent Lieutenant Colonel Rutland Beard, down from the deputy chief of staff's slot to act as deputy commander for Clark, to keep track of details and permit Clark the time he needed to be a field commander. The scheme had worked well, and the 1st Brigade team was getting better every day.

The reason Harlow Clark was apprehensive about extending his brigade too far to the west was that there was ample evidence that the NVA were still in and around the hospital area in some strength. The cavalry scouts were turning up evidence of continued NVA presence. Despite being overshadowed by the more spectacular exploits of the Blue teams, the White (scouts in H-13s) and Red (gunships) teams were doing a thorough job of scouring the jungles for traces of the enemy. The 2/12 Cav had made small contacts throughout its search area, located about five kilometers northeast of the hospital. Gene Fox's Alpha Company had marched and countermarched on November 2 and 3, with various minor contacts. He had a brief run-in with an NVA platoon and sustained one wounded, but he captured a wounded man who turned out to be a battalion sergeant major. Alpha also captured a 75-mm recoilless rifle. Bravo Company had run across a medical and arms cache, and Charlie Company had had brief skirmishes with small groups of NVA. It was clear that there still were North Vietnamese in the area, but allied intelligence officers had no real handle on the identity of the units. In fact, many intelligence summaries still referred to the NVA's 33rd Regiment as the 101B, which was the regiment's infiltration designator. Brigade and division headquarters were operating under the assumption that the contacts being made by the Second of the Twelfth north and east of the hospital were with the unit that had fought there on November 1. They were wrong.

At the 33rd's headquarters, orders were received from Field Front to move out of its mountain sanctuary, Hill 732 in the Chu Pong Massif, and take up positions with its battalions on the eastern slopes of the Chu Pongs, with one wing of its defensive line taking in the regiment's assembly area of ANTA Village. The fact that the regiment didn't really have any battalions remaining apparently didn't faze the order givers at higher headquarters. The one battalion, the 2nd Battalion, that had made it to the sanctuary had been chewed up so badly at Plei Me as to be nearly ineffective. By November 4, the first stragglers from the hospital fight were arriving, bearing the bad news. The balance of that battalion, approximately two understrength companies, was still about four kilometers from ANTA Village, holed up on a wooded ridge above a stream bed, waiting for nightfall before setting out on the last leg of their odyssey. One unit of the regiment, the 3rd Battalion, was still reasonably intact, and it had acted as a rear guard. Starting its trek to the west later and moving more slowly than the others, it was still east of the main cavalry positions. Thus, the contacts being made by 2/12 Cav were with the advance elements of the 3rd Battalion.

In the 2/8 Cav area of operations west of the hospital, the units were widely dispersed. The battalion command post, co-located with A Battery, 2/19 Arty, and initially secured by Charlie and Delta companies, was on a base called LZ CAV-ALAIR. Located on a small plateau which provided firm footing for the artillery pieces, it was only four kilometers west of the NVA assembly area at ANTA Village! At first light on November 4, Charlie Company air assaulted into a LZ up near Duc Co along with B Battery, 2/19 Arty to provide artillery support for the 1/8 Cav, which had taken control of the embattled ambush patrol base across the Drang River. With Charlie Company gone, a platoon of Alpha Company was pulled in from its search location about six kilometers east of CAVALAIR to become command post security. With additional security present, Lieutenant Colonel James Nix, the battalion commander, concurred with a request from his S-2, Captain Richard Slifer, to take a closer look at a suspected camp about 800 meters north of CAVALAIR. Nix directed the Delta Company commander, Captain Samuel P. Linton III, to send the reconnaissance platoon into the area. The Executive Officer of the company was First Lieutenant Franklin Trapnell, who recalls that the Recon Platoon leader, Lieutenant William A. Ward, split his platoon into two parts, going out himself with seventeen men and leaving his platoon sergeant, Sergeant First Class Clint R. Marshall, and one squad of the platoon at CAVALAIR. At 10:15 A.M., after moving north by northeast for about six hundred meters and just after crossing a small stream, Ward's force discovered and captured one sick NVA soldier. Across the stream was a long, low ridge line that ran from southeast to northwest. The hill mass was dominated by two crests, each perhaps 150 meters wide and rising twenty-five to fifty meters higher than the remainder of the ridge. Between the two peaks was a densely forested saddle covering about 250 meters. The patrol started moving up the hill from the stream bed and had covered about another 150 meters when it began receiving light fire from the hill on their right front, the northernmost of the peaks. Nix landed his command chopper to evacuate the prisoner and told Ward to maintain contact. The platoon then veered into a northeasterly course, orienting on the enemy fire. As the two squads of the platoon began moving up the hill, they took more fire, and then an estimated thirty-five to forty enemy soldiers began to flee the area in all directions, many of them seemingly unarmed.

Ward ordered Staff Sergeant Harold G. Rose to keep moving up the hill to secure the high ground and sent Staff Sergeant Jones to pursue in the direction where most of the NVA soldiers seemed to have gone. This was due north, and within

100 meters, Jones's squad overran a camp hidden in a small, heavily wooded depression. There, he found ten sick and two unarmed NVA soldiers. Jones tied up all of the prisoners and sent half of his squad back up the hill to help Rose, who was now yelling for help. In the process of clearing the hill, Rose's squad began to take sniper fire in sufficient strength to begin suffering casualties. With help from Jones's people, Rose's squad went into an immediate action drill, forming into a skirmish line and assaulting up the hill. Rose led his men in a hand grenade assault, dashing this way and that as he made his way up the slope. Once the objective was taken and the NVA driven from the ridge line, Rose began taking care of his dead and wounded. Two of his men were killed and two wounded. One of the wounded was his assistant squad leader, Sergeant Robert E. Wilson, who had been instrumental in wiping out a sniper's nest with hand grenades before being hit in the leg by an AK-47 round. The assistant squad leader of the second squad, Sergeant Richard Coffey, wasn't as lucky. He had led his squad to within thirty meters of the NVA positions when the attack bogged down. While trying to inspire his men to cover the final distance, he was mortally wounded when struck in the head by a sniper round.

The two Recon Platoon squads paused on the objective to take stock of the situation. The platoon leader notified the battalion of the results of the contact, including the capture of twelve NVA soldiers in the camp. He also requested reinforcements and medevacs. At 11:00 A.M., Linton ordered the balance of the Recon platoon under Sergeant Marshall, with an additional ten men from Company B attached, to move to the contact area and reinforce Ward's force. Marshall arrived at the NVA campsite just as the NVA forces were filtering back into it. He took light fire as his group moved forward and then swept through the camp, killing ten NVA in the process. The prisoners were still tied up, and Marshall kept his force in the camp to secure it, sending the balance of Jones's squad on up the hill to reinforce Rose.

Concurrently, Lieutenant Trapnell was told by Linton to take the 2nd Platoon of Company A, four men from Delta's Anti-Tank Platoon, and a medic and move to the camp and hill area. Captain Richard Slifer, the battalion intelligence officer, and his interpreter, Sergeant Be, also were to accompany the group. Trapnell's mission was to organize the forces already in the camp and on the hill, ensure that the area was secured, and begin to evacuate casualties.

The force moved out and, at 12:30 P.M., just as it was crossing the little stream, came under sniper fire from an area just in front of the camp, on the western slope of the ridge. Obviously, the NVA had again filtered back into the area and were prepared to contest the movement of anyone coming up from the west. The Alpha Company platoon deployed on a line and rapidly swept up the ridge and into the camp. But then, when the unit began moving up the slope of the hill, it began taking heavier fire. Once again, a strong NVA battle element had slipped in between Ward's two squads at the peak and the NVA rest camp. The distance was only about two hundred meters, but it was densely wooded, with tall grass and bushes obscuring vision.

The proximity of the enemy force to the friendly elements ruled out any kind of indirect fire support. Neither cavalry force had enough combat power to make any decisive movements, and the two antagonists remained in position for the better part of the afternoon, trading shots.

Trapnell was able to evacuate the wounded down the hill to a point where there was some degree of cover. Linton sent an M274 (Mechanical Mule) and litter bearers out from CAVALAIR. The vehicle got to a point just south of the stream bed, and the litter bearers went forward by foot from there. The NVA began reinforcing their sniper force, bringing increasingly heavier volumes of fire against the squads.

Back on CAVALAIR, Nix was frustrated by the inability to bring in ARA, tube artillery, or Tac Air in support of his Recon Platoon, so he directed reinforcement on the ground to shoe horn some sort of maneuverability back into the battle. Alpha Company was told to take two platoons and attack from the southeast. Its skipper, Captain Roger McElroy, soon had his platoons moving on a northeast heading from CAVALAIR. At about 1:15 P.M., just after they crossed the stream bed, their lead elements came under fire from NVA riflemen concealed along the ridge line southeast of Recon's position. Alpha's platoons hit the ground and started fire and movement up the slope toward the direction from which they were receiving fire. By 2:00 P.M., the fight was raging in three locations along the slopes of the ridge: with Alpha Company's two platoons on the southern side of the ridge; with Trapnell's force just east of the NVA rest camp but down the slope from the ridge line; and with Lieutenant Ward's bobtailed platoon, which was holding out at the northernmost peak of the ridge line.

The two Alpha platoons spent nearly three hours struggling up the two hundred or so meters from the stream bed to about halfway toward the top of the ridge line. Platoon Sergeant Norman G. Welch and his radio operator, Private First Class Ronald Luke, both won Silver Stars that afternoon, but only Welch lived to collect. Welch set up a squad as a base-of-fire element and started to maneuver with two other squads. The intensity of NVA fire increased and stalled the advance about a hundred meters up the hill. No one had been killed yet, but half a dozen men were wounded. Welch received notification of impending fire support and pulled his point and flank men back into the cover of a small ravine. It was no easy task, taking the better part of an hour to get all of the men back to cover while pulling the wounded to a location where they could be evacuated. The fire-swept ridge was so hot that a Huey slick from one of the lift battalions that attempted to land and take out wounded was hit and had to make a precautionary landing about twenty-five hundred meters to the east. As Welch ran back and forth to collect the wounded, the NVA snipers began concentrating their fire on him. This was when

Luke stood up, still carrying his radio, and deliberately drew fire to himself by blazing away with his M-16. Although his radio was hit eleven times, Luke continued to draw fire while Welch pulled two more wounded troopers to safety. As Welch was moving the third man, Luke's luck ran out and a machine-gun burst cut him down. Another man whose luck ran out that day was the ARVN interpreter, Sergeant Be, who caught a sniper round in the head as he was moving around Trapnell's portion of the battlefield to interrogate prisoners.

Although the infantry fight had become stalemated, there was a window of opportunity through which Nix could get in some fire support. The strip of the ridge line that the NVA held was about two hundred meters in depth, more than enough to safely bring in aerial rocket artillery and mortars from CAVALAIR. Nix used the 105-mm howitzer battery on CAVALAIR to fire concentrations on the northern, eastern, and western sides of the battle area. Because the range was just under one thousand meters, he was reluctant to risk close-in support with the extreme high angle of fire that would be required of the howitzers. Finally the mortar barrages and gunship runs, combined with the steady firing from all three cavalry positions, began taking their toll on the North Vietnamese on the ridge line. By 5:30 P.M., the NVA had had enough and, having discovered that there was no opposition on the northern side of their position, began breaking contact, moving north and then west toward ANTA Village.

The proper thing to do from a doctrinal standpoint would have been to maintain contact with the fleeing enemy, but the cavalrymen were exhausted and content to stay where they were. Nix sent in Charlie Company, which was now back under his direct control. But by the time C Company relieved the two Alpha platoons and then linked up with Ward's Reconnaissance Platoon and Trapnell's force, it was nearly dark and everyone was content to stand fast, evacuate wounded, and wait until morning to sweep the battlefield. Only twenty-two NVA bodies were left on the ridge line, but there was ample evidence that perhaps as many as forty or fifty more had perished in the fight, many from aerial rockets and mortar fire. The 1st Battalion of the 33rd Regiment had ceased to exist as a viable tactical unit.

Just about the time that Harlow Clark was considering sending in elements of the 1/8 Cav as a reinforcement for its sister battalion, Bravo Company of the 2/12 Cav made a sharp contact in a river bed seven kilometers northeast of the hospital. Captain Graham Avera's company was on a search mission, generally heading north toward the Tae River. At around 4:00 P.M., his lead platoon approached the river. The point man for the lead squad, Private First Class Laris White, spotted a flash of khaki along the river bank and opened fire with his M-16. The single weapon drew a violent response from a series of rock and trench fortifications on the southern bank of the river. White dropped instantly, riddled by rifle and machine-gun fire. The team leader of the squad closest to the river, Sergeant Walter B. Oliver, immediately began deploying his fire team. As he struggled to get movement in the face of withering fire, Oliver saw an NVA machine gunner draw a bead on the platoon radio operator, and he leaped in front of the man, knocking him to the ground. Oliver then opened fire with his M-16, charging forward as he did so. He was struck in the chest with a burst of machine-gun fire, but even as he was dying he was able to squeeze off another burst of automatic rifle fire at the machine-gun bunker. This allowed the grenadiers in the platoon to lob grenades into the position, eliminating it. Avera quickly maneuvered the other two platoons into position to support his lead element and assaulted the stream line, but the NVA force melted into the jungle. When the troopers hit the bottom of the river bed, they discovered that the security force had defended what appeared to be a regimental supply dump. The NVA had left a dozen dead in the area and a substantial amount of weapons and equipment. There were six 12.5-mm machine guns, three 75-mm recoilless rifles with forty-four rounds of ammunition, two 82-mm mortars with 108 rounds of ammo, fifteen AK rifles, four light machines guns, and a rocket launcher. There were mortar sights, recoilless rifle sights, night-firing devices, a bunch of packs, food supplies, and thousands of rounds of 7.62-mm and 12.5-mm ammunition. Best yet, a prisoner informed intelligence officers that the main force of the rear guard battalion had just passed through on its way west to the Chu Pongs.

The cost to B Company was three men killed, fifteen wounded. A medic from Headquarters Company was also killed. The estimated strength of the NVA in the cache site was about two platoons, indicating once again that in a straight-up firefight without the interference of artillery or air support, the elements of the 33rd Regiment could inflict fearsome casualties in a hurry.

With two fair-size contacts occurring well within his AO, it is a small wonder that Clark declined to venture further west to the far side of the Ia Drang. Sometimes, in looking back at a campaign, it is easy to forget the clouds of mystery and uncertainty that hang over a battlefield. Once all of the enemy prisoners were interrogated and the captured documentation translated, it was relatively easy to figure out what Field Front had been up to. But at the time, there still was monumental groping for a clue to the enemy's location, much less his intentions. Thus, Clark and Knowles still believed there was an enemy force due west of the old ambush site on the road from Pleiku to Plei Me and kept the 1/12 Cavalry flailing about in the bushes in a fruitless search for the NVA. Further south, however, Clark ordered his battalions to tighten what he believed to be a noose around the necks of a substantial enemy force. The 2/12 sent Charlie Company, under Captain William O. Childs, to help out Bravo at the cache site. It took until nearly 3:00 P.M. on November 5 to get all of the materiel either sorted, backhauled, or destroyed.

Further west, reacting to the intelligence that the enemy force that had just left the cache site was heading toward the Chu Pongs, 2/8 Cav was maneuvering its forces to intercept the NVA battalion. The artillery base was moved about five kilometers east, from LZ CAVALAIR to an LZ called FALCON, which was about two thousand meters due west of the old hospital area. Alpha Company closed out the old landing zone and took over the security of LZ FALCON. Charlie Company spent a good part of the 5th searching the battlefield north of CAVALAIR, and just before nighfall was airlifted into LZ FALCON. Captain John Richardson's Bravo Company continued sweeping north along the drainage of the Tae River. At a point about three thousand meters north of the hospital area, the Tae River, which flowed in a general north-south pattern by the hospital, began angling toward the northeast. The Tae River is part of the Meur River basin, a distinctly different drainage area from the Ia Drang, which, while flowing northeast to southwest, empties into the Seprok River in Cambodia around the northern side of the Chu Pongs. The Meur River, on the other hand, drains the southern part of the western plateau and empties into the Seprok from around the southern reaches of the Chu Pong Massif. The Seprok empties into the giant Mekong.

Each of the main drainage rivers has major tributaries, and each of these has smaller feeder streams. It was on one of those Tae River feeder streams that the hospital site was found. Late in the afternoon of the 5th, Bravo crossed the Tae River, traversed a small ridge, then crossed another feeder stream and set up for the night on some high ground that straddled an old Montagnard trail. The trail ran from an abandoned village on the Tae to the northwest. As soon as the company began setting up night defensive positions, Richardson told the 1st Platoon leader, Lieutenant John Meyer, to send an ambush squad back down toward the feeder stream. Staff Sergeant Steve Coulson, the leader of the First Squad, got the mission and headed toward a location about 800 meters south and slightly west of the company position. Coulson's squad had an uneventful night, although they could hear movement and voices across the stream to their west. His squad was delayed in getting back to the company base the next morning because, after getting about halfway back, one of his men discovered he had left a .45 pistol at the ambush site.

By the time the weapon was retrieved and the squad was back inside the company perimeter, Richardson had already deployed the remainder of the company in a two-pronged sweep toward the southwest. He sent the 1st Platoon, minus Coulson's squad, on the northern loop and his 2nd Platoon, augmented by two squads and the platoon leader of the 3rd Platoon, on the southern loop. The Mortar Platoon, one squad of the 3rd Platoon, and one squad from the 1st remained at the company base to provide security. Meanwhile, Charlie Company, under Captain Manley J. "Jim" Morrison, had started at dawn on a search operation oriented generally north and slightly west out of LZ FALCON.

A few minutes after 10:00 A.M., Bravo's 1st Platoon reported taking small-arms fire from its left flank and had three men wounded. Lieutenant Meyer told Richardson that he was pulling back slightly, reorienting his platoon toward the south, and was calling in artillery fire. Almost simultaneously, the 2nd and 3rd platoons, moving southwesterly almost one thousand meters south of the 1st Platoon, also reported taking fire, this time from the north. It was clear that Bravo had caught an enemy force between its pincers. What was not clear was its size and disposition. The 2nd and 3rd platoons reoriented their direction and began bringing the NVA under fire. The NVA broke the initial contact, pulling back into a heavily jungled north-south ridge line separating the Meur and Tae river drainages. Lieutenant Colonel Nix ordered Charlie Company to change directions and head east overland for the firefight. At 10:15, the company still was three thousand meters of heavy jungle away.

As all three Bravo platoons began pressing forward, heading toward each other, hoping to squeeze the enemy between them, they began taking higher volumes of fire. This time the fire was from well-prepared, camouflaged, and concealed positions, where automatic weapons had interlocking fields of fire down gently sloping and open terrain. It was obvious now that the initial contacts had been with the NVA flank security elements, that now the platoons were butting up against a dug-in enemy, and that the force was at least a battalion in size. Moreover, during the reorientation of the two platoons, the 2nd, which was in the lead at the outset, got separated by about two hundred meters from the 3rd. All three platoons were quickly pinned down by the violent fire, and the NVA launched a counterattack by a reinforced platoon that temporarily split the 2nd and 3rd Platoons and threatened to envelop the 2nd. In organizing his platoon to defend against the attack, the 2nd Platoon leader, Lieutenant James A. Castle, was struck in the shoulder and chest by rifle fire. Castle crawled to a vantage point where he could direct his platoon's efforts. He called for an air strike, carefully plotting his position with the forward air controller, and had his platoon mark their flanks with red smoke. The strike by F-104s, which included a napalm run, brought about a slacking of the fires from the NVA positions, but the platoon still was in jeopardy from the attacking force which was too close to call in fire support. Sergeant First Class Payton Watson, Castle's platoon sergeant, ran to one of the platoon machine-gun crews and led it to a position on the platoon's right flank where they could place effective fire on the attackers. Exposing himself frequently, Watson killed at least ten NVA infantrymen with his M-16 before the attack began to fizzle and the North Vietnamese survivors began pulling back.

Meanwhile, the 3rd Platoon leader, Lieutenant Felix King, realizing the danger in which the attack had placed the platoon and learning that Castle had been hit, led his bobtailed platoon across the fire-swept slope to cover the two hundred meters between the platoons. His attack from the flank, coupled with the 2nd Platoon's machine-gun fire that had been set up by Watson, broke the back of the NVA assault. In trying to reach Castle to coordinate the defense of the two platoons, King dashed across fifty meters of open ground. Castle, who had refused first aid during the heated stages of the fight, now consented to King's bandaging his wounds. He indicated to King that Watson would probably be running the platoon for the rest of the day, then passed out from shock and loss of blood. As King started to return to his platoon sector, he was cut down by a burst from a North Vietnamese machine gun and died almost instantly.

By this time, Captain Richardson, an aviator, had been given an H-13 and was trying to direct the firefight from overhead. Fire support in the form of air strikes and ARA sorties, plus the determined defense of the infantrymen in the two platoons, broke the back of the NVA counterattack, but both platoons had sustained multiple casualties. Artillery support was a bit harder to get. The guns at LZ FALCON were only four kilometers away, which meant the tubes were set at a very high angle. One gun in the cluster of six kept throwing out, and Nix was afraid to use the battery in close-in support because of that one erratic tube. Eventually B Battery at LZ FALCON was augmented by C Battery, located on an LZ in the 1/12 AO about nine kilometers to the northeast.

It was now becoming abundantly clear that this NVA outfit was a particularly truculent lot that was not about to break contact quickly. The superior positions and preponderance of firepower kept both the 2nd and 3rd Platoons pinned in place, and the loss of leadership in the early stages of the fight had sapped them of any desire to try advancing further up the hill. So on the southern flank, things were at a stalemate.

On the northern flank, where the 1st Platoon had first made a contact, things were somewhat better in that the casualties taken were less severe. But when the hail of fire from the NVA's prepared positions stopped their advance cold, the men of the 1st Platoon had to drag their wounded back into a small ravine, where they would be sheltered from the withering rifle and automatic weapons fire. Sergeants Robert Padilla and John Baer and Privates First Class James J. Crafton and Rodrigo Gonzalez were particularly conspicuous on the fire-swept slopes as they tugged and pulled wounded comrades to safety, bandaged their wounds, fired suppressive fires from their weapons, and went back out for more. Like their comrades to the south, the 1st Platoon could neither advance nor withdraw, and there it stayed through another hour and a half, waiting for the arrival of Charlie Company.

At 12:55 P.M., the lead platoon of Morrison's company had reached the western bank of the Meur River. The river bed itself was densely jungled, but twenty-five meters out of the bed the terrain began sloping upward toward the long ridge line occupied by the NVA. The terrain was open and the sight distances for the enemy gunners were incredible. All in all, it was not a promising position for Company C. But the situation with Bravo dictated a movement to relieve the pressure, so Morrison urged his company forward. He planned to bring his 2nd Platoon on line with the 1st and attack with two platoons abreast, but the 2nd got bogged down crossing the river and moving to the left flank of the 1st. And the 1st got too far ahead and was starting up the hill before Morrison was ready to move out on the assault. The NVA let it get about seventy-five meters up the slope before opening fire. The effect was devasting. Soldiers were dropping everywhere, and the advance was stopped immediately. Once again, the Americans had the unenviable task of retrieving wounded in the face of enemy fire. Privates First Class Donald Pond and Willie Pierce accepted the challenge and raced out to pull back four wounded comrades, probably saving their lives. Private First Class James L. Allen of Headquarters Company, a medic assigned to the First Platoon, died that afternoon tending to wounded, refusing to take cover while some comrades remained in the open needing treatment.

Morrison got taken out of the fight when he ran forward to see what he could do to move the platoons up the hill. By the time he got to the rear of the 1st Platoon, the company began taking fire from the flanks, as NVA security elements at the cache sites along the river had begun firing at targets of opportunity. One such target was Morrison. A round hit him in the head, knocking him down. Major Jim Bachman, the S-3, was talking to Morrison on the radio when he was hit. Realizing that he could no longer direct the fight, he called for the Weapons Platoon leader, Lieutenant John Weiss, and turned the active leadership of the company over to him. The company was now beset by enemy on three sides; fortunately for Morrison's charges, the NVA forces on the flanks were of little more than nuisance value, and the 2nd and 3rd Platoons were able to eliminate that threat fairly quickly.

Unfortunately, the elimination came too late for Private First Class Thomas Maynard. But he proved once again that the American fighting man can and will sacrifice his life for his comrades. While trying to resupply forward elements of his platoon with ammunition, Maynard was wounded in the leg. Despite his wound, he continued forward with the ammunition until he found cover near a tree. While Maynard and a badly wounded comrade were behind the tree, an enemy grenade landed between the two soldiers. Maynard immediately attempted to push the seriously wounded man away from the grenade, but then realized that his fellow soldier would be unable to move to safety in time. Maynard fell on the grenade, smothering the explosion with his own body and saving the life of his comrade. Naturally, Maynard was recommended for the Medal of Honor for his sacrifice, but somewhere in the mountains of red tape something got dropped through the cracks, and there is no record of Maynard having received so much as an Army Commendation Medal.

Even though C Company was unable to move further up the ridge, its fire and the heavy volume of fire support—more than forty sorties of Tac Air alone during the afternoon—began sapping the NVA strength, and the bullets came less frequently from the enemy positions. The fire had slackened enough to permit slicks from the lift battalion to land close enough to bring in ammunition, water, and other supplies and to start evacuating wounded. It wasn't a cake walk by a long shot, as snipers kept the small, temporary LZ's under fire, wounding members of the carrying parties and hitting several birds.

By 6:00, it appeared that the NVA battalion was breaking

contact; only sporadic sniper fire was coming from the positions on the ridge line. Nix ordered the companies to link up, essentially at a location down the slope from where Bravo's 2nd and 3rd Platoons were located and where lift ships were coming in for resupply and medical evacuation. Someone dubbed the landing zone "LZ WING," and the name stuck. The Bravo's 1st Platoon, stuck out like a sore thumb on the northern flank of the fight, disengaged without further casualties, worked its way west down the slope to the Meur River, and then eased along the river bed to link up with Charlie Company's elements. C Company began sliding to its right at the same time that Bravo's 2nd and 3rd Platoons began moving to their left toward LZ WING. The full linkup occurred at about 7:00 P.M., and as the various platoon leaders and sergeants began forming a perimeter, the survivors began to breathe easier and relaxed their vigilance. Many of Charlie Company's wounded had not yet been evacuated, and a couple more of the men got clipped during the consolidation movement. Once again, slicks of the 229th Assault Helicopter Battalion were called on. In the growing darkness, one bird was still on the LZ, loading litter patients. Specialist Five Joseph F. Bishop, the crew chief, and Private First Class Louis J. Cunningham, a member of the 11th Pathfinder Company who had volunteered to be a door gunner on this mission, were on the ground helping a wounded soldier wrestle a litter into the aircraft. Suddenly the LZ was brought under heavy fire from the northern and eastern sides. The NVA had sent a platoon down the slopes on a mischief-making trip to keep the American forces well pinned down while the rest of the unit truly broke contact. Surprised, the cavalrymen on the perimeter blazed away and the pilots of the aircraft, blinded by muzzle flashes and a crescendo of tracers, pulled pitch, leaving Bishop and Cunningham alone in the middle of the landing zone with the wounded soldier. There they remained, fighting as infantry soldiers until the attack was beaten back and the aircraft could safely return to police them up. This time, there was complete quiet on the battlefield.

The NVA had slipped away to the southeast, initially, passing south of the Bravo company base and then swinging westward toward the Chu Pongs. At the Bravo base, Coulson remembers a number of probes during the day, but always they were quickly beaten back by the defender's fire. The NVA apparently were more interested in locating a safe way out of the contact zone than in tackling another apparently well-prepared position.

The night passed without incident; a few shots were fired from the perimeter, but more than likely they were the result of tired warriors, rather than NVA contact. The nights in the western plateau could be very spooky, even without contact. Shortly after daybreak on the 7th, Richardson moved the balance of his company to LZ WING and, with Charlie Company, conducted a sweep of the battle area. Colonel Nix was walking with Coulson's squad through the NVA positions, which were littered with bodies, when they came face-to-face with a very live NVA machine gunner. Coulson said they stared at each other for what seemed like an eternity, then Coulson and Nix realized that the man was wounded and, since he had had the drop on them, that he either would not or could not shoot the machine gun. As it turned out, he probably would have, but he was out of ammunition. Division headquarters credited Nix with the capture, but the good colonel always tended to get embarrassed about it, noting that as battalion commander he probably shouldn't have been down there with a squad anyway.

The booty taken out of the battlefield filled three Chinooks: three heavy machine guns, three light machine guns, two automatic rifles, twenty-three AK's, one hundred hand grenades, a B-40 rocket launcher, forty-five individual packs, and about a ton of ammunition. This time the NVA left some bodies on the battlefield to count—seventy-seven total, with clear evidence that a couple hundred more had been hurt badly, probably many of them fatally. The cost to the 2/8 also was high. The battle resulted in the largest number of casualties yet taken in the campaign. The battalion had twenty-six killed—seventeen from C Company, seven from Bravo, and two from Headquarters Company. An additional fifty-three men were wounded.

The next morning, the brigade commander took actions designed to squeeze the NVA, but it was a case of being a day late and a dollar short. He sent two companies of the 1/12 Cavalry marching southwest from their overnight positions about seven kilometers from the battle site. Had he started them out at 3:00 P.M. the previous day, even if they moved by foot, as they did on the 7th, the companies would have arrived in the battle area in time to make a decisive difference. Had Clark cranked up some airmobility and moved the companies by chopper to a point fifteen hundred meters from the battle, the impact would have been greater. But the 1st Cavalry was still feeling its way in this campaign, not only with intelligence, but also with tactics and techniques. The Cav of 1966 and later, with its "find the bastard and then pile on" approach, had yet to evolve. Commanders were still thinking in terms of conventional tactics and movements and they totally underestimated the ability of the NVA to quickly break contact and evade further action.

Clark also had the 2/12 Cav move all three companies into blocking positions about three kilometers due east of the battle area, in the mistaken belief that the NVA had fled to the east. The only unit that had a remote chance of policing up stragglers was Alpha 2/8, which had a couple of platoons in a position about one thousand meters west of LZ Wing. The only contacts during the day were by the 1/12 Cav companies as they ran across isolated North Vietnamese soldiers moving westward. By nightfall, these skirmishes had accounted for nine more NVA killed, with only two cavalrymen wounded. At LZ FALCON, an NVA soldier, a cook with the 3rd Battalion, 33rd Regiment, walked in, carrying a safe conduct pass. Visiting the brigade base at the time was South Vietnamese Premier Nguen Cao Ky, who talked to the young prisoner. It turned out that he was from the same home district in

North Vietnam that Ky had come from. They chatted about the homeland, and Ky promised to take the young man back to North Vietnam with him when he returned to the North in triumph. Needless to say, the young prisoner never made the trip.

Regimental cadres were now gathering the last of the 33rd's stragglers from across the valley and beginning to count noses. There were many missing. The regimental muster showed 890 men of the original 2,200 killed, more than 100 missing, and hundreds more suffering from incapacitating wounds. Materiel losses also were heavy, with the antiaircraft company losing thirteen of its eighteen guns and the mortar company losing five of its nine tubes. In addition, six more mortars were lost by the battalions. The ammunition, food, and medical supply losses also had been crippling. The 33rd Regiment had been dismantled by the 1st Cavalry and airmobility.

These are the NVA casualty figures that were reported by the regiment to Field Front:

Units	Approximate Strength Prior to Plei Me	Percent or Number of Men Killed or Missing in Action
1st Battalion	500	33% KIA
2nd Battalion	500	50% KIA
3rd Battalion	500	33% KIA
Regimental Mortar Company	120	50% KIA 60% KIA
Regimental Antiaircraft Company	150	

Units	Approximate Strength Prior to Plei Me	Percent or Number of Men Killed or Missing in Action
Regimental Transport Company	150	50% KIA
Regimental Medical Company	40	80% KIA OR MIA
Regimental Signal Company	120	4 KIA, 16 MIA
Regimental Engineer Company	60	15 KIA OR MIA
Regimental Reconnaissance Company	50	9 KIA

The chart does not include the Regimental 75-mm Recoilless Rifle Company because captured documents did not have these figures. However, since the regiment reported losing all of its recoilless rifles, it is safe to assume that the company sustained about the same level of casualties as did the mortar and antiaircraft companies.

If ever an outfit was spent, it was the 33rd. The regimental commander asked Field Front for a month for the regiment to reequip and to integrate and train replacements. But the request was denied. Field Front had a new plan, one that required the services of the 33rd, battered as it might be.

9

CHANGING THE BRIGADES

It was a Sunday in Vietnam. A Sunday in most places in the world is a time of leisure, of contemplation, of serenity. But in Vietnam on this day, November 7, two generals were formulating plans and making decisions that ultimately would result in two epic clashes in tiny clearings in the midst of trackless jungles. For one of the generals, Harry Kinnard, it was a fairly routine decision—to send in the 3rd Brigade to replace the 1st Brigade. For the other, Chu Huy Man, the decision was breathtaking in its audacity.

The reason that rest and recuperation were not in the cards for the 33rd was that Field Front had made a decision, a decision that likely was masterminded by General Nguyen Chi Thanh, the architect of the Tay Nguyen Campaign. The decision: attack! The target, incredibly: Plei Me! The date of the attack: November 16. And the decimated 33rd figured into the plans. The commander was directed to form what was left of the three battalions into a composite fighting unit, essentially a battalion combat team, given the amount of regimental support assets still available. This time, Field Front wasn't going to fool around with a lure-and-ambush tactic. General Man intended to take out the camp with one massive blow and then move on to other targets.

The forces available to Field Front, in addition to the depleted 33rd, was the 32nd Regiment which, despite the casualties sustained during the ambush of the ARVN armored task force on the road to Plei Me, still remained a cohesive fighting force. Field Front directed that it remain in its staging areas on the northern bank of the Ia Drang, south of Duc Co, until time came to begin the march to Plei Me.

The real cutting edge for the attack, however, was the newly infiltrated 66th Regiment, fresh off the trail and spoiling for a fight, particularly after one of its companies got its nose bloodied in the cavalry's ambush on November 3. It would be in the van of the three-regiment effort against Plei Me. The 66th was ordered to move south from its initial staging areas on the eastern bank of the Ia Drang, where it flowed south to north around the Chu Pong Massif to the eastern slopes, just above ANTA Village, where the 33rd was resting.

To add punch to the attack, Field Front also decided to commit a battalion of 120-mm mortars and a battalion of 14.5-mm twin-barrel antiaircraft guns. These two units were en route down the infiltration trail and were scheduled to arrive in time for the attack. The period between the issuance of the attack order and its execution would be spent in preparation and then movement to the target. Thus, for the first time, a full NVA division would be committed offensively against a target in South Vietnam.

After the 1st Brigade battalions generally lost contact with the remnants of the 33rd Regiment on November 7, Kinnard said, in *Army Magazine*, that, "I had been planning to replace the gallant, but spent, First Brigade with the Third Brigade, commanded by Colonel Thomas W. Brown, and this seemed a logical time to do so." The general might have been indulging in a bit of hyperbole. The units of the 1st Brigade unquestionably were gallant, but spent? The 2/12 Cav had spent the longest period in the field, eighteen days total—but its days in contact numbered about five. The 2/8 had fourteen days in the valley and only two days of hard contact. The 1/8

Cav's one company had one day of contact, while the others had none. And the 1/12 Cav had only its reconnaissance platoon truly get shot at in anger. Compared to times in the field by units later in the war, this was a walk in the park. The friendly casualty figures were commensurately moderate, with fifty-nine killed and one hundred ninety-six wounded or injured during the first eighteen days of the campaign.

Kinnard was generally satisfied with the results of the 1st Brigade's operations. Remarking on the first phase of the campaign, Kinnard said, "This phase saw a North Vietnamese regular army regiment, operating in its own trackless 'stomping grounds,' found, engaged and nearly destroyed by a new unit which had landed in Vietnam the month before." And this was not hyperbolic. The 33rd Regiment had just about ceased to exist as a tactical entity.

The 1st Cavalry's 3rd Brigade was commanded by Colonel Thomas W. "Tim" Brown, a thin, sandy-haired, bespectacled West Pointer. He had graduated from the academy in the wartime accelerated class of 1943. Brown's older brother, George, already was a brigadier general in the U. S. Air Force; thus, a great deal was expected of little brother. And, going into this campaign, Tim Brown had not disappointed. He had commanded the 3rd Brigade during AIR ASSAULT II in the Carolinas and, despite not having had any real battalions to maneuver, was considered to have done an outstanding job in preparing his staff for the one exercise that they were able to run with troops. He had been given an up-and-coming lieutenant colonel, Edward C. "Shy" Meyer, as his deputy, and had an experienced staff surrounding him.

The 3rd Brigade had only two "assigned" battalions, given the reality that no battalion in a 1965 vintage division was truly wedded forever to a brigade headquarters. The two units were the 1st and 2nd Battalions of the 7th Cavalry. It was not surprising, then, that the brigade and its battalions began calling themselves the "Garry Owen" brigade. The name came from a drinking song that was once sung by the Irish

Lancers and adopted by George Armstrong Custer's 7th Cavalry Regiment. Legend has it that the 7th's troopers sang it as they rode to the Bighorn in Montana. Although a marching version of the song was played by the division band at all divisional functions, "Garry Owen" was a particular mark of *esprit* of the units bearing the Seventh Cavalry colors.

The 1/7 Cav was commanded by Lieutenant Colonel Harold G. Moore, a West Pointer from the class of 1945. He was one tough hombre with extensive combat experience in Korea with the 7th Infantry Division. Already selected for promotion to full colonel, Moore was only a couple of months away from pinning on his eagles. This would be the last time he would campaign with the battalion he had led for nearly two years. Moore was unarguably the most experienced and, probably, the best battalion commander in the division. The 2/7 Cav, on the other hand, had one of the most inexperienced. Lieutenant Colonel Robert McDade had changed jobs with the previous commander, Lieutenant Colonel John White, only a week prior to being deployed to Plei Me, coming down from the division G-1 slot.

To give the brigade some added punch, Kinnard assigned a nominal 2nd Brigade battalion, the 2nd Battalion, 5th Cavalry, under Lieutenant Colonel Robert Tully. The normal supporting elements for the 3rd Brigade also were deployed to Pleiku Province. The 1st Battalion, 21st Artillery, the normal direct support 105-mm howitzer battalion, was brought in to supplant the 2/19 Arty and the 2/17 Arty. The 3rd Brigade decided to use the 1st Brigade command post at Catecka. It had borne the name of STADIUM during the 1st Brigade's tenure, and the 3rd Brigade went along with the original for the most part. But generally, most everyone started calling the brigade base by the name of the nearby tea plantation, whose eastern boundary was, in fact, the western perimeter of the command post. The Catecka plantation was the largest of its kind in Vietnam and was owned by French interests. It was like a world of its own, a tranquil park in the middle of a war zone, with row upon row of four-foot-high tea bushes, covering thousands of acres, tended by hundreds of workers. Trees had been planted in and among the bushes so that the tender leaves would be sheltered from the blistering dry-season sun. The plantation house was a typical colonial mansion with its own water and power systems, and its landscaping made a sharp and vivid contrast to the wildness of the country surrounding it.

The plantation was operating at full capacity, with big trucks filled with cases of tea rolling down the macadam private road toward Route 19 and the north-south route, Highway 14, that would take them to the port of Saigon. The fact that these trucks operated with impunity on roads that otherwise had little or no vehicular traffic was a puzzlement to the troops gathered at the brigade base. Some of the immunity to Vietcong mischief was explained one day at a party given by the French manager, when he noted that just the other day he had been "kidnapped" on a trip from Kontum to Pleiku and won his release only after payment of a "ransom" of one million piasters (about $80,000). Apparently, the manager was quite accustomed to these "kidnappings" and generally carried the requisite ransom with him when its cyclical due date drew near.

Because the operation of the tea plantation was important to the South Vietnamese economy, it was also important to the U.S. economic advisors to the Vietnamese. The members of United States Overseas Mission (USOM) who worked the area had made it clear, with the obvious backing of the embassy, that American forces were in no way to take any action that would endanger the operation of the plantation, war or no war. That should have been enough to scare away American forces, but the location had so many plusses—an airstrip, a nearby hard-surface road, and excellent access by helicopter to any part of the area of operations—that Clark and, now, Brown, overlooked the political restraints. Ultimately it would cost American lives.

Besides the brigade headquarters, there were a number of other organizations stashed at Catecka: Charlie Battery of the 2/20 Arty, the aerial rocket artillery battalion with its twelve B-model gunships; and a battery of the 6th Battalion, 14th Artillery, a 175-mm self-propelled howitzer outfit that was attached to the 1st Cavalry. The 175 could hurl a 174-pound shell nearly thirty-two kilometers. While this helped provide good mutual support for the battery of the battalion that remained in Pleiku, most of the fighting in the western plateau that had gone on thus far was just out of the range of the big guns. But, since Plei Me camp was well within the range of the 175s, the presence of the long-range artillery provided a degree of comfort to the Americans manning the defenses at the camp. The men were still a bit skittish, particularly after the cavalry moved farther west. Additionally, there was a signal team, an interrogation team (IPW) from the military intelligence company, a military police team to provide security for the command post as well as to guard prisoners of war, a long-range patrol team from the 54th Infantry Detachment, and a team from the 10th Radio Research Unit, a cover designation given to the radio intercept people of the Army Security Agency.

As part of the brigade's settling-in process, the deputy commander, E. C. Meyer, sent the assistant S-2 to visit II Corps and 24th Tactical Zone intelligence types, as well as to visit the G-2 shop at the forward DTOC in the II Corps compound. Captain John Pritchard talked with ARVN Colonel Phouc of the 24th Tactical Zone and Captain Luong of the II Corps IPW Team. Luong stated categorically that he had several prisoners who told him the NVA's 66th Regiment was in the vicinity of the Chu Pong Massif. Pritchard telephoned the information back to brigade headquarters, and it was placed in the November 11 intelligence summary. When he got back to Catecka, he personally briefed the brigade commander and his staff and the intelligence officers of the 1/7 and 2/5 Cav, the first two battalions in. He also placed a large red star in the middle of the Chu Pongs on the S-2's situation map. It was similar to the red star he had seen on both the ARVN and division G-2's intelligence maps.

Despite this plethora of intelligence to the contrary at the field command level, Kinnard, acting on the orders from Task Force Alpha (the American command's euphemism for a corps headquarters), told Brown to begin his search south and east of Plei Me. For some reason, Swede Larsen and his staff, and probably the operations and intelligence people up the line at MACV as well, were convinced that some of the North Vietnamese had slipped away to the south and east to the hill country about fifteen kilometers from the Plei Me camp, and they were adamant that the Cav should start turning over rocks in that area. Accordingly, the initial battalions in from An Khe were directed to search areas in that vicinity. This meant that the 1st Brigade battalions would not be relieved in place and that they would have to extract from each of their locations and return to Camp Holloway for transit back to An Khe.

If a combat assault into a suspected hostile area is what the Cav was all about, extraction ran a very close second in its requirement for carefully orchestrated activities. With an assault, the troops on the ground know there was always more folks scheduled to arrive right behind them. In an extraction, the combat power on the ground steadily declines until, finally, there is just one platoon left in defensive positions around the pickup zone. The most critical moment of vulnerability is when that platoon gets into the aircraft. Every commander has different variations on this theme, but the technique used most often would be to have the next-to-last platoon out act as an "Eagle Flight," that is, orbiting and ready to go back in if the platoon on the ground is in danger of being overwhelmed. Also orbiting would be the gunships that were escorting the lift birds. The infantrymen on the ground would let loose a burst of fire as they sprinted toward the aircraft which were waiting very light on the skids. When the infantrymen boarded, the door gunners would hose down the edges of the clearing and the gunships would start their firing runs. The lift ships would clear up and out of the pickup zone and the extraction would be complete. While no extraction in the campaign was opposed, lessons learned from early airmobile operations in other parts of the country kept everybody's pucker string in a very taut condition until the operation was complete.

The changeover of units went on for a period of three days—November 9, 10, and 11. Brown's S-3, Major Henri-Gerard "Pete" Mallet, drew out neat little search areas on the situation map—blocks of terrain northwest, west, and southwest of the Plei Me camp. These were code-named with colors—red, gold, white, blue, and brown—and each battalion was assigned a search area. Basically, it was the same technique used by the 1st Brigade when it blocked out areas Jim, Earl, and Shoe. Except that this time the search areas were in a part of the plateau never touched by the North Vietnamese.

The clouds of mystery that shrouded this battlefield were but thin veils as compared to the density at higher headquarters. It seemed the higher the headquarters, the more murky the intelligence waters. No one, particularly at the division and corps level, or even at the higher commands, had a real handle yet on the identity of NVA units in South Vietnam. A communiqué issued by Military Assistance Command (MACV) on November 5 stated:

ARVN and MACV now accept the presence of five PAVN [Peoples Army of Vietnam] regiments in South Vietnam as of 1 November. Three of the regiments are: the 18th, 95th and the 101st. All three are further identified as belonging to the 325th PAVN Division. The other two regiments are identified as the 32nd and the 250th. The 32nd and 250th are known to be operating in Western II Corps.

Of course, the 250th was in fact the 66th, and the 101st

was the 33rd. And these, along with the 32nd, were operating as the combat units of a provisional division headquarters called Field Front. The NVA's 325th Division, one of the conquerors of Dien Bien Phu, never came south and continued to operate as an incubation organization for NVA units that would later be transferred to the southern theater of operations.

With time, the allied order of battle experts got a better feel for the devices of the NVA, including their hanging all sorts of unit identifiers on the infiltrating units to confuse and obfuscate. The NVA high command cared not a whit about unit history and heraldry. What mattered was deception and the ability to keep American and ARVN intelligence experts off balance' as well as to keep up the myth that the battle in the south was fought by native revolutionaries. Again, the propaganda war was as important as the shooting war. And it wasn't limited to Hanoi either. Under pressure by the embassy, MACV had issued rules that prisoners of war were to be called ralliers, to reinforce the image that the government of the south was issuing a siren song to the recalcitrant brethren in the Vietcong. Even when the enemy clearly were North Vietnamese regulars, as was the case during the Pleiku Campaign, the rule was rigidly enforced. Those NVA troops taken by the 9th Cavalry at the hospital were all called "ralliers," to the great amusement of the troops. At any rate, miscalculation about the enemy was not limited to the field. *The New York Times* asked Secretary of State Dean Rusk about the significance of the new NVA regiments in the south, and he replied in the November 6 issue that he did not see the appearance of new regiments in the south as "any major new decision" by the Hanoi government to change the strategy or escalate the war in response to the American military buildup.

On November 12, the last of the 1st Brigade's units departed the area of operations, bound for An Khe, and the third of the 3rd Brigade's three maneuver battalions arrived.

All three battalions now were working the color-coded search areas generally between Plei Me camp and Highway 14. It had been a dry hole for everyone, and General Knowles and Tim Brown were getting impatient and starting to look longingly toward the west. Knowles had long wanted to stage some kind of operation inside the Chu Pong Massif and, earlier in the campaign, had suggested that Bob Shoemaker's 1/12 be tasked to handle the action. Something came up—Knowles can't remember exactly what—and the proposed operation was scrubbed before it had gotten very far in the planning process. Knowles unabashedly considered Shoemaker and Hal Moore to be the battalion commanders who best understood the nuances of the use of airmobility. In fact, it was to get Moore into the fight that Kinnard had tilted toward the nomination of the 3rd Brigade as the follow-on unit in the campaign when it could just as easily have been Ray Lynch's 2nd Brigade.

That day, General Larsen was visiting the division's forward command post at the II Corps compound. He asked Knowles how things were going. Knowles briefed him on the attack on Catecka the night before and then told him the brigade was drilling a dry hole out east of Plei Me. Larsen said, "Why are you conducting operations there if it's dry?" Knowles's response was, "With all due respect, sir, that's what your order in writing directed us to do." Larsen responded that the cavalry's primary mission was to "find the enemy and go after him." Shortly thereafter, Knowles visited Brown at the 3rd Brigade command post and told him to come up with a plan for an air assault operation near the foot of the Chu Pongs.

The most significant action on November 12 came just before the day ended, at 11:30 P.M. An estimated battalion of either NVA or main force Vietcong staged a violent attack on the brigade base at Catecka. It kicked off with a heavy barrage of mortar fire; nearly one hundred rounds of 82-mm and 60-mm mortars fell on the base. The mortar fire was aimed at the petroleum, oil, and lubricants (POL) dump and the laagered aircraft. The firing positions were located on the high ground some four hundred fifty meters to the north. But a good part of the ground attack came out of the west, right out of the rows of carefully manicured tea bushes. Clearly, not all of the workers in the tea plantation had been busy clipping tea leaves; some obviously were occupied in placing direction signs, plotting distances to targets, and otherwise making themselves useful to the Vietcong.

The base had not retained a rifle company as palace guard. Instead, it relied on a provisional company made up of the artillerymen, military policemen, Support Command people, and anyone else who could carry a rifle to a perimeter position. The provisional company was led by Captain Riley J. McVeay, commander of Battery B, 6th Battalion, 14th Artillery. His second in command was a second lieutenant from the same battery, Billy G. Wilson, who was serving as an infantry platoon leader. Wilson was hit by fragments from an enemy mortar round very early in the fight, yet he refused medical treatment and crawled from position to position to steady the defense on the northern perimeter. Finally, bleeding badly from his wounds, Wilson directed a counterattack against the VC assault that had penetrated the thin line on the northern sector. He refused to leave the scene until finally ordered to do so by McVeay, who then took over the leadership of the counterattack. When the defensive lines were restored, McVeay returned to his company command post but en route was also wounded by mortar fragments.

The VC/NVA knew exactly what targets to hit with their sapper and infantry probes. The northern section of the perimeter was closest to the aircraft that were parked along the strip. The western portion housed the brigade command post and the POL dump was in the southern portion of the perimeter. Major Roger Bartholomew, the commander of Charlie Battery, 2/20 Arty, rushed his pilots out to their helicopters. Amid the crashing of mortar rounds and the snapping of AK and machine-gun slugs, the distinctive whine of the Hueys' gas turbines in a start mode signaled big trouble for the attackers. Nearly every ship took hits as they wound up the heavy blades to the required RPM for takeoff, but once airborne, it was an unequal match. The ARA birds split, with half heading for the mortar positions, easily identified in the dark by the spitting muzzles. Within minutes, the mortar positions were silenced by the aerial rockets, and the defenders had only to deal with the ground attacks. The other half of the ARA flight worked over the outside of the perimeter, especially the northern edge, where the penetration had taken place, and on the western sector, where rockets ripped tea plants asunder along with small men in black pajamas.

The attack was broken off about fifteen minutes after midnight, with the command post, the aircraft, and the POL dump still intact. Seven men had died defending the perimeter and twenty-three more were wounded. A sweep of the area the following morning revealed only six enemy bodies, all clad in the traditional black pajamas of the VC. There were numerous blood stains around, particularly where the mortars were located, but nothing was found in the area. Patrols did find some 100 demolition charges that had been destined for parked aircraft or fuel bladders. With no prisoners, it was impossible to tell whether the attack was by local force or main force VC (the H-15 Main Force VC Battalion was supposed to be operating in the western plateau), or whether these were NVA regulars dressed up as guerrillas and using local force folks as guides. The attack shook up the brigade staff, though, and Brown made it a point thereafter to have an infantry company for night security at the brigade base. Of course, the usual defense for a fixed base, the first light—last light patrols, the H & I artillery fire, was not possible at Catecka because of the civilian population close by and the thousands of acres of sacrosanct tea bushes.

On November 13, after the brigade staff settled down to planning for new operations, Pete Mallet took his grease pencil in hand, walked over to the acetate-covered situation map, and drew in new areas of operations for the brigade. He started adding search zones like building blocks, working his way westward, with one zone, code-named MAROON, just south of Plei Me Camp. To its west was another zone named BRONZE, which included the site of the old 2/8 Cav's fire base FALCON. And, finally, to its west, at the foot of the Chu Pong Massif, Mallet drew in an oval-shaped zone covering about fifteen square kilometers and named it AREA LIME.

The 1/7 Cav was ordered to perform company-size search missions in AREA MAROON. Two companies, A and C, air assaulted into LZs about four thousand meters apart and about seven klicks south of Plei Me camp. Alpha Company worked over an area three kilometers north of the camp and the battalion headquarters and Battery A of the 21st Artillery were located adjacent to the camp itself. In order to be ready for the long jump to the west, Brown ordered that LZ FALCON, located on a plateau between the Meur and Tae Rivers about three kilometers west of the old hospital site, be reopened by the 2/5 Cav. By noon on November 13, Battery C of the 21st Arty was set up and firing from LZ FALCON while two companies of the 5th were patrolling south along the Tae River. Now a cavalry checker had been placed in the next square to the west, AREA BRONZE. The next step was to move into AREA LIME at the foot of the Chu Pongs.

At 5:00 P.M. on the 13th, Brown flew down and met Moore at the A Company command post south of Plei Me and told Moore to conduct an airmobile assault into AREA LIME the following morning. As was his practice, Brown allowed his battalion commanders to select their own landing zones and to work out their schemes of maneuver. The brigade commander's guidance was that Moore was to conduct the search operation along the edge of the mountains through at least November 15. Brown was concerned about the possibility of heavy contact in the area, although there had been no American forces that far west; the closest the 1st Brigade came was the battle on November 4 about four kilometers northeast of ANTA Village. Now Brown intended to send forces directly to the eastern slopes of the Chu Pongs. Looming in the back of his mind was that big red star on the G-2 and S-2 situation maps, and for this reason, he told Moore to keep his rifle companies within very close supporting range of one another. Brown and Moore were both keenly aware that, although a veteran of the air assault maneuvers and already exposed to some field duty, first in Operation SHINY BAYONET in early October and now, while flailing away in dry holes east of Plei Me, the battalion was still untested in a real combat situation. Brown also allocated sixteen helicopters to the 1/7 for the assault. The 3rd Brigade had a total of twenty-four choppers assigned for its use, but each of the other two battalions needed four each for resupply purposes and for local movements of squads and platoons. In addition, Brown planned to augment the firepower already on FALCON with another battery of the 21st Arty. That battery was on orders to move at 8:00 A.M., November 14.

After receiving the brigade commander's guidance, Moore swung into action. His S-3, Captain Gregory "Matt" Dillon, began an extensive map reconnaissance of the target area, looking for possible landing zones. Moore decided to change his normal approach for this operation; rather than landing the companies in smaller, separated LZs, he planned to put the entire battalion into a single LZ and then patrol out from there. He radioed his two companies still in the field—Bravo Company had been lifted to Catecka to play palace guard for the night—to concentrate their men at first light on the 14th for pickup and movement to the landing zone. The company commanders were to be ready to be picked up after first light to make a reconnaissance of the area. Moore arranged to have Company B moved by Chinook helicopters from Catecka to the Plei Me strip early on the 14th. Since it would be fully assembled, he decided to use Bravo as the lead company in the assault.

While pondering the tactical moves, Moore also considered his personnel assets. Of the twenty-three officers authorized for his three rifle companies and one combat support company, twenty were available for duty and many had been with the battalion since it was the 23rd Infantry in the Second Division. Some of the second lieutenant platoon leaders, however, had joined the unit after graduation from officer candidate school in the summer of 1965—just prior to shipping out to Vietnam. On the enlisted side, the picture was more gloomy. Most of the companies were operating at two-thirds strength; malaria and other tropical diseases were taking their toll. To further complicate matters, the so-called ninety-day deployables were departing every day. The depletion of enlisted strength was so bad that General Knowles gave orders that no man could leave the field until the day before his actual DROS date—the day he was supposed to leave Vietnam!

Moore wasn't unduly concerned about the strength situation though—the companies had been operating at less than full strength since arriving in Vietnam, and the commanders were growing adept at compensating for the shortages. The advantage the Americans had was an unending supply of firepower potential. Not only was the artillery support plentiful, but the skies were filled with warbirds, ranging from the F4C's, F-100's and A1E's of the Air Force, to the aerial rocket artillery gunships of the cavalry. The battalion SOP (standing operating procedure) dictated that each rifleman carry at least three hundred rounds of M-16 ammunition, and each grenadier was ordered to bring two to three dozen high-explosive shells for his 40-mm grenade launcher. Machine gun crews were to carry at least 800 rounds of linked 7.62-mm ammunition—many carried as much as a thousand rounds—and every man was to carry at least two fragmentation grenades plus one smoke grenade. Each company was to bring in one 81-mm mortar tube with twenty-four rounds of ammunition; Delta Company would carry three tubes and a basic load of ammunition. Every soldier was to have two canteens of water and a day's C-rations. The rations usually were stuck inside black GI socks and slung from the web gear. On the ground, light and swift the cavalryman definitely was not. But he had staying power even when resupply was initially difficult. Past battles had proven that he who shoots last, wins. And Hal Moore had always been a winner.

Often called flamboyant by other officers, Moore was, in fact, a very controlled man who was capable of fierce concentration one minute and a genuine affability the next. He was often impatient with the shortcomings of others. Born in Bardstown, Kentucky, on February 13, 1922, he went to work at the age of seventeen for Senator Happy Chandler and later received an appointment to the U.S. Military Academy. He graduated in 1945, soon became a paratrooper, and spent his early years in Japan with the 11th Airborne Division. During the Korean War, he served as company commander of K Company, 17th Infantry Regiment of the 7th Infantry division. He also was the regimental S-3 for the 17th Infantry and, later, assistant G-3 for the 7th Division. Moore had earned a master's degree in international affairs at George Washington University, writing his thesis on Laos. Legend has it that, shortly after arrival at An Khe, Moore went out on Highway 19 to the site of the ambush of the French Groupement Mobile 100 by the Vietminh. He took Bernard Fall's book *Street Without Joy,* which describes the battle, and, sitting by the roadside, read the chapter, picking out terrain features as he read.

If Moore had a weakness as a commander, it was involving himself in the most minute details of his command instead of leaving them to his staff so that he could concentrate on the bigger picture. But this tall, blond, fiercely competitive officer compensated for this overattention to detail by engendering incredible loyalty among his subordinates. Given his almost larger-than-life stature and the heritage of the unit he commanded, it was almost inevitable that the men, behind his back, of course, began calling him "Yellow Hair."

Sunday the 14th dawned bright and clear; it would be another hot, dry day on the western plateau. A couple of H-13's delivered Captains Robert H. Edwards (C Company) and Ramon A. "Tony" Nadal II (A Company) to the Plei Me strip, where they joined Captain John D. Herren, the B Company commander, and Captain Louis R. LeFebvre, the D Company commander. Also on the dusty strip were Captain Dillon, the S-3; Major Bruce P. Crandall, the commander of Company A, 229th Assault Helicopter Battalion; and a scout section leader from Charlie Troop, 9th Cavalry. The group gathered around Moore and a map that showed the target area. Based on the map reconnaissance and input from the 9th Cavalry scout section, Dillon had marked tentative landing zones on the map. These were coded by letters of the alphabet, in this case, a gaggle from the latter part of the alphabet—T, V, W, X, and Y. But, as is the procedure in the Army, the letters were designated by the names in the phonetic alphabet. Thus the proposed landing zones were named TANGO, VICTOR, WHISKEY, XRAY, and YANKEE. The officers were briefed quickly by Moore on the battalion's mission, the flight route, and what to look for.

Then, using two Huey choppers and escorted by two gunships, the reconnaissance party lifted off. Moore's plan was to fly at 2,500 feet and follow a pattern that would provide some deception and allow for maximum viewing of the target. The small formation headed southwest to a point about eight kilometers south of the Chu Pongs, then headed due north and flew a straight pattern to up near the Duc Co Special Forces camp, where they orbited for about five minutes, reversed course, and flew a north-south pattern across the target area. By 8:15 A.M., the reconnaissance party was on the ground at Plei Me. The recon had revealed only three LZs close enough to the Chu Pongs to be of use. Only two of the three, XRAY and YANKEE, were large enough. Moore immediately dispatched the scout team on a low-level reconnaissance of the slopes of the Chu Pongs and a closer look at the two candidate landing zones.

The scout section was back in forty minutes. Although the pilots had seen several trails during their low-level flight, they had drawn no enemy fire. LZ YANKEE, they reported, was usable but risky because of high tree stumps. LZ XRAY, on the other hand, was large enough to take up to ten birds in formation. And just a couple hundred meters north of it, on an east-west trail, they had spotted communication wire. This final bit of intelligence cinched it for Moore. He would land his battalion at LZ XRAY. The map coordinates were YA935019. If a North Vietnamese were plotting those same coordinates, he would not have called that spot XRAY; its proper name, as far as the NVA were concerned, was ANTA Village! A North Vietnamese regiment and an Air Cavalry battalion were now, inexorably, on a collision course.

10

XRAY—
THE FIRST DAY

"**F**ew units that have a rendezvous with destiny have an inkling of their fate until the historical moment touches them. So it was with the 1/7 Cav on the morning of November 14th." That was the way the 1st Cavalry's official after-action report on the Pleiku Campaign led off the section dealing with LZ XRAY. It was to be a routine operation, in so far as any operation deep within enemy territory can be termed routine. Not for Hal Moore, of course. He had seen the menacing red star on both the G-2's and S-2's intelligence maps and he was too wise and experienced a warrior to be lulled by past inactivity. But it was different for the troops. The monotony of the dry holes encountered thus far tended to take the edge off the rush of adrenaline that usually surges when a combat assault is contemplated.

After selecting the LZ, Moore assembled his commanders, staff, and representatives of supporting forces to hear his operations order. He told the group that, according to the latest available intelligence, an enemy battalion was located five kilometers northwest of XRAY. Another hostile force of undetermined size was suspected to be just southwest of the landing zone itself and the so-called secret base of the enemy was located about three kilometers to the west of the LZ,

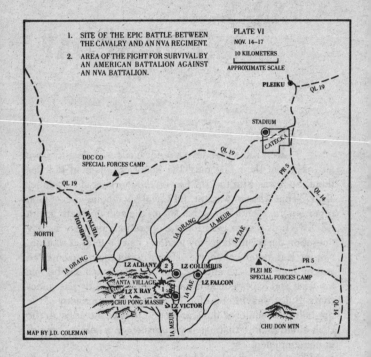

1. SITE OF THE EPIC BATTLE BETWEEN THE CAVALRY AND AN NVA REGIMENT.

2. AREA OF THE FIGHT FOR SURVIVAL BY AN AMERICAN BATTALION AGAINST AN NVA BATTALION.

PLATE VI

NOV. 14–17

10 KILOMETERS

APPROXIMATE SCALE

PLEIKU

QL 19

STADIUM

CATECKA

QL 19

DUC CO SPECIAL FORCES CAMP

QL 19

PR 5

QL 14

NORTH

CAMBODIA

VIETNAM

IA DRANG

IA MEUR

IA TAE

IA DRANG

LZ ALBANY

2

LZ COLUMBUS

PLEI ME SPECIAL FORCES CAMP

PR 5

ANTA VILLAGE

LZ X RAY

1

LZ FALCON

IA TAE

CHU PONG MASSIF

LZ VICTOR

IA MEUR

QL 14

CHU DON MTN

MAP BY J.D. COLEMAN

somewhere in the Chu Pong Mountains. To exploit these targets, the battalion would conduct an air assault on LZ XRAY, then search for and destroy any enemy forces found in the area, with the search concentrating on stream beds and wooded high ground.

Recognizing that the low-level reconnaissance may have alerted the enemy that something was up, a deception plan was cranked up. The 21st Artillery would fire eight-minute diversionary preps on LZ TANGO and LZ YANKEE. Then the guns would shift to XRAY and the preparation would rain steel on that landing zone and the surrounding woodlines for twenty minutes. Special emphasis was to be given to the slopes of a finger that jutted down off Chu Pong toward the LZ. Gunships of the 2/20 ARA would fire rockets at the borders of the LZ, concentrating on the western and northwestern portions closest to the mountain, as well as to a grove of trees jutting into the center of the LZ from the north. Finally, the gunship escort birds for the lift battalion would hose down the LZ with rocket and machine-gun fire just as the lift ships flared for landing.

Moore's order called for Herren's Bravo Company to be the assault company, using the sixteen available lift ships, and then to secure the LZ. Bravo would be followed by Companies A, C, and D. Moore's maneuver plan after the LZ was secured was to have Companies A and B search to the north and northeast with Alpha Company on the right. Company C was to assume the LZ security mission on landing and, once Company D with its mortars and reconnaissance platoon were in, be prepared to search west to the slopes of Chu Pong. Moore told each company that the mortar tube they were bringing in with them would revert to Company D control for a massing of mortars once Delta was on the LZ.

The brigade commander arrived just as Moore was completing his attack order and was briefed separately on the scheme of maneuver. Brown agreed with the tactical plan and the selection of XRAY as the primary LZ, and was satisfied that Moore had followed the brigade's operational guidance. Brown also agreed to Moore's plan for securing the LZ. This operation would be different than the usual air assault. Normally, the platoons of the assaulting company fan out to all points of the compass to secure the landing zone. In this case, only one platoon was to send out squad-size patrols in sweeps to the tree line, while the balance of the company was grouped in a central location as a massed reaction force.

At 10:17 A.M., the preparatory fires on XRAY began. Minutes later, with a thunderous roar of turbines and rotor blades, sixteen choppers lifted off from the Plei Me strip in a cloud of red dust. Twelve of the birds, four platoons, were from Company A of the 229th, the "Snakes," and four were from Company B, the "Preachers." The 229th birds were identifiable by the blue company markings on their noses—a triangle for A Company, a square for B Company, and a circle for C Company. At the controls of the lead ship, Snake Yellow One, was Major Bruce Crandall, whose basic officer branch was Corps of Engineers but whose very life was flying. His copilot was an infantry captain named Jon Mills.

The formation was a platoon in column and flew southwesterly at around two thousand feet. About two kilometers out and due south of the LZ the flight began turning to the north and dropping in altitude just as the white phosphorous round burst on the LZ, signalling the end of the artillery prep. The ARA gunships then made two firing passes, followed by the 229th escort gunbirds making rocket and machine-gun passes at the edge of the LZ. Finally, the lead choppers skimmed over the edge of the clearing, slowing, mushing through the air in a noses-up, tails-almost-touching-the-ground attitude, the rotor blades making that distinctive whop-whop-whop sound. Just as the lead birds began setting down on the skids among the holes, splintered stumps, and waist-high grass, with dirt and leaves whirling everywhere, the door gunners unleashed volleys of machine-gun fire. The men off the first lift, led by their battalion commander, charged from the aircraft, snap-firing at possible targets in the trees and tall grass. The sound of each lift platoon roaring in, then pulling pitch and departing, was deafening. Then, suddenly, the choppers were gone, and there was a strange silence on the landing zone as smoke curled upward from the dozens of shell holes left from the preparation.

Relatively flat and open as seen from above, LZ XRAY took on an altogether different appearance from the ground. It was typical of the terrain the cavalry had been confronted with all during the campaign. LZ XRAY was covered by yellowish-brown, waist-high plateau grass that provided concealment for attackers and prevented good communications between defensive positions. The LZ itself was in the shape of an east-west oval, almost pinched off in the middle by a grove of trees. This created two side-by-side landing zones, each capable of handling four or five ships. Near the center of the grove, the typical plateau hardwoods, was a giant anthill, about ten feet high, a dozen feet in girth at the base, and as hard as concrete. Because of its key location on the LZ, this area had taken some serious prep fires, and it was where Moore, who had come in with the first lift, chose to place his battalion command post.

The trees along the edge of the clearing were fairly sparse, but along old creek beds and up the slopes of the mountain the trees were thicker and higher and there was more underbrush. And there was the mountain itself, five hundred meters up from the valley floor. It didn't look terribly imposing from the air; on the ground it was a different story. The sky troopers gazed upward and a veteran noncommissioned officer spoke for all of them: "My Gawd, that son of a bitch is big." The LZ was right in the shadow of the mountain, and it was clear that if there were North Vietnamese up on its slopes, getting up there after them would be a tough go indeed.

And the helicopter landing had been spotted by the NVA. Even now the Field Front commander, General Chu Huy

Man, was making a fateful decision. The attack on Plei Me would have to wait; right now there were Americans at the very doorstep of the NVA sanctuary. The 66th Regiment, now with two battalions virtually overlooking the LZ, and the composite battalion of the 33rd Regiment, in an assembly area no more than five hundred meters from the Cavalry outpost, were ordered to attack. By noon, the NVA units were in position.

At XRAY, at about 11:20 A.M., B Company's First Platoon, under Second Lieutenant Alan E. Deveny, probing west from the LZ into the trees, flushed out a Vietnamese. Clad in black shorts and a dirty khaki shirt, he bolted but was overtaken and tackled by one of the platoon members. Notified of the catch, Moore, his S-2, Captain Thomas C. Metsker, and their civilian interpreter, a Mr. Nik, rushed to the spot. Preliminary questioning revealed that the prisoner was a North Vietnamese regular who had deserted and had been subsisting on bananas for the past five days. He also told the interpreter that there were three North Vietnamese battalions on Chu Pong Mountain that allegedly were anxious to kill Americans. Moore radioed his S-3, who was circling above the landing zone in the command chopper, to come in and pick up the prisoner and fly him to 3rd Brigade headquarters for additional interrogation.

Moore told Herren to intensify his search and to prepare to assume Charlie Company's mission of exploring the ground at the foot of Chu Pong, giving special attention to a sloping ridge that pointed like a finger at the heart of the landing zone. Moore also was understandably anxious about getting the rest of his battalion in. The forty-minute round trip for each lift was worrisome. However, within minutes of giving B Company its adjusted mission, Tony Nadal's Alpha Company was landing. Moore promptly gave him the job of securing the LZ until C Company arrived.

Herren decided to move up toward the finger ridge with two platoons abreast—Devany's 1st Platoon on the left and Second Lieutenant Henry T. Herrick's 2nd Platoon on the right.

Positioning Second Lieutenant Dennis J. Deal's 3rd Platoon behind the first as a reserve, Herren moved his company off of the landing zone and up toward the mountain. It was 12:30 P.M., and on the LZ, troopers of Alpha Company had broken out some C-rations for lunch. The quiet of the day was broken only by shouts of squad and team leaders positioning their people and by the whop-whop-whop of the command chopper circling monotonously overhead.

Deveny had moved slightly ahead of Herrick's platoon in crossing the dry creek bed and was moving up the left side of the finger. At about 12:45 P.M., about 150 meters from the creek bed, his platoon ran straight into an NVA assault force, which immediately pinned the 1st Platoon down with withering fire from the front and flanks. The platoon immediately started taking casualties and Deveny radioed Herren for help. The battle on LZ XRAY was joined.

Herren contacted Herrick by radio and told him to move up to relieve the pressure on Deveny's right flank. The 27-man 2nd Platoon began moving northwest along the finger, basically along the right slope, orienting on the sound of firing to its front and left, when it came to a clearing on the northern side of the finger. Herrick asked his company commander for guidance: should he push straight through the clearing, possibly exposing the platoon to enemy fire but maintaining visual and sound contact with the 1st Platoon, or should he veer off to the right and circle the clearing? Herren, taking the conservative approach, told him to stay out of the clearing. Normally a sound decision, but in this case, because of the onrush of the attacking NVA, it doomed Herrick and his platoon.

Herrick maneuvered his platoon to the right and slightly downhill to skirt the edge of the clearing. Just as he reached its far northern edge, his lead element bumped into a squad of NVA infantrymen trotting down a trail that was parallel to the platoon's advance. The two foes spotted each other almost simultaneously; the NVA squad reversed course, hustling back up the trail and snapping off some quick shots as they went. Herrick radioed to Herren that he had made contact and pressed forward eagerly now with all three squads on line and his machine guns on the flanks. The firing from the retreating NVA squad had ceased, but Herrick knew they were somewhere in front of him and continued the advance. Suddenly his left flank squad made contact again, this time with a platoon of NVA moving along the crest of the finger. Just as his left squad opened fire, a blistering volley of enemy fire erupted from the front of the squad, killing a grenadier and pinning down the rest of the squad.

Deploying his two machine guns toward the beleaguered squad, Herrick yelled to the Third Squad leader, Staff Sergeant Clyde E. Savage, to pull back under cover of the machine-gun fire. Herrick also called Herren to tell him of the worsening situation. Even as he was talking, fire began sweeping across the platoon's position from all points of the compass. Normally, the NVA dislike firing from all points, preferring an L-shaped attack position, which ensures that grazing fire won't hit their own troops. The two soft sides opposite the L usually are manned by snipers tied in trees, just to make sure the quarry doesn't slip away. But today, in the heat of battle and because of the flow of NVA soldiers toward the LZ, the position of the small American unit was not unlike a large rock suddenly placed in a swift-flowing brook, with streams of NVA soldiers eddying on both sides and around the platoon.

Covered by the M-60s, Savage managed to withdraw his squad back toward the platoon, which by now was being formed by Herrick into a hastily created twenty-five-meter perimeter. The machine gunners were not so lucky. The closer team managed to make it back, but the far team—all four men—were killed by the blistering fire. Then the NVA seized the machine gun and turned it on the perimeter, raking the prone infantrymen with fire until the ammunition was exhausted.

Farther back on the finger, the 1st Platoon's situation was not as critical. It was still in contact, but as yet not surrounded, and Deal's 3rd Platoon was hustling forward to reinforce. Herren's command group had been moving with Deal, but Herren stopped in order to relay the 2nd Platoon's situation to Moore down on the LZ. He had precious few assets to do much about the situation. He decided to reinforce Deveny with Deal and then, with the two platoons, make an effort to break through to Herrick. His lone mortar tube, unlimbered and cranked into action as soon as the 1st Platoon made contact, had exhausted its basic load of ammunition. That left the artillery. First Lieutenant William O. Riddle, the company forward observer, had moved on with Deal's platoon when Herren stopped to render his report to the battalion commander. Just as Herren finished his transmission, he looked up and saw a North Vietnamese soldier aiming an AK at him. Herren ducked, snapping off a couple of rounds from his M-16 as he fell to the ground. Then he tossed a grenade in the direction of the attacker.

At the landing zone, the third lift had just arrived with the last platoon of A Company and the first elements of Charlie. The lifts no longer were the large, majestic air armadas of sixteen ships. Because of the scattered locations of the other companies, all lifts after the first big one were gaggles of four and six birds at a time. Thus the companies were arriving on XRAY in piecemeal fashion. The time was 1:30 P.M. Enemy mortar rounds were beginning to feel out the landing zone for American positions. Moore told Nadal to rush a platoon to Herren to be used to push through to Bravo's isolated platoon. Nadal was to follow with his remaining two rifle platoons and anchor Bravo's left flank. Turning to Edwards, he told him to take what he had of Charlie Company and occupy positions just inside the tree line west, southwest, and south of XRAY, taking care to cover Alpha's left flank. Moore was deeply concerned about committing his reaction force to a linear position because he virtually had no one left on the LZ to defend to the east and southeast. When Delta arrived, he would have to plug them into the hole and also reserve some force for a central reaction unit. But right now, in view of the rapidly developing situation, the threat was from off the mountain to the northwest, and that is where he had to orient the bulk of his forces. No one knew it yet, but some NVA scouts had already crawled through the high grass to breach the thin security line surrounding the LZ.

By this time, Dillon had returned from Catecka, having delivered the prisoner and refueled the command chopper. Moore directed him to coordinate the supporting fires from the chopper. With Dillon in the aircraft was Captain Jerry E. Whiteside, the artillery liaison officer, and First Lieutenant Charles Hastings, the Air Force forward air controller. Moore directed that fires be concentrated on the lower portions of the Chu Pong slopes initially, and then, later, to ring the entire landing zone with a curtain of steel. Priority of fires, of course, would be given to requests for support from any of the engaged infantry units. Within minutes, A1E's from Pleiku were overhead, sending five-hundred-pound bombs crashing into the slopes of the mountains, and, later, on the valley floor just to the north and northwest of the LZ, the suspected location of the 33rd Regiment.

The artillery fire also came, but accurate delivery of concentrations was difficult at first. Already a heavy pall of smoke and dust had risen over the platoons in contact; there were no well-defined terrain features for the forward observers to use in adjusting rounds. Ultimately, the artillery FO's used the technique of walking the rounds down the mountain until they were close enough to the perimeters to be of assistance to the troopers. By this time, Brown and his key staffers were over the battle area. He spotted the artillery rounds going in high on the mountain and called Moore to tell him to bring the fire down. It was a fairly redundant command, the kind made by a combat leader who is absolutely helpless to influence the fight on the ground. At this time, the situation was serious but by no means critical, and Moore had not yet called for reinforcements.

Nadal had dispatched his 2nd Platoon, led by Second Lieutenant Walter J. "Joe" Marm, to assist Herren's company, while Nadal, himself, moved his 1st and 3rd Platoons northwest off the LZ toward positions in the dry creek bed. Unable to consult directly with Herren, Marm decided to move directly out and connect with Deal's platoon. Just as he crossed the creek bed, two North Vietnamese soldiers appeared to his front and surrendered. Marm had a noncommissioned officer and a couple of troopers take the prisoners back to the battalion CP, and pressed on toward Deal's platoon. Just as Marm reached Deal's position, the troopers of both platoons spotted a large force of khaki-clad NVA cutting across their front, left to right. They had met some of the advancing enemy that was attempting to get behind Deveny's platoon. The combined firepower of the troops of Marm and Deal decimated the ranks of the NVA. They broke contact momentarily, then began shifting and sliding to the left of Marm's platoon.

As this flanking force headed down the slope of the finger, it came upon the dry stream bed where it originated on the side of Chu Pong. At this point, the bed ran west to east and then, as the terrain flattened, curved to flow to the northeast. That northeastern leg of the stream bed was where Nadal now had one of his platoons. Also, Marm and, earlier, all of Bravo Company, had departed a bit further northeast of this position. Nadal used the shelter of the stream bed until it made its bend away from the landing zone and then put his 3rd Platoon on the flat ground angling away from the stream. As the NVA poured down the stream bed, they came in contact with the 3rd Platoon, led by Second Lieutenant Robert E. Taft. The first volleys of fire killed a squad leader. When Taft went to the sergeant's aid, he was shot in the throat and died instantly. The fires from the 1st Platoon beat back the thrust by the NVA down the stream bed. The North Vietnamese assault force recoiled and restarted their incessant flanking to the

American left. When the cavalrymen counterattacked and reclaimed their positions, they found Taft's dog tags on the body of a North Vietnamese infantryman.

Now it was Charlie Company's turn. Lying prone on the ground, Edwards's troopers poured fire into the wave of NVA soldiers advancing toward the LZ. Edwards radioed Moore: "We are in heavy contact. These guys are good! They have on helmets, camouflage, and good webbing." It was about 2 P.M. when some of Second Lieutenant Neil Kroger's 1st Platoon folks captured an NVA soldier. He had been wounded, and Edwards could tell it was not a fresh wound.

Now the fifth lift was arriving, carrying lead elements of Delta and some more of Charlie Company. Snake Yellow One, with Crandall and Mills at the controls, was the lead ship, carrying the Delta Company commander, Captain Louis R. LeFebvre, his radio operator, First Lieutenant Raul E. Requera-Taboada, and his RTO plus a couple other Delta Company troops. Just as the choppers were settling on their skids on the western half of the landing zone, Mills said he saw two NVA soldiers pop up out of the grass to the left of the aircraft and start spraying AK-47 fire in their direction. LeFebvre leaned forward to unhook his seat belt and felt a bullet crease the back of his neck. He glanced to his right and saw his RTO slump against his seat belt, dead from a wound in the temple. LeFebvre grabbed the dead man's radio and leaped out the right side of the aircraft. He yelled at a small group near him to follow him, and sprinted for the tree line north of the LZ. Under fire all the way, they reached the relative safety of the dry creek bed.

Lefebvre heard firing in front of him as well as on both sides. His small band of soldiers had moved into position on the right of Nadal's two platoons, which were still battling the NVA force that was trying to slip behind Marm's platoon. Lefebvre radioed Staff Sergeant George Gonzalez, the leader of his antitank platoon, which had been reorganized for this fight as an infantry platoon, to bring his men and join him along the creek bed. He also yelled for Lieutenant Taboada to send him the lieutenant's radio operator to replace the RTO who was killed in the chopper. As the radio operator joined him, LeFebvre looked up to see Herren approaching from the right. Herren told him there were NVA to the east and south of their position, then took up a firing position along the bank. The combined fires stopped the advance of some two dozen enemy soldiers, but in the exchange of bullets, Herren's radio operator, Private First Class Dominic Deangelis, was killed, LeFebvre's right arm was shattered, and Taboada was wounded in the leg. Herren paused in firing long enough to place a tourniquet on LeFebvre's arm.

The fire on the LZ now was so heavy that Moore waved off any further helicopter lifts. The LZ now was awash with bullets and the crashing of artillery and air strikes blended with the claps of incoming high-explosive rounds to create a deafening cacophony. Brown was now certain that Moore was going to need help in the form of additional infantry. He arranged for Company B, 2/7 Cav, which had been moved to Catecka to take over the mission of CP security, to begin assembling at the Catecka strip and be prepared to board choppers at a moment's notice. He also told Bob Tully to start assembling his battalion for a possible march into XRAY. Old "Yellow Hair" hadn't yelled for help yet but Brown was going to be ready when he did.

Up on the mountain side, the 66th Regiment's antiaircraft company had unlimbered its 12.5-mm machine guns and were challenging every low pass being made by the Air Force fighter-bombers. At around 2:30 P.M. a skyraider from Pleiku, making a low-level firing pass at the NVA positions northwest of the LZ, took hits from the heavy machine guns. Smoke flumed out of the big engine and the bird never pulled up, crashing in flames about three thousand meters north of XRAY. Dillon, in the battalion command chopper, made a low pass across the wreckage to see if the pilot was still alive and determined that he had died either from the crash or from the slugs that brought down his aircraft.

The enemy was still keeping pressure on the western side

of the landing zone, and Edwards realized that he was going to need some help on his left flank. He went back to the LZ and found Sergeant Gonzalez, who had not yet begun to move toward LeFebvre's position. He obtained Moore's permission to move Gonzalez into a slot on his company's left flank. Edwards also tried to get all the mortars on the LZ under a central control until the Delta mortar platoon leader arrived with his fire direction center. He did get some central control, but the noise, smoke, and confusion along the edge of the battle area made it difficult, if not impossible, for the young forward observers to accurately adjust fire.

It was now nearing 3:00 P.M., and Moore, recognizing that he was being attacked by at least two battalions of NVA, asked Brown to send him another rifle company. Although the eastern portion of the LZ was receiving sporadic sniper fire, the western portion, which had been subjected to violent grazing fire, was growing quieter. Moore deemed it safe enough to permit the landing of the next lift of troops. This brought in the last squads of Charlie Company and Delta's reconnaissance platoon. It also cost two aircraft, disabled by NVA fire. One of them had to make a precautionary landing immediately after takeoff in an open area just off the northern edge of the LZ. The other had had a major blade strike on the way in and was unable to fly at all. The crews were uninjured and were soon evacuated.

The matter of evacuation of the wounded, which now were piling up in an emergency aid station near the command post anthill, was becoming a matter of concern. Even though the wounded were being tended by four aidmen and the battalion surgeon, who had landed with medical supplies earlier in the afternoon, some of the wounded needed surgical attention. Several of the slicks, which were slated to bring in water, ammunition, and other supplies, braved the NVA firestorms to carry out the wounded. Captain Metzger, who had been slightly wounded in the shoulder earlier in the day, was out on the LZ helping load seriously wounded on the choppers when he was struck in the chest by a sniper round and fell dead across the skids. The crew chief reached down and pulled him into the aircraft as it departed.

General Knowles had been at the division's TOC when the first news of the contact came in. He piled into his command chopper and headed for Catecka, where Brown briefed him. Both commanders realized that they had stirred up a hornet's nest that would take more troops to quell than Brown had available. Knowles got on the horn and called Harry Kinnard back at An Khe, asking for another infantry battalion, more artillery, and both troop- and medium-lift helicopters. Kinnard replied, "They're on the way, but what's going on?" Knowles responded, "We've got a good fight going. Suggest you come up as soon as possible." After setting the reinforcement wheels in motion, Kinnard choppered over from An Khe and met Knowles at Catecka. When he arrived, Knowles showed him the situation map he had propped up against a palm tree. Kinnard took one look and said, "What the hell are you doing in that area?" Obviously, someone hadn't kept the boss informed about Larsen's guidance to get after the enemy even if it meant walking away from the dry holes in the east. Knowles told Kinnard, "The object of the exercise is to find the enemy, and we sure as hell have!" Knowles remembers an awkward pause before Kinnard said quietly, "Okay, it looks great. Let me know what you need."

By 4:00 P.M. Moore had his full battalion on the ground and the first enemy thrusts had been beaten back. The two Bravo platoons, Deal's and Deveny's, and Joe Marm's platoon, had finally linked up and, on orders from Moore, had withdrawn to the creek bed, under cover of intense artillery fire, bringing their dead and wounded with them. But Herrick's platoon positioned some 200 meters up the finger ridge was still cut off. The cavalrymen on XRAY were facing an aggressive, well-trained, well-armed, and highly motivated enemy force that could shoot extremely well and obviously was not afraid to die. But Moore had to give one more try to extricating his lost platoon. He ordered Companies A and B to prepare for a coordinated attack to reach the platoon.

During the afternoon, the platoon's situation steadily worsened. While fires on the LZ below would ebb and flow, the NVA never relented in their pressure on the tiny perimeter, and it was taking the inevitable toll. The North Vietnamese rifle and automatic-weapons fire crossed the perimeter so close to the ground that it was causing casualties even among those who were hugging the ground. If a man so much as raised up on one elbow in order to try to wield an entrenching tool on the rock-hard earth, a bullet would find its mark. By mid-afternoon, Lieutenant Herrick was dead, struck by a bullet that ripped through his body. As he lay dying, he turned command of the platoon over to Platoon Sergeant Carl Palmer. He told Palmer to redistribute ammunition, call in artillery fire, and, at the first opportunity, try to fight his way back to the LZ. Palmer had no such opportunity. Within minutes, he too was dead. The chain of succession moved rapidly thereafter. The Second Squad leader, Sergeant Robert Stokes, took over but made the mistake of getting up on his hands and knees, mumbling something about leading the platoon to safety. He was struck in the head with a slug and sank back to the ground. Killed in the same volley of bullets was the forward observer for the mortar platoon. The artillery forward observer liaison sergeant was shot in the neck and could no longer function. Now, finally, it was up to Sergeant Savage. He hadn't exactly been unoccupied during the early part of the afternoon, killing at least a dozen of the NVA who ventured into the sights of his M-16. But now he grabbed the artilleryman's radio and began calling in and adjusting artillery fire. Within minutes, he had ringed the perimeter with concentrations, some as close to the position as twenty meters. Without the artillery there is little doubt that the NVA would have overrun the perimeter, because, for some inexplicable reason, they were concentrating resources all out of proportion to the strength of the tiny American outpost. Of the original twenty-seven men who started out, eight had been killed and twelve were wounded. Only seven were still unscathed and effective warriors. During the afternoon, the platoon occupied the exclusive attention of at least one and probably two NVA rifle companies, units that never made it down the mountain to join in the early attacks on LZ XRAY. Herren later said the platoon was like a Bastogne in microcosm. He may not have been far from the truth.

The coordinated attack ordered by Moore to extricate the platoon would have the two platoons of Bravo on the right and three platoons of Alpha on the left. Herren had no choice but to move out with two platoons abreast, but Nadal elected to put two platoons abreast with the third, echeloning to the left rear. He reasoned that because of the mountain on his left—the direction from which so much of the NVA pressure had come during the afternoon—it would be prudent to have that degree of flank security. Nadal gathered as many men as he could in the creek bed and quietly told them that an American platoon was cut off and in trouble and that they were going after it. The morale of the troops was high and they responded with yells: "Let's go get 'em" and "Garry Owen."

The line of departure for the attack would be the now familiar landmark—the stream bed. The artillery prep for the attack was landing one hundred to one hundred fifty meters in front of the stream bed, too far away to be of real use to the assault forces. Within fifty meters of the stream bed, the two companies ran into a hail of fire from North Vietnamese that had used the past hour or so to dig hasty positions. They were burrowed into the ground in "spider" holes, dug into the tops and sides of anthills, and tied in trees. Nadal was leading his two platoons when they hit the enemy resistance. Almost immediately, the leader of the 1st Platoon, Second Lieutenant Wayne O. Johnson, fell with a chest wound and Sergeant Raymond Bernard, a team leader, was killed. The platoon sergeant, Troy L. Miller, took over and tried to keep the platoon forging ahead in the face of the NVA fire. On his right, Marm's men moved ahead until enemy machine gun fire, which appeared to have come from an anthill about thirty meters to their front, stopped them cold. Deliberately exposing himself to the fire in order to precisely locate the machine-gun position, Marm fired an M-72 antitank round at the anthill. The explosion caused some casualties, but the main nemesis, the machine gun, kept chattering, scything the grass in front of Marm. He then directed one of his men to dash forward and throw a hand grenade at the position. But the sergeant nearest him misunderstood the command and, simply flung a grenade from his position. It landed well short of the anthill. So Marm told the platoon to cover him, and he dashed across the bullet-swept grass, hurling grenades as he went. The last grenade silenced the machine-gun crew. As Marm was firing his M-16 at the dazed survivors, he was struck in the jaw by a bullet from another anthill. For this action, Marm subsequently was awarded the Medal of Honor, the first from the 1st Cavalry Division to receive one.

But despite Marm's heroics and the gallantry of other members of both A and B companies, it was obvious to Nadal that they were not going to be able to advance and that to stay in their present exposed location would subject the units to being picked to pieces. All of Nadal's platoon leaders now were either dead or wounded, and four of his men, including Sergeant Jack E. Gell, his communications sergeant, had been killed within six feet of him. It was now just past five o'clock. Here, on the eastern side of the mountain, it would soon be getting dark. Accordingly, Nadal called Moore and asked permission to pull back to the stream bed and set up positions for the night. Herren, who had moved even less than Nadal, monitored the radio message. Although he was anxious to reach his platoon he was realistic enough to recognize that he had little choice.

The decision grated on Moore's psyche. By nature an attacker, the idea of being forced to defend ate at him. But he was also a pragmatist and he recognized that at present his battalion was fighting three separate actions—one force was defending LZ XRAY, two companies were attacking, and one platoon was cut off from everybody. To continue blindly into the night would risk having his entire force defeated in detail if the enemy discovered and capitalized on Moore's situation. And, given the actions of the NVA during the afternoon, it was clear that the enemy had the strength to do just about anything it wanted if Moore gave them the opening. So Moore agreed to the withdrawal and, still under fierce fire, both companies prepared to pull back, bringing their dead and wounded with them.

But a withdrawal under fire is one of the most difficult of maneuvers. Nadal's 1st Platoon was having difficulty extracting from its position with its dead and wounded, so he committed his 3rd Platoon to relieve some of the pressure and to assist with the casualties. He still was having trouble, so he called Moore and asked him to order in smoke rounds to screen his withdrawal. When Whiteside, the FO in the command chopper, called the 21st Artillery's Fire direction center at FALCON, he learned that there were no smoke rounds available. Moore recalled from his Korean War experience that white phosphorous (WP) often provided the same degree of cover initially that conventional smoke rounds could. The down side was that it could injure friendly troops when fired in close. But Moore was willing to take the risk and ordered in the fire. He called Nadal and told him that Willie Peter was on the way, but no one in the company realized exactly what it meant. White phosphorous rounds explode with huge geysers of white smoke trailing the burning particles of phosphorous. The phosphorous burns as long as it is exposed to the air, and wounds by white phosphorous, while they may not be fatal, are extremely painful and debilitating.

When the rounds burst in the midst of the 1st and 3rd Platoons as well as the NVA positions, Nadal said, "I was upset, to say the least. However, miraculously, no one was hurt and it was extremely effective." All of the firing died down from in front of the positions and the troopers of both companies scurried about pulling the dead and wounded back. But the action bought only a little bit of time. Too soon, the NVA guns were beginning to hammer again. This time it was Nadal's call. Weighing the risks, he had his troops hug the ground when the second volley of WP rounds whistled in. Again, no friendly troops were hurt and again, the NVA fires stopped, during which time both companies disengaged. Nadal, who still had a bit of tidying up to do in his sector, briefly contemplated a third volley, but decided against pushing his luck and used conventional weapons to complete the extrication of his platoons.

Getting his two companies back safely made Moore feel a lot better. Also, while the withdrawal was occurring, the first elements of Bravo, 2/7 Cav, commanded by Captain Myron Diduryk, began arriving on the LZ. Diduryk, in the lead bird, climbed out and ran up to Moore, snapped off a salute and growled, in his typically gruff voice, "Garry Owen, sir." Moore initially had Diduryk place his company in the center of the landing zone, to act as a mobile reserve. Later, as he thought about the frontages being faced by his companies, he told Diduryk to attach one platoon to C 1/7. Bravo 2/7 had come in with one hundred and twenty men who, like the troopers in the companies of the sister battalion, were carrying heavy loads of ammunition. Each rifleman brought in an average of twenty magazines of M-16 ammo, and every M-60 machine gun crew had at least four boxes of ammunition. The M-79 grenadiers carried thirty to forty rounds each. Diduryk also brought in two 81-mm mortars with forty-eight HE rounds each.

Diduryk assigned the mission of reinforcing C 1/7 to Second Lieutenant James L. Lane's 2nd Platoon. When Edwards got the platoon, he fed the force into the right flank of his perimeter where he could tie in with Alpha's left flank. Edwards directed his men to dig prone shelters, but he did not place listening posts out in front of the perimeter. He reasoned that the tall plateau grass would cut down on their effectiveness and he planned to register final protective artillery fires with a hundred meters of his positions.

As Moore planned his LZ defenses, he realized that his Recon platoon would likely be sufficient mobile reserve and

directed Diduryk to take his remaining two platoons and occupy the northern and northeastern sectors of the perimeter,
tieing in with Bravo 1/7 on his left and the platoon of Delta
1/7 on his right. Thus, when looking at the LZ as if it were a
clock, with due north as twelve o'clock, Bravo 1/7, with two
platoons had the portion from ten to eleven; Bravo 2/7 had
from eleven to one; Delta 1/7 had from one to five; the reinforced Charlie 1/7 had from five to eight; and Alpha 1/7 filled
in from eight to ten. Thus far, the most severe NVA pressure
was off the mountain, generally in the eight to eleven o'clock
sectors. Nadal placed most of his forces in the stream bed,
but at the point where it bent sharply toward the mountain, he
had four or five dug in positions on top of the bank and tied in
with Lane's platoon. Herren, on the other hand, elected not to
use the stream bed, instead placing his two depleted platoons
forward of the bed in dug-in positions, with his CP located in
the creek bed.

By 7:00 P.M. the perimeter was secure and all weapons
sited and registered. Accompanied by Command Sergeant
Major Basil Plumley, Moore walked around the entire perimeter, visiting with troopers, spot-checking fields of fire and
ammunition resupply procedures, and generally satisfying
himself that the battalion was ready for the night. Just because the firing had died down and the LZ no longer was
under direct pressure, Moore did not delude himself that the
fight was over. The fact that the NVA were dug-in so close to
the perimeter, as evidenced by the reception they had given
his two attacking companies earlier, made it clear the enemy
had definite plans for LZ XRAY.

As darkness fell over the LZ, some of the dead and most of
the wounded were evacuated from the battalion collecting
point to FALCON, where the larger Chinooks would carry
them back to Camp Holloway, the dead to the graves registration point at Holloway and the wounded to surgical hospitals
at An Khe and Qui Nhon. The lift ships, guided in by members of the pathfinder platoon with flashlights, came into a
portion of the eastern landing zone. They brought in all sorts

of resupply—water, food, ammunition, medical supplies. The aid station had run very low on critical supplies such as morphine, Dexedrine, and bandages, and the water supply was so low that some soldiers had eaten C-ration jam just for its moisture content. Soldiers in firefights rarely get hungry when the bullets are flying, but they tend to dehydrate rapidly under the stress, so water was a critical item on the resupply runs. Moore also directed that his command chopper land, bringing in Dillon, the S-3, plus the artillery liaison officer, the forward air controller, and two more radio operators. Except for refueling stops, the command chopper had been in the air continuously since the assault began that morning. As Dillon's helicopter began its approach in the darkness, he looked out to his left at the mountain and spotted four or five blinking lights on the slopes of Chu Pong. He surmised that they were signal lights of the North Vietnamese moving down the mountain toward the landing zone. After he landed, he gave the information on the lights to Whiteside and Hastings to use in the future as target data.

During the evening, Field Front headquarters ordered its units in contact to maintain pressure on the Americans and directed that the 8th Battalion of the 66th move from its assembly area along the Ia Drang and be prepared to attack on order. General Man also ordered the Vietcong H-15 battalion, in positions well south of the scene of the fighting, to move north and make contact with the Americans. Inexplicably, he did nothing about the 32nd Regiment, which had never moved from the assembly area it had occupied for nearly all of November, almost thirteen kilometers northwest of XRAY. The heavy antiaircraft and heavy mortar battalions had not yet closed into assembly areas in the Chu Pong Massif. Nevertheless, despite the failure to commit the 32nd Regiment, Field Front had no intention of leaving the battlefield to the Americans.

XRAY—
THE FINALE

Late in the afternoon of November 14th, Brown firmed up plans for additional reinforcement of LZ XRAY. He directed Lieutenant Colonel Robert Tully's 2/5 Cav to position itself just south of XRAY and move overland early on the morning of the 15th. Brown even selected the jumping off point for the battalion, an open area about thirty-five hundred meters southeast of XRAY, which he called VICTOR. Two of the 2nd of the 5th companies, using four Hueys in relays, had assembled on VICTOR by nightfall. It was a real drill for Charlie 2/5. Captain Edward A. Boyt's company was in such dense jungle that it took his troopers thirty pounds of plastic explosive and seventeen shattered entrenching tools to clear a modest two-ship pickup zone. The third company, Bravo, remained on FALCON to secure the two batteries of artillery. Also moving that evening was A Company, 2nd of the 7th, shuttled into Catecka to provide security for the brigade base. And arriving at Camp Holloway by nightfall by Air Force transport was a brand new battalion, the First Battalion of the Fifth Cavalry under Lieutenant Colonel Frederic Ackerson. It would move to Catecka by Caribou and Chinooks at first light on the 15th.

Brown's S-3, Pete Mallet, worked long into the night coming up with a scheme of maneuver for the following day. Brown intended to send A 2/7 into the LZ by air as early as possible, with the Tully's full battalion moving overland from the southeast. In order to beef up the artillery support, Kinnard had dispatched another battery of 105-mm howitzers—C 2/17 Arty. Brown intended placing that battery along with the third battery from the 21st Arty on a firebase to the north of XRAY. This he named MACON and directed the remainder of the 2/7 Cav to conduct an air assault and secure the base as soon as the airlift had delivered Alpha 2/7 to XRAY. To spring Bravo 2/5 from guard duty at FALCON, Mallet and Brown intended to bring in Charlie 1/5 from either Holloway or Catecka, depending on where the unit was at the time the lift was available. It was an extremely complicated series of aerial moves, requiring exquisite timing on the part of air and ground commanders alike.

It was because so much of Brown's available lift was being expended on these establishing moves that he decided to move Tully's battalion overland. Another cogent reason was that a move by foot might surprise the NVA, which would, after all, be expecting to see a steady stream of helicopters coming into XRAY. Brown hoped to put an element of surprise back into the game. He could have gone through the entire division and not come up with either a battalion or a battalion commander better suited for the task than Tully and his men. The 2/5 Cav had been the 2nd Battalion, 38th Infantry, at Fort Benning and had brought a serious reputation as a straight-leg line infantry battalion into the air assault arena when it was "loaned" to the 11th Air Assault Division in December 1963 for the air assault tests. Tully had joined the battalion in February 1964 and had been its commander since. A tall, lanky West Pointer from the class of 1946, Bob Tully was easily the peer of Hal Moore as an infantry commander. Tully had served with the 187th Airborne Regimental Combat Team in Korea, making two combat jumps and commanding both a platoon and a rifle company. He was blessed with a boisterous sense of humor and a leadership style that engendered fierce loyalty on the part of his subordinates. He also was cursed with a speech impediment that caused him to stammer at inopportune times. Yet, when the chips were down, Tully's voice was icy calm and without a hint of a stutter. He constantly preached to his officers and noncommissioned officers that a leader's main job in combat is to accomplish his mission while working hard at saving the lives of his troops.

On LZ XRAY, there wasn't any sleep for the defenders and, for the men of Bravo 1/7 who had spent the previous night with the skittish brigade base at Catecka, it was a case of near exhaustion. The NVA tried numerous squad-size probes of the defenses, with every sector of the perimeter save that of Delta 1/7 getting probed. In every instance, final protective concentrations from the two batteries of artillery on FALCON discouraged the enemy. During the day and on into the night, the two batteries on FALCON had hurled more than four thousand rounds around the landing zone and up on the finger that ran down from Chu Pong. Tactical air support continued on into the night along with Puff, the Gatling gun bird, and, overhead, Smokey, the flare ship, was kicking out flares on request.

Up on the finger, the remnants of Bravo's Second Platoon continued to be a mini-Bastogne. Three times during the night the NVA attacked with at least a reinforced platoon, and three times the combined fires of artillery, tactical air, and small arms from the perimeter beat back the assault waves. The enemy still was expending an incredible amount of time, effort, and human lives to eradicate a redoubt that was tactically insignificant. At the helm within the tiny perimeter was the doughty Sergeant Savage, who manned the artillery radio and called in protective fires within twenty-five meters of his position. The first attack came shortly after midnight. At 3:45 A.M. came the second assault, stronger than the first. Savage could hear the NVA soldiers talking to one another as they moved into position. He used the sounds as a guide for a fifteen-minute artillery saturation of the area to his northwest and then followed it with a tactical air strike under illumination. Savage noted that the flares lit up his perimeter as well, and, thereafter, illumination was not used close to his position.

The wounded in the perimeter who could still shoulder a rifle were used in the defense. The third and final attack came around 4:40 A.M. and it was as unsuccessful as the first. Savage and his comrades could hear the NVA dragging their dead and wounded away through the underbrush of the mountain when the last attack failed. Through it all, Specialist Five Charles H. Lose, the senior aidman in the company, whom Herren had placed with the platoon because of a shortage of medics, moved among the wounded, ministering to their needs. Although wounded early on, his diligence and ingenuity throughout the day and night saved several lives. When he exhausted the supply of bandages in his first-aid kit as well as the men's individual first aid packets, he used C-ration toilet paper packets to staunch the flow of blood on some of the wounded. And, of course, in order to treat his patients he exposed himself to enemy fire time after time. Both Savage and Lose were to win Distinguished Service Crosses for gallantry under fire for these actions.

During the night, Moore discussed with Dillon plans to extricate the isolated platoon. He said that all that night his thoughts were dominated by two things—how to save that platoon and how to hold on to the landing zone. Both Moore and Dillon were convinced that the enemy clearly had the capability of attacking the LZ and hitting the platoon concurrently. He had toyed with the idea of staging a night movement to the platoon, but because the enemy also had a night attack capability and because the LZ was his lifeline, he discarded that proposal. Finally he came up with a plan for a daylight attack. His preliminary plan was to use all three of the 1/7 rifle companies in the attack. He would attach a company from Alpha to Bravo, giving that company three full platoons, and use Bravo as the lead force again. Moore and his command group would follow Herren's company and A and C companies would echelon left and right behind Herren, ready to assist the lead unit if necessary. The S-3 was to remain on the LZ with B 2/7 and Delta Company as security. Although the enemy did expend a disproportionate amount of energy on the platoon the preceding day, there was no guarantee that he would continue that course. So Moore had to be prepared again to fight on two fronts—on the mountain and on the landing zone.

At ten minutes after first light, Moore directed all company commanders to meet Dillon and him in the vicinity of the Charlie Company command post. There he would give the attack order for extricating the platoon and review the attack route with them. He chose the C Company CP, which was on the southwestern edge of the LZ, because it was easy to get to and provided an excellent view of the attack objective. In the interim, Moore directed all companies to patrol forward of their perimeter positions to look for possible snipers. He also told them to sweep their rear areas for possible infiltrators.

Upon receiving these instructions, Edwards told his C Company platoon leaders to send at least a squad-size force out to a distance of two hundred meters. It was about 6:40 A.M. when the patrols moved out. They hadn't moved much more than fifty meters from their positions when heavy enemy fire shattered the stillness of the morning. The two platoons on the left of Edwards's position (at the five and six o'clock positions on the landing zone), Second Lieutenant Neil Kroger's 1st and Second Lieutenant John L. Geoghegen's 2nd, were taking the heaviest fire, although all of Charlie Company's positions began getting longer-range small arms fire. Edwards tried to raise his platoon leaders on the radio but got no answer from the two on the left. There was a good reason: both were dead, as were a substantial number of their patrols. They had run headlong into a quietly advancing NVA company crawling on their hands and knees. The patrol sweep had prematurely triggered the enemy assault. It was with tremendous relief that Edwards was able to contact his 3rd platoon leader, Second Lieutenant William W. Franklin, and the leader of the attached B 2/7 platoon, Lieutenant Lane. Both had been able to pull back their squad patrols when the firing erupted to their left. Edwards feared the worst from his left flank.

Edwards took a chance and stood up in order to see over the tall grass. He spotted a dozen or so NVA soldiers about 200 meters to his front, moving toward him. He called Moore, briefed him on the situation, and had his forward observer request artillery fire. Then he, along with four others in his command group, commenced firing their rifles at the advancing enemy. He called Moore again, this time requesting commitment of the battalion reserve to bolster his left flank. Moore refused. He and Dillon were not yet convinced that this was going to be the enemy's main effort. They knew the NVA had the capability of staging a two-battalion effort against the LZ. And since the enemy had shown an uncharacteristic desire for offensive combat against a fixed base, Moore and Dillon had no real choice but to hang tough for a few minutes more to see how the situation developed.

The situation in the C Company sector grew steadily worse. Despite a pounding from artillery and tactical air and deafening volleys of rifle and machine-gun fire from the company's defensive positions, the North Vietnamese, disregarding hideous losses that ripped huge holes in their ranks, kept pressing forward. Some of their more intrepid soldiers now were within hand-to-hand combat range of the prone shelters that had been scooped out by the defenders. Since most of the pressure still seemed to be coming from the south and southeast, Edwards told Franklin to push his Third Platoon to the left to reinforce the flank. Just as he finished giving the order, he spotted two NVA soldiers within thirty meters of his hole. He stood up and tossed a grenade at them, and as he did so, he felt what he said was like a hard slap on the back. He had taken an AK slug in the back. Edwards did not lose consciousness and again asked Moore for reinforcements. He also asked Moore to send up his executive officer, Second Lieutenant John W. Arrington, from the central resupply point by the battalion CP, to take over command of the company.

This time, Moore agreed to reinforcement, but he still wasn't touching his precious battalion reserve, the recon platoon. Instead, he ordered Tony Nadal to detach one of his platoons and send it to Edwards's aid. As Arrington approached his company CP, an NVA machine gun, using an anthill barely fifty meters from the front-line trace, brought low, grazing fire to bear on Edwards's position. Arrington was hugging the ground, receiving instructions from his wounded commander, when he was struck in the chest by an RPD round. Notified that both his commanding officer and his executive officer had been wounded, Lieutenant Franklin began crawling toward the company command post from his platoon location. In short order he too was hit and seriously wounded. It was now 7:15 A.M.; the fight had been raging for nearly forty-five minutes, yet the other sectors of the perimeter remained unscathed. Now it was the turn of the Delta Company sector. Manned on the line by the Antitank platoon, now serving as infantry, and backed up by the Mortar Platoon, it was struck by a company-size assault.

In response to Moore's directive to reinforce Charlie Company with a platoon, Nadal detached his 2nd Platoon—Marm's Platoon, minus Marm, of course—from the right flank of Alpha Company, and had his 3rd Platoon stretch across the gap. The 2nd Platoon had just started across the clearing, which was, in effect, the western edge of the landing zone, when heavy, grazing fire swept across the LZ from the west. The platoon simply couldn't move and formed a prone line of skirmishers just behind A Company's left flank and C Company's right flank. There it remained for the balance of the firefight.

By 7:45 A.M., the fire criss-crossing LZ XRAY was killing

and wounding men on the far side of the contact area. A man was killed in the battalion CP near the big anthill; several others were wounded. Anyone who moved toward the C Company sector drew immediate and heavy fire. Platoon Sergeant Glenn A. Kennedy, who had made a quick trip to the battalion supply point, had to brave scathing fire to get back to his company. He arrived at the company CP just in time to nail two NVA soldiers who were sniping at the command post. Then he stood up and ran forward with grenades to eliminate another group of attackers. Incredibly, he was not touched by the hail of bullets. Now Moore alerted the recon platoon to be prepared to go to either the Delta or Charlie Company sectors on order. He also radioed Brown that he needed reinforcement. Brown told him he had Alpha 2/7 saddled up at Catecka ready to send in as soon as the fire slackened enough to permit choppers to land. In the meantime, he was pushing Tully's battalion overland from the south. Bravo 2/5 had been relieved from artillery base guard duties and flown to VICTOR, and that set the stage for the battalion move.

The 2/5 Cavalry pushed off from VICTOR at around 8:00 A.M. It was not to be a speed march. Despite the urgency of the situation at XRAY, Tully was not about to sacrifice security for the dubious advantages of speed, so he used artillery rounds to mark the course of the battalion. The rounds accomplished two things: they kept the lead companies firmly on course, in an area where land navigation was difficult because of the lack of distinguishing terrain features, and they discouraged enemy ambushes. And should the enemy strike the battalion, the artillery FOs had immediate firing data to use. It was a sound system for movement in the jungle, yet for the most part, only 2nd Brigade battalions tended to use the technique.

The battalion moved overland with Alpha and Bravo abreast and C Company echeloned to the left rear. The line of march put the battalion through a saddle of a long ridge line that ran down off the Chu Pong Massif and curled to the northeast. The saddle itself was about a hundred meters high and perhaps a thousand meters wide. Its western side sloped up rapidly to nearly five hundred meters of the mountain mass itself. To the east and northeast, the ridge line sloped up another two hundred meters. Its furthermost extremity formed the eastern ridge of the basin in which LZ XRAY was located.

At the same time that Tully started overland, Moore directed his units to throw colored smoke grenades so that the air and artillery observers could get the fire support as close to the perimeter as possible. Overhead in Brown's command chopper was Captain Dudley Tademy, the 21st Artillery liaison officer to the 3rd Brigade. He took over the fire coordination, as he was able to see all parts of the landing zone, and started bringing 105-mm HE shells within fifty meters of the front-line trace. They were coming so close, in fact, that the artillery FOs with the companies were shouting at the top of their lungs, just before each volley, "Get down!" Within seconds, the troops would hear the shwoosh of the shells as they rocketed past their holes, then the awesome and earsplitting *crack* of high-explosives and the whirring and whizzing of shrapnel. The Air Force, which had had a fighter-bomber on station over the LZ an average of one every fifteen minutes since the contact was made on November 14, brought the support in extremely close—in one case, too close. An F-105 dropped two canisters of napalm right on the LZ and some of the burning gasoline jelly reached the battalion command post in the anthill area, killing one man, burning a couple others, and exploding a pile of M-16 ammunition. As Jerry Hastings, the Air Force FAC, screamed into the radio to wave off the second jet of the flight, Matt Dillon sprinted across the bullet-swept clearing to the center of the LZ to lay out an aircraft recognition panel.

Despite the ferocity of the fire support, the NVA infantry kept pressing forward, keeping the LZ awash with bullets. Company A had repulsed an attack at its position, but company D was in danger of being overrun. Moore finally committed the reserve to help reinforce the Antitank Platoon, and then had Diduryk assemble his command group and one platoon at the battalion CP to act as a reserve. This left Diduryk only one platoon on his sector of the perimeter. He directed the platoon leader, Lieutenant Vernon, to slide across and fill the gaps, and told the 1st Platoon leader, Second Lieutenant Cyril R. "Rick" Rescorla, to assemble the platoon by the battalion command post. So violent was the grazing fire coming in from the opposite side of the landing zone that Rescorla lost two men—one killed and another wounded—before he even got out of his platoon positions.

Eventually, the fire superiority of the Americans began to beat back the NVA and by 9:00 A.M., the volume of fire directed on the LZ had slackened to the point that Moore could permit the first birds of the reinforcement lift to come in, using the easternmost portion of the landing zone. As soon as the first elements of Company A, Second of the Seventh, landed, Moore directed its commander, Captain Joel E. Sugdinis, to take two platoons and occupy Diduryk's old perimeter position. This freed up Vernon's platoon to join B 2/7 at the center of the LZ. By now the NVA had begun withdrawing, employing the now-familiar technique of employing snipers in trees to cover the withdrawal.

Moore decided it was time to rearrange the units in his perimeter. He directed Diduryk to take over the positions occupied by Charlie 1/7 which now, in the absence of all other C Company officers, was being run by Diduryk's platoon leader, Lieutenant Lane. Because that part of the perimeter was a four-platoon sector, Moore added the Third Platoon of Alpha 2/7 to Diduryk's three platoons and returned to Nadal his Second Platoon. Company C was in bad shape, sustaining more than thirty killed and another forty wounded in the three-hour battle. Moore brought the shattered remnants back to his CP area to act as battalion reserve.

Brown meanwhile was juggling airlift to position more artillery to support the embattled perimeter. The remnants of the

2nd Battalion, 7th Cavalry, air assaulted into a position called MACON, about five kilometers due north of XRAY, close to the banks of the Ia Drang. It was to be a base for two batteries of artillery, but when the redlegs tried to emplace the tubes they found the soil too unstable to support the firing platforms. So Brown decided to reopen what had been CAV-ALAIR under the 2/8 Cav a week earlier; but this time it would be called COLUMBUS. By late afternoon the LZ was secured and B 1/21 Arty and C 2/17 Arty were adding their fire to the steel curtain around XRAY. COLUMBUS was only five klicks northeast of XRAY.

Shortly after noon, Tully's battalion reached the south perimeter of XRAY. The trip overland had been mostly uneventful, except that just as the battalion was crossing the saddle about fifteen hundred meters south of XRAY, Capt. Larry Bennett's Alpha Company started receiving small arms fire. This stalled the advance temporarily while Bennett maneuvered his platoons forward, using pure infantry school fire and movement techniques, augmented by the ubiquitous artillery fire. The NVA resistance quickly shattered and Bennett's company policed up two prisoners, both armed with AK's.

Brown had made Moore the commander of all ground forces in the landing zone, so when the 2nd of the 5th was completely within the perimeter, Tully conferred with Moore about the disposition of his troops. Uppermost in Moore's mind, now that the NVA attack had been beaten off, was the rescue of the platoon. Because Tully's battalion was already formed up, it made good sense to keep it in attack formation and use Herren's Bravo Company as a guide to the platoon. Bravo 2/5 would remain behind on XRAY and start relieving Delta 1/7 in place.

Tully's guidance to Herren was simplicity: "Here are our radio frequencies; my A Company will be on your left flank; move out when you're ready. We'll guide on you." At 1:15 P.M., the attack force moved out, preceded by artillery and aerial rocket prep. Herren's company was on the right, moving up the right slope of the finger, with Bennett's company abreast to his left and Boyt's company echeloned to the left and rear. The relief expedition advanced cautiously up the hill, harassed by sporadic sniper fire. As Herren's troops neared Savage's platoon, they found the captured M-60 machine gun, smashed by artillery fire. Close by were the bodies of the crew, along with the bodies of successive North Vietnamese crews. They also found the body of the grenadier, the first man in the platoon to die the previous day. Minutes later, the relief column broke through to the platoon. The emotions of the moment included tears of thankfulness. Incredibly, the platoon had not incurred a single additional fatality after Savage had taken command of the platoon the preceding afternoon. Herren attributed this to extraordinarily good fortune, to the enemy's ignorance of their precise predicament, to Specialist Lose's first aid to those already wounded, and, most of all, to Savage's incredible use of artillery fire.

Tully did not tarry long to make a thorough search of the area. Now that he had reached the platoon, his mission was to evacuate the survivors and casualties back to XRAY with all possible haste. Herren's company provided the bulk of the litter detail—four men, with crude poncho litters for each of the dead and many of the wounded. Tully surrounded Bravo 1/7 with his companies for security. Just before the expedition was to start down the mountain, a sniper's bullet crashed into Bennett's chest, seriously wounding the Alpha commander. The trip down the mountain was made without incident, and by 3:00 P.M., everyone was back inside the XRAY perimeter.

While Tully was up on the mountain, Moore had directed that all units on line screen out to a distance of three hundred meters. They quickly discovered that the NVA had paid a hideous price and still had failed to overrun a single American unit. Enemy bodies littered the battlefield, many stacked like cordwood behind anthills; body fragments on the ground and on bushes were mute testimony to the devastation of the air strikes and artillery fire. Trails littered with bandages and spotted with blood spoke of the many other bodies being dragged away. The violence of the close-in fighting was attested to by the number of NVA killed with M-16s and M-60s who were scattered among the American dead. One rifleman from Company C was found with his hands clutched around the throat of a Hanoi soldier. Lieutenant Kroger was found surrounded by five enemy dead. Weapons and equipment were scattered all over the landscape. Tenderly, the search parties lifted their dead comrades onto poncho litters and brought them back to the main landing zone for their final helicopter flight out of XRAY.

And if the North Vietnamese thought the destruction wrought by the American artillery and tactical air was bad for their morale, they were about to be introduced to a a new weapon. Shortly after noon, at a distance of about seven kilometers due west of XRAY, suddenly and without warning a large area erupted with hundreds of thunderous explosions that moved across the ground like a giant carpet being unrolled at whirlwind speed. The B-52 bombers had struck. For the first time, the big bombers worked as a partner in the ground scheme of maneuver, their bombs plowing up large areas of the Chu Pong Massif. The NVA soldiers were terrified of these raids, because they believed that each attack covered a twenty-kilometer area and that ordinary trenches and foxholes were of no protection.

During the morning, just prior to the arrival of Tully's battalion, Knowles flew into XRAY with Lieutenant Colonel John Stoner, the Air Force liaison officer for the division. Knowles said he brought a cigar in for Moore and listened to his briefing on the situation. As Moore finished his briefing, an air strike hit a target on the side of the perimeter closest to the command post. The ground trembled and a bomb fragment flew into the CP area, about ten or fifteen feet away from where they were standing. Knowles had been gently pinging on Stoner about bringing Tac Air in close and tight. So Stoner walked over and gingerly picked up the smoking fragment, came back, and handed it to Knowles, saying, "Is this close enough, General?" Knowles briefed Moore on the activities going on around the landing zone and told him that on November 16 he would have Brown pull the 1st of the 7th and attached units out of XRAY and fly them back to Camp Holloway for a couple days of R & R.

By this time, word of the big fight at the foot of Chu Pong had become big news. On the afternoon of the 14th, the MACV press briefing, popularly known as the "Five O'clock Follies," announced a major contact with North Vietnamese forces. By noon of the 15th, the tiny press tent just outside the forward Division Tactical Operations Center at II Corps in Pleiku was swarming with reporters and photographers clamoring for transportation to the fight. Knowles's guidance to the captain running the press center was explicit: there would be no "charter" flight to XRAY on November 15. But if a reporter was ingenious enough to hitchhike into the LZ, no one would particularly care. A number of them did. Joe Galloway of United Press International came in with Dillon on the evening of the 14th and stayed until it was over.

Although the NVA had suffered cruelly, the sporadic sniper fire to all parts of the LZ was ample evidence that they had not abandoned the field altogether. The night of November 15 was cloudless with bright moonlight and all four batteries of artillery poured in constant fire all night long. At 1:00 A.M., there was a very light probe of the northwestern section where Bravo 1/7 still was manning a piece of the perimeter. A flurry of small arms fire drove off the North Vietnamese, who left behind two dead. Things went quiet around the perimeter, save for the incessant crashing of artillery rounds. At 4:00 A.M., a series of short and long whistle signals was heard from out in front of Diduryk's position, the same section that had been manned twenty-four hours earlier by Edwards's company. Trip flares were ignited and anti-intrusion alarms were sprung, some as far out as three hundred meters. The main enemy effort appeared directed at the platoon from A 2/7, which was anchoring Diduryk's left flank, between the five and six o'clock positions on the LZ. The platoon leader, Second Lieutenant William H. Sisson, asked for permission to fire when he saw a large group of NVA soldiers advancing toward his position. He opened fire and the response from the enemy quickly spread throughout Diduryk's entire frontage, from southeast to due west. It appeared to be at least a company-size assault.

The attack was finally broken up, but not before the NVA had penetrated to within five meters of the foxhole line. A great deal of credit for smashing the attack was given to First Lieutenant William L. Lund, the forward observer for Bravo 2/7. Lund had each of the four artillery batteries fire different defensive concentrations, with a mix of point-detonating and time fuses of high explosives, and white phosphorous shells. Then Lund adjusted each battery in one hundred-meter increments laterally. And finally, each was adjusted to within fifty meters of the foxhole line.

At 5:30 A.M., the North Vietnamese tried it again, inexplicably always coming from the south or the west. In all of the firefights, Diduryk and his platoon leaders and key noncommissioned officers ran a virtual clinic on fire discipline, point targeting, and final protective fires. By dawn of November 16, the enemy attack had run its course. Diduryk's company had sustained only six men slightly wounded, while outside the perimeter were heaps and mounds of dead enemy soldiers. At one firing position they were stacked so high that the men had to go out and move NVA bodies in order to clear a field of fire. The scene reminded old timers from Korea of the Chinese human wave attacks and their inevitable end in the face of American firepower.

Still apprehensive about the enemy's potential for attack, Moore directed all companies to spray the trees, anthills, and bushes in front of their positions to kill any snipers or infiltrators—an innovation the men of the Cav would eventually call the "mad minute." Seconds after the firing began, a forty-man NVA element that had been creeping forward in the tall grass suddenly leaped to their feet about 150 meters in front of Sugdinis's position and began milling in confusion, apparently thinking they had been spotted. They made an excellent artillery target and were cut down in minutes. It was the first time any real threat had been directed against the north-eastern portion of the LZ. During the mad minute, an NVA soldier dropped out of a tree right in front of Herren's command post; the riddled body of another fell and hung swinging from the branch he had tied himself to in front of the leftmost platoon in Diduryk's company.

After the mad minute was over, Charlie Company and the recon platoon, the battalion reserve units, made a detailed sweep of the interior of XRAY. There were still three American casualties unaccounted for and Moore was adamant that every American soldier who came to XRAY would leave—that no mother's son would be left behind. He also was still concerned about infiltrators. The search, which took the better part of an hour, turned up nothing.

It was now 9:55 A.M., and Moore wanted to push away from the perimeter in a coordinated sweep out to five hundred meters. After covering from fifty to seventy-five meters, Diduryk's company was hit with a large volume of fire, including hand grenades thrown by wounded NVA soldiers still lying in the area. The lapse between the mad minute and the sweep of the landing zone interior may have allowed the relentless enemy an opportunity to return to firing positions, or they may never have left their positions, simply lying low until the mad minute was over. It's something no one will ever know for sure. At any rate, in a twinkling, Diduryk had lost his weapons squad leader and had nine other men wounded, including the platoon leader and platoon sergeant of his 2nd platoon. Under artillery cover he withdrew back to the foxhole line.

There, Moore and Lieutenant Hastings, the forward air

controller, joined him. Minutes later, fighter-bombers were unloading bombs, napalm, rockets, and cannon fire on the target area. Then, behind a wall of artillery fire, Bravo moved back out, using the time-honored infantry tactics of fire and movement, and quickly reduced the pockets of resistance that were left from the cannonade. The sweep revealed twenty-seven more NVA freshly killed. But more important, the troopers found the bodies of the three missing Americans.

By 10:30 the lead elements of the 2nd Battalion, 7th Cav, augmented by Alpha company of the 1st Battalion, 5th Cavalry, arrived after moving overland from COLUMBUS. The battalion was placed under the control of Tully, who was directed by Brown to secure the LZ and relieve all of the 1st of the 7th Cavalry units, plus B 2/7 and the 3rd Platoon of A 2/7. Those units would be lifted by Huey and Chinook back to Camp Holloway for a well-deserved rest.

As his battalion was consolidating for a move, carrying captured arms and equipment back to the command post for either destruction or evacuation, Moore had to face the press corps. Knowles had given permission for the assistant Public Information Officer to lay on a Chinook to carry the clamoring media into XRAY. All three networks had crews, as did the wire services and a number of other news organizations. There was even a photographer from *Life* in to get some final pictures of Ed Boyt for an upcoming magazine spread. But Hal Moore was the center of attention; suddenly he was catapulted from an obscure Army lieutenant colonel to a national news figure. As articulate in front of the cameras as he was brave in front of the NVA, Moore made a number of memorable statements. In one shot he held up an M-16 and said: "Brave men and this little black gun won this victory." That statement, when repeated in Pleiku to an audience that included General Westmoreland, had a profound impact on the arming of the U.S. Army. It erased any doubts the high command may have had about the efficacy of the M-16, when compared to the communist AK-47. Westmoreland began pressuring the Department of Army to get M-16s for every soldier in Vietnam and, ultimately, for the ARVN.

In another interview, with tears running down his cheeks, Moore told a TV newsman, "I've got men in body bags today that had less than a week to go in the Army. These men fought all the way; they never gave an inch." The newsman, Lou Cioffi of ABC, said he knew he had a real bell-ringer of a piece and thought he had an exclusive—until later, when he saw the black-and-white kinescopes of all of the network pieces. "I'll be damned if Hal didn't cry on all three networks," Cioffi lamented. He by no means meant that Moore was insincere; that the American fighting man still was the best in the world was a message Moore would lay on anyone who would listen. He had profound respect for the fighting qualities of the NVA soldier, but never wavered in his belief that in straight-up battle, the American would triumph.

That sentiment also was shared by some hard-bitten newsmen. Galloway, who had been in the Plei Me camp when it was under siege and had seen all of the heroics at LZ XRAY, told Charlie Black, "Charlie, these are the greatest soldiers that have ever gone into a fight! There hasn't been any outfit like this one before. It's something I wish every American in the world could understand, what these kids did. Look over there, doesn't that make you feel good?" Galloway was gesturing to a shattered tree with a tiny American flag flying from its broken top, about ten feet off the ground. True, it was a cliché camera shot from every war movie ever made, but there on LZ XRAY, in the midst of death, destruction, and unbelievable heroism, its impact transcended the stereotype.

While the media was in XRAY, Knowles held an impromptu press conference, announcing that the cavalry was going to move off LZ XRAY the next day. He said the purpose was to "expand the killing zone" but, for security reasons, couldn't tell the media what the real reason was—that B-52s would be hitting the entire valley where XRAY was located on November 17. The announcement that the Cav was going to simply abandon a piece of real estate that cost seventy killed and a hundred twenty-one wounded touched off a series of sharp and hostile questions by the press. The reporters simply couldn't understand that the landing zone, in and of itself, was worthless; that its value was its luring the NVA into crashing onto the reefs of high explosive and deadly small-arms fire. When the NVA pulled back away from the landing zone, its *raison d'être* disappeared. At the heart of the problem was the inability of the media to understand that Vietnam had become a war of attrition and that airmobility made it unnecessary to spend quantities of resources occupying worthless ground. It was a lesson that few reporters ever mastered.

But other than the troublesome matter of withdrawal, the media had a field day interviewing the troops and officers; shooting pictures of squad and platoon sweeps, which both battalion commanders kept going, regardless of how peaceful the scene had become; and taking pictures of the incredible booty won by the Cav. Captured enemy equipment included fifty-seven AK-47 rifles; fifty-four SKS carbines with bayonets; seventeen Degtyarev automatic rifles; four Maxim heavy machine guns; five RPG-2 rocket launchers; two 81-mm mortar tubes; and enormous amounts of ammunition. There also was the individual equipment that, after being picked over for souvenirs, was destroyed in place. The official body count for the battle at XRAY was set at 834 dead, with an estimated 500 more killed, mostly by tactical air and artillery, countless wounded, and six prisoners. Later, revisionists would sneer at the body count, but no newsman who visited XRAY on November 16 would ever doubt that the 66th and 33rd Regiments had been in a blood bath. And, certainly, no trooper of the Seventh Cavalry ever had any doubts that a lot of men from the North died there in the valley of the Ia Drang.

All of Moore's battalion had already extracted when he clambered into the aircraft to fly to Holloway, and he was delighted to see that it was being flown by his old friends from the 229th—Bruce Crandall and Jon Mills. When they got to Holloway, Moore asked them to fly him over to his command post where his command chopper was parked. Mills recalls that after they shut down, Moore suggested, "After the last few days, I think I could use a drink. Where can we get a drink around here?" There was a small officer's club close by, so the three set out, still carrying their weapons, with Moore still wearing the scroungy World War II–type herringbone fatigues that he had spent the last three days in. When they walked up to the bar, the bartender told them he couldn't serve them because Moore was too dirty. Mills remembers how Moore patiently explained that they had just come out of the field and would really appreciate a drink. The bartender replied, "You're in the First Cav. This club doesn't belong to you; you'll have to leave." Mills says that was when "Hal started to lose his patience. He said, 'Go get your club officer, and we'll settle this. But right now, I'm here and I'm going to have a drink. And I would like to have it in the next couple of minutes." The bartender beat a hasty retreat to summon the club officer but still refused the trio service. So, Moore unslung his M-16 and laid it on the bar, Mills and Crandall solemnly following suit with their .38s. Moore then said, "You've got exactly thirty seconds to get some drinks on this bar or I'm going to clean house." The bartender got smart and served the drinks. By this time, the club officer had arrived. He had heard all about the fight in the valley and knew who Moore was. And, as it turned out, so did most of the customers in the club. From then on, the trio couldn't buy a drink. That was when they knew that the fight on LZ XRAY was finally over.

12

AGONY AT ALBANY

The night of November 16 passed without incident at LZ XRAY; the NVA had decided it was too tough a nut to crack and the three battalions pulled back northwest along the base of Chu Pong to lick their wounds. Essentially, the battle at XRAY was fought with the equivalent of a regiment—the 7th and 9th Battalions of the 66th and the composite battalion of the 33rd, plus the normal supporting regimental arms. Field Front had put the 8th Battalion of the 66th Regiment in motion toward the battlefield late on November 15, but it had barely gotten started when its mission and direction of march were changed. Field Front concluded that if XRAY was too tough, there was a good chance that the artillery bases were vulnerable. The landing zone at LZ MACON early on the 15th confused the NVA, whose scouts spent valuable time flailing around the area, only to discover that the artillery had been there only a very short time before being moved to COLUMBUS. Now the 8th Battalion was en route to COLUMBUS from the west, while the H-15 Main Force VC battalion was headed its way from the south.

The impending B-52 strikes—they were called "arc lights"—were due within a couple hours and there had to be a minimum three-kilometer safety zone between the strike and friendly troops. The two battalions on XRAY, after local security patrols off the landing zone revealed a total lack of enemy in the area, quickly organized for an overland march. Led by the 2/5 Cav, the two battalions would move quickly over the ridge line that formed the eastern boundary of the basin in which XRAY was located. Once on the eastern side of the ridge, a distance of about three kilometers, the 2/5 would continue on in the last fifteen hundred meters to CO-LUMBUS, and the trailing 2/7 Cav would swing toward the northwest and sweep toward a map location called ALBANY, a distance of about twenty-five hundred meters.

The movement off XRAY was part of a larger maneuver being designed by division headquarters to put the NVA in a nutcracker. Now that some sort of victory could be anticipated on the western plateau, the ARVN wanted a piece of the action. In order to be in on the kill, the ARVN high command was even willing to commit a couple of its palace guard battalions in Saigon, the Airborne Brigade. Initial plans were to have these battalions operate south of Duc Co toward the Ia Drang while the cavalry worked its way west and north, driving the NVA ahead of it. Knowles would have preferred to assault directly into the heart of the Chu Pong Massif, but the Air Force had dropped a number of five-thousand-pound bombs in the interior that had delay fuses set to go off over a two-week period. Putting American troops into that area would have been hazardous to their health, so the 3rd Brigade would have to settle for skirting the base of the mountain. Brown's first move was to have the 2nd of the 7th sweep the area between COLUMBUS and a map location about four kilometers north and slightly east of XRAY. From there the battalion was supposed to set up a perimeter and send out company-size patrols toward the mountains as well as up through the Ia Drang Valley. The mission was to find and destroy the enemy; essentially the same mission that was given the 1st Battalion, 7th Cavalry four days earlier. The next step for the brigade would be to air assault a battalion into an LZ further north. That would be the 2nd Battalion, 5th

Cavalry and it was being planned even as the two battalions prepared to leave XRAY.

At 9:00 A.M., the 2/5 began its march off XRAY. As was his custom, Tully had artillery crashing in front of his lead unit, Boyt's Charlie Company, as it moved through the jungle toward COLUMBUS. When they reached a point where the artillery couldn't fire any longer, Tully called the 2/7 commander, Lieutenant Colonel Robert McDade, and offered to have his fire support coordinator hand off the firing data to McDade's artillery guy so that the 2nd of the 7th could have the same kind of march support. McDade declined the offer. That decision, when combined with several others of questionable validity, doomed the battalion.

The 2/7 Cav started the march with one of its companies, Bravo, and one of the platoons from Alpha, the 3rd, already at Camp Holloway getting some well-deserved rest after the fight at XRAY. To make up for the loss of the company, Brown had assigned Alpha 1/5, but A 2/7 still was a platoon short. For the march, McDade assigned the battalion reconnaissance platoon to Alpha to give that company three full rifle platoons. That's about the only thing about the ALBANY affair that is clear-cut and well-documented. Things get hazy after that. For example, the order of march: one eye witness said it was A, C, Hq, D 2/7, and A 1/5. The company commander of Charlie Company said it was A, Hq, D, C 2/7, and A 1/5. The battalion after-action report lists it as A, C, D, Hq element, and A 1/5, as does the article by Kinnard in the September 1967 issue of *Army* magazine. Based on how things played out, Charlie Company was probably farther back in the column than was officially recognized. The real question, though, was not the order of march, but that it was a battalion column formation to begin with. Remember that two days previously, the 2nd of the 5th moved to XRAY with two companies abreast. Most experienced battalion commanders would not have moved anywhere in the Ia Drang in just a simple column formation.

But that was the problem. McDade was very inexperienced. He had taken over the battalion less than three weeks before it was deployed to the western plateau. His major work experience in the Army had been in personnel; he had been the division G-1 for more than two years before coming to the battalion and at that, by all accounts, had done an outstanding job. Although he had been a platoon leader in the Pacific in World War II and a company commander in Korea, he had not been with troops for ten years. Why McDade was put into the slot remains a mystery. Kinnard says he was the best man available for the job at the time; more than likely it was the measure of the loyalty Kinnard evidenced for his hard-working subordinates. What makes his contention suspect were the hard-nosed and experienced lieutenant colonels like Shy Meyer, John Hemphill, Ray Kampe, Rutland Beard, and Robert Litle who were waiting in the wings. All, eventually, would successfully command battalions in the Cav. A measure of Kinnard's concern about McDade's capabilities was the fact that he placed his former aide, Major Frank Henry, in the battalion as executive officer. And unlike most infantry battalion executive officers, who rode herd on the rear areas, Henry followed McDade like a shadow.

The battalion itself was a 2nd Infantry Division battalion, the 2nd of the 9th, that came to the 1st Cav when it was formed in July 1965. Like another Indianhead Division battalion, the 1st of the 23rd, which became the 2/12 Cav, the 2/7 had had little true airmobile training before getting on the ship to Vietnam. But it was a solid infantry battalion, supposedly well-schooled in basic infantry tactics. Its company commanders, particularly Diduryk and Sugdinis, were considered to be among the better captains in the division, and had brought their companies over from Fort Benning. The battalion's Charlie Company was commanded by a brand new captain, John Fesmire, who had taken over only a month earlier. Delta Company was commanded by Captain Henry Thorp, who also had been deployed with his company. The companies had strong leadership at the noncommissioned officer level, with many of the senior noncoms having combat experience in Korea. The private soldiers were a mixture of volunteers and draftees; in 1965, draftees were, on average, two years older than those who fought later in the war.

McDade, a tallish, sandy-haired, freckle-faced man, was certainly not without merit. He had replaced a lieutenant colonel who was something less than beloved by his troopers and, in the very short time that McDade had been in the saddle, had taken several steps to begin improving the battalion's morale.

After splitting away from Tully's battalion, McDade headed the column to the northwest. The lead company, Alpha, commanded by Sugdinis, was exhausted after manning the perimeter at XRAY the night before. Even though no direct thrusts had come at the Alpha sector of XRAY, the men had been one hundred percent alert since arriving early on November 15. Sugdinis had each man take two APC tablets, a combination of aspirin and a mild stimulant, before moving out, in the hopes that it would increase alertness on the move. The company moved out in a wedge formation with the recon platoon at the point, 1st Platoon on the right, and 2nd Platoon on the left. The command group marched in two fire teams abreast in the midst of the formation and the mortar platoon in trail behind the command group. Sugdinis placed the battalion reconnaissance platoon on point for the move because it was fresh and well-led. Second Lieutenant James Lawrence was a crackerjack leader and Sugdinis had confidence in him. He had only one other platoon led by an officer—the 2nd, under Second Lieutenant Gordon A. Grove. The 1st Platoon was normally led by Second Lieutenant Michael N. Mantegna, but he had remained at base camp when the battalion deployed, and the platoon now was led by Platoon Sergeant James L. Fisher. The Mortar Platoon was led by Sergeant First Class Braden.

One of the best witnesses to the action at the head of the

column was First Lieutenant S. Lawrence Gwin, the company executive officer. A graduate of ranger school, he had been stationed in the Delta (IV Corps) for six weeks before being transferred to the 1st Cav in September. He wrote a detailed chronology of the battle after he came back to the States to work in the ROTC Department of Northeastern University. Gwin said that the company formation looked very good and tight nearly all the way toward the clearing they were told was going to be LZ ALBANY. Sugdinis, his radio telephone operators, and Second Lieutenant Hank Dunn, the artillery forward observer, were in the right of formation's interior, while the left was controlled by Gwin, two radio telephone operators, and First Sergeant Miller.

It was a formation right out of the manual for moving through hostile territory. But Alpha was the only company in the battalion with a march posture that presented any degree of readiness for combat. The trailing companies of the 7th were almost in an administrative column, and there was no indication that any of the trailing companies were putting out flank security during the breaks, much less marching through the jungle with such security. Part of the problem may have been how the commanders perceived the mission of the battalion. Although the brigade order was clear that the battalion was to sweep through to ALBANY, a mission that implied combat actions en route, the march order given by McDade was ambiguous. The order that was relayed by company commanders, or at least by Captain Sugdinis, as remembered by Gwin, was: "Enemy situation is presently unclear, but there are definitely PAVN units in the area. Terrain is high grass, ant hills and heavy undergrowth. 2/7 is moving from XRAY to LZ ALBANY to prepare a landing zone for *probable pickup and evacuation back to Pleiku*" (emphasis is the author's). With that guidance, and given the general inexperience of the units following Alpha, it's no wonder that it was treated as just a walk in the sun.

Another witness to the action was Private First Class Jack

Smith, son of ABC news commentator Howard K. Smith. Earlier, when division headquarters learned that young Smith was in a line outfit, it sought to have him transferred to the public information office, but he refused to leave his friends in Charlie Company. Smith's vision of the larger picture was, of course, diminished by his position in the company—riflemen generally have what old soldiers call "three mil vision": an extremely narrow point of view. Nevertheless, some of Smith's observations are instructive. He recalls that as the march wore on through the morning and into the heat of the day, the men in his company were visibly drooping.

At about 12:40 P.M., approximately 200 meters short of the ALBANY clearing, the Recon Platoon, on the point of the company wedge formation, called and said they had captured two NVA soldiers. No shots had been fired; they had virtually tripped over the men. When the word was relayed back to the battalion command group, McDade ordered the column to halt. His command group moved forward, along with an interpreter. The prisoners were dressed in khaki uniforms and had SKS carbines. But they were sick and feverish. They told the interpreter they were part of a group of about half a dozen men who, sick with malaria, had deserted. The regimental designations given by the men made absolutely no sense at all; one said he was from the 35th Regiment and the other from the 180th Regiment. The 2/7 after-action report laconically discussed the two prisoners: "In view of later developments, it appears that these two men were an outpost of an enemy force occupying an assembly area."

The capture and interrogation of the prisoners took about twenty minutes. McDade had his S-2 notify brigade of the capture and had the two NVA soldiers moved back into the column for security. He then ordered Alpha to proceed to the clearing and stayed with A Company during the move. Behind the lead company, the rest of the battalion had become disorganized. March discipline is difficult enough to maintain in open terrain when there are frequent stops. In the grasslands and forests of the plateau, tactical unity had virtually disappeared. Private First Class Smith said the platoons of Charlie Company sprawled in the grass, dropping where they halted. Canteens, which had been refilled at a tributary of the Ia Drang about 500 meters back, already were being drained. Particularly exhausted were those carrying mortars in the rifle companies as well as the combat support company. The weight of the mortar tubes, plus the ammunition on top of each individual's own pack, was staggering. It had been a long walk. Airmobility was supposed to have cured all of this; it was supposed to deliver the soldier to the battle fresh and ready to fight. But, for whatever reason, 3rd Brigade chose not to use available lift to maneuver the battalion.

At any rate, none of the men of Charlie Company or the lead elements of Delta heard anything that would indicate disaster was about to strike. Even perfunctory flank security would have given warning of a NVA company moving silently and swiftly, parallel to the battalion's route of march. The two men captured by Alpha were in fact part of a flank security patrol of the 8th Battalion, 66th Regiment, which, at the moment of their capture, was enjoying a rice break along the banks of the Ia Drang, about fifty meters beyond the far edge of the ALBANY clearing. The NVA battalion column was almost perpendicular to the oncoming American column; in fact, viewed from the air, it would have looked like a giant T. When his flank scouts brought him word about the oncoming American Force, the NVA battalion commander assumed, logically, that it was an American rifle company moving through the jungle. His plan was the classic hasty ambush used by the North Vietnamese Army since the days of the war with the French. The maneuver would be in the form of an L, with the base at the nose of the American advance, and the long axis parallel to the right of the American column. He ordered his lead rifle company to swiftly move to the Americans' flank, staying about 100 meters out from the line of march. He kept one company in reserve, slightly to the west and north of the clearing. The signal to stop the easterly march and wheel to the right and attack would be mortars hitting somewhere among the Americans. The commander knew he didn't have much time, and he was willing to let the advance elements of the column penetrate very close to his own column in order to give the flanking forces time to get into position. He had slightly more than twenty minutes but not more than thirty. Not enough time to dig in. And besides, the noise of entrenching tools would have been a sure tipoff. So hasty was the departure of the lead company that some still had their forage packs on. At the base of the ambush, the automatic weapons crews deployed along the base of anthills and hardwoods, snatching grass and twigs to camouflage themselves and their weapons. This was the battalion that had had one complete weapons platoon wiped out in the brutal night ambush just as it was arriving in Vietnam fourteen days earlier, and it thirsted for revenge against the Americans. The stage was set.

The battalion column lurched forward again and, as the combined command groups of Alpha and McDade hit the southeastern edge of the clearing, McDade called for his company commanders to come forward. Later, this action would bring criticism on McDade's head, but in an interview with Charlie Black shortly after ALBANY, McDade was quoted as saying that because Alpha was securing the landing zone, he wanted his commanders forward so that he and Major Henry could show them the sectors their companies would occupy. It was a fairly normal action for a normal situation. Meanwhile, Sugdinis set about to secure the clearing. He sent the recon platoon forward through the clearing to set up on the northwestern side. The 1st Platoon was sent to the right of the clearing; the 2nd Platoon was sent to the left. He ordered the Mortar Platoon to set up its tube near a cluster of anthills and a grove of trees near the center of the clearing. Gwin doesn't remember how long it was before they heard firing from the direction of the 1st Platoon. Within seconds, though, there was the "crump" of mortar rounds exploding on the left side of the LZ, at about where the 2nd Platoon had disappeared into the tree line.

The first bit of firing seemed to Gwin to be snipers, but after the mortars, the volume picked up, and suddenly the entire clearing was buzzing with bullets. Captains Thorpe (Delta) and Fesmire (Charlie), heeding the call for a commander's meeting, had just shown up at the battalion command group when the firing began. Fesmire had no way of knowing that the main flanking thrust of the NVA was directed at the heart of his company. Nor was he ever able to get back to lead his company; his leadership was limited to radio conversations with his executive officer, First Lieutenant Donald C. Cornett, and all too soon those ceased, when Cornett was killed. At the sound of the mortar rounds, the NVA company wheeled and assaulted the American column. The men of Charlie Company and the mortar platoon of Delta were just staggering to their feet when the blow fell, from the middle of the column forward. As the assault wave came in close on the ground, other NVA soldiers scrambled like monkeys up the trees bordering the line of march, tied themselves in, and began sniping at anyone who moved in the tall grass. The men of Charlie began firing back, wildly at first, and then with more discipline as some of the noncommissioned officers began to exert leadership. Up ahead, Delta Company's mortar platoon was being struck a mortal blow. Its members were also firing wildly—so much so that Grove's platoon from Alpha, which was fighting for its life on the western edge of the LZ, was taking casualties from M-16s.

At the rear of the column was Alpha company, 1/5 Cavalry, commanded by Captain George Forrest. Unlike the units ahead of him, Forrest hadn't been taking any chances. He had a platoon at the head of his column march with two squads abreast and well-dispersed. The right flank squad began pouring M-16 and M-60 machine gun fire into the left flank of the attacking NVA force. The NVA commander quickly realized that the American column was much larger than a single company, and committed his third company to the battle, sending it down the western side of the column to reinforce the flanking unit. Forrest, himself heeding the call for commanders, was with his RTOs partway up through the Charlie Company column when the firing broke out. Forrest never bothered to ask permission to return to his company; he just turned and bolted back through Charlie Company, bullets nipping at his heels and those of his radio operators. As he passed through the lead elements of Alpha, he yelled at the platoon leader to start pulling back into a perimeter. In short order, Forrest's company was being assaulted by platoon-size elements from the west side of the column. Nevertheless, there was enough tactical integrity in the company to permit it to coil into a hasty perimeter. The lead platoon, because of its wide dispersion, sustained the heaviest casualties, but they bought the time necessary for the survival of the rest of the company.

About this time along the rest of the column, the battle ceased being a fight of cohesive tactical units and turned into a melee in the jungle—a series of individual and small-unit fights. None of the commanders, from platoon on up, had any inkling of what was happening. For more than twenty of Charlie Company, death came within seconds after the NVA assault. For the others, and twenty-one more from that company died that day, the agony stretched on through the afternoon and into the night.

Up on the LZ itself, Sugdinis and Gwin were struggling to get a handle on the action. The clearing was now surrounded on three sides by the enemy, and anyone who moved in the open was being shot at. They ran forward, found cover by a large anthill, and finally had a report from the 1st Platoon, that it was surrounded and taking heavy casualties. Sugdinis told the platoon sergeant to try to maneuver back toward the center of the clearing. The company had one more radio contact with the platoon, someone saying they were all dead or wounded and being overrun. Then the radio was silent. Sugdinis looked at Gwin and said, "I've lost the 1st Platoon." Grove's platoon still was functioning, although it had lost a number of its members. And Grove was still pleading with someone to keep the friendlies from firing into them.

Gwin remembers looking back at the path the company had just traveled to see NVA soldiers moving behind them. He also spotted some American soldiers running from that direction. They came sprinting into the anthill where Gwin was located—the Air Force liaison officer, the battalion command sergeant major, and a young private first class who had been gutshot. Gwin also remembers clearly the reactions of McDade, who was close by. "He thought all the incoming rounds were friendly fire and kept screaming for everyone to cease fire. Quite frankly," Gwin said, "McDade starting losing it right there." His analysis coincides with others: McDade was ineffective as a battle commander during the crucial stages of the fight. Within minutes, they looked up to their left front and saw a group of about twenty NVA soldiers trotting toward their anthill complex. The small group of defenders opened fire and, with deadly accuracy, killed or wounded every attacking soldier. For the moment, enemy movement to their left front ceased.

Shortly after that group of NVA was eliminated, Lawrence started maneuvering his recon platoon back toward the anthills, bringing their wounded with them. Miraculously, even though they had been virtually in the center of the enemy battalion, good fire discipline and solid maneuvering kept them from being overrun. Lawrence had lost three killed during the initial burst of fire, but at the time the platoon was probably the most cohesive tactical unit between the anthills and Forrest's company. He put his men in a defensive perimeter on the northwest side of the anthills, using the big mounds as anchors. A few of Delta's men had straggled in, and Gwin put them on the recon's left flank. Alpha's mortar man finished off the perimeter on the east side. It was small and tight and crude but, for the first time at the forward part of the column there was a cohesive tactical unit capable of a unified defense. Shortly after the perimeter was formed, Lieutenant Grove and a couple of men from the Second Platoon fought their way back to the anthills. Grove wanted immediately to go back with a reinforced group and bring his men out. But there was no one who could be spared, and Grove finally had to be given a direct order to stay put.

At brigade headquarters, the duty officer monitoring the radios in the operations center had only the slightest hint of trouble out in the valley. The transmission had come shortly after the message about the prisoners, and in fact, at brigade, the concern was about who to send out in a chopper to bring them back for detailed interrogation. Brown was visiting FALCON at the moment and was just taking off and heading for Catecka when the radio transmissions from ALBANY began getting both hysterical and incoherent. Casualty figures were transmitted and the numbers were so unbelievable that they were initially dismissed as the products of a hysterical operator.

Notified of the contact, Brown flew over the area. It was impossible to make out any details on the ground. Tademy, his fire-support coordinator, was with him and wanted to bring in artillery fire, but there just was no way to distinguish friend from foe. Meanwhile, the Air Force guy on the ground had gotten together with Major Henry, the executive officer, who was an army aviator, and the two of them got through to order in air strikes. The only place they could really direct the strikes safely was the area on three sides of the clearing. There also was a call out for aerial rocket artillery. Bartholemew's Charlie Company, 2nd Battalion of the 20th Artillery, gunbirds got to the scene first and, under direction from Henry, worked over the area to the north, northeast, northwest, and west of the column. The ARA strikes were followed by napalm runs by a flight of A1E's from Pleiku. Henry had everyone around the anthills throw out colored smoke grenades to mark their positions. Gwin remembers watching in fascination as the silver canisters came loblollying across the front and sides of the clearing. They broke on tree tops and splashed burning napalm through large groups of the NVA. Then he watched in horror as two canisters splashed in directly over the area where the remnants of the 2nd Platoon were thought to be. The air strikes continued, and finally the back of the NVA attack was broken. The men from Hanoi stayed around all afternoon and through the night, committing some unspeakable atrocities on the hapless cavalrymen they caught, but there never again was a concerted thrust against any of the two perimeters.

Brown had reinforcements on the way. At 2:00 P.M., Lieutenant Colonel Ackerson, who commanded the 1st Battalion, 5th Cavalry, was directed to detach a company from his force at COLUMBUS and send it overland toward ALBANY. Ackerson, his S-3, and Captain Walter B. Tully, commander of Company B, a cousin of the 2/5 battalion commander, were in the command chopper, routinely reconnoitering for future landing zones, when the call came in. They immediately flew to the scene of the action. They got there in time to watch an airstrike come in and saw the smoke of battle along a stretch of jungle more than a thousand meters in length. Tully radioed back to COLUMBUS and had the company saddled up and waiting for him when he arrived. The company kicked off the move at 2:42 P.M. It took the better part of three hours to cover the distance, and around 6:00 P.M., his advance elements made contact with Forrest's perimeter. Tully reported that Alpha had taken many casualties and still was missing men who had been out on point. The two companies now expanded the perimeter to create a single-ship LZ and called in slicks to evacuate the most critically wounded.

Brown also alerted Bravo 2/7 at Camp Holloway for immediate movement by air into the clearing called ALBANY. Diduryk had to police up a number of his soldiers from the enlisted men's and noncommissioned officers' clubs; they had, after all, been sent to Holloway for rest and relaxation. Brown got enough choppers to bring the entire company in with one lift. Henry was on the radio to Diduryk telling him that the birds would be landing from the south and east and that his troops should fire to their left and run to the woods and anthills on their right. The flight made three passes. Each time heavy NVA fire drove them off, and gunships from the lift battalion as well as ARA birds would punish the NVA. Finally, the fire diminished enough to get the company in. The lift ships took hits, but no one was wounded and all aircraft were flyable.

Gwin remembers how Rick Rescorla, platoon leader of 1st Platoon, Bravo Company, came swaggering into the tiny perimeter, toting an M-79, an M-16, and a bugle he had captured two days before on XRAY. Gwin said his enthusiasm and high spirits were infectious, and before long, the original defenders were feeling better and more full of fight. By 6:30 P.M. Diduryk had his full company into ALBANY, about ninety men total—and had expanded the original perimeter to encompass the entire clearing. Henry gave him operational control of all ground elements on the LZ, and Diduryk integrated the survivors into his platoons, rather than having separate unit boundaries. It was probably just as well; most of the leaders had reached a point of incoherency. Sugdinis dug his hole for the night next to Diduryk, and Gwin teamed up with Grove. Gwin remembers the poignancy of watching Fesmire digging in for the night with the surviving members of his company—nine in number.

At the eastern position, Tully and Forrest had evacuated their wounded. With Bravo in the lead, the two companies started moving toward where they believed the rest of the Seventh Cavalry was located. Bravo, moving in a company wedge, had covered only about four hundred meters to the northwest toward ALBANY when all three platoons were brought under very heavy small-arms, automatic weapons, and RPG fire. The fire was coming from a tree line to their front. Sergeant Mack Cox and Private First Class Ralph Ernst were killed and three others wounded in the first volley. Tully rushed to the front and realized that he had no alternative but to assault the wood line; to stay in place invited more casualties, and to withdraw also would endanger his command. Bravo, using fire and movement, and in particular using the M-79 grenade launchers to blow the snipers out of trees, assaulted the tree line and drove the NVA back into the jungle. One of the wounded men in the assault was Private First Class Frank Martin. He had burned his hands badly the night before at COLUMBUS while handling a flare and had been evacuated. At Camp Holloway, he talked the doctor into leaving his trigger fingers exposed when he bandaged his hands. Then he skipped out of medical channels and hitched a ride on a Chinook back to COLUMBUS just in time to join his company. He told a reporter who was riding with him that he had just twelve days left to go in the Army, but that it just wasn't right to go off and leave his buddies. He was leading the attack on the tree line when an NVA slug caught him in the hip. This time when he got to the hospital, he stayed put.

Tully was going to start consolidating his position when Forrest radioed that more survivors had straggled into the clearing Alpha was holding and that they would need to be evacuated. Although both companies were technically under the operational control of the 2nd Battalion, 7th Cavalry, Ackerson was, in effect, running the show on the eastern perimeter. He directed the two companies to establish a solid defensive position around the single-ship LZ and be prepared to sweep to the northwest to link up with the 2/7 at daybreak. The perimeter was established at about 7:00 P.M., just after the time that Diduryk was closing on ALBANY. There were still twenty-two wounded men inside Tully's perimeter, but Ackerson did not want to risk night medevac from that tiny landing zone and directed the two company commanders to make the men as comfortable as possible for the night.

The choppers that brought Diduryk's force into ALBANY were able to carry out some of the wounded from the forward perimeter, but none of the dead. As a result, the number of wounded evacuated through Camp Holloway the night of November 17 probably did not exceed forty in number. As yet, no one at division headquarters had any inkling of the severity of the fight.

On ALBANY, all during the night, the defenders could hear North Vietnamese patrols moving about the area. There would be screams of "no, no . . . . please," then a gunshot. And then more. And still more. It was clear that the NVA were systematically searching the battlefield for wounded and were shooting them. The shootings were, in fact, pure executions. One noncommissioned officer, found the next day, told of having a 9-mm pistol shoved into his mouth and the trigger pulled. The bullet missed striking his spinal cord and he survived to tell about it. None of the others who were caught were so lucky. They were found the next day with the backs of their skulls blown away. There has never been a logical explanation for this kind of savagery; a freshly committed unit usually does not have the storehouse of hate that veteran outfits sometimes accumulate. Nevertheless, any illusions the young American soldiers may have had about the honor of warriors and the rules of warfare were shattered that night at ALBANY.

It was sometime just before midnight in the perimeter established by Alpha and Bravo, 1/5, that an unidentified station was heard on the radio. Calling himself "Ghost 4-6," the voice sounded as if its owner was going into shock. He said that he and about fifteen others were wounded and cut off from their unit. Forrest talked to him, trying to calm him down and learn his position. Finally, Forrest and Tully decided to send a patrol. Since he was generally familiar with the terrain to their front, Platoon Sergeant Fred S. Kluge of Alpha volunteered to lead the 1st Platoon back toward ALBANY. Kluge had taken over the platoon when his platoon leader, Second Lieutenant Larry L. Hess, had been killed early in the fight. Specialist Five Daniel Torrez, the senior aidman in Alpha Company, also volunteered for the patrol.

Within minutes, the twenty-one men of the platoon, taking seven litters, threaded their way through the darkness. They made radio contact with "Ghost 4-6" and had him fire his pistol as a directional aid. Sergeant Alfred Montgomery, who was with the point squad, finally located the group. There were actually about forty-five men scattered about the area with one large group near one of the big anthills. Kluge put the most critically wounded on the litters and got the walking wounded on their feet and headed back toward the 1/5 perimeter. Kluge said he couldn't go off and leave the remaining eighteen or so men by themselves—they were all wounded and couldn't walk, but with treatment, would survive the night. So Torrez again volunteered, this time to stay with the survivors, all members of Charlie Company, 2/7 Cav.

Kluge departed with his patrol, promising to return at daybreak. Torrez crawled about the jungle floor, gathering the men tightly around the anthill and began treating their wounds. He began treating the eighteen men, emptying his medical bag and the bags he found on two dead medics who had been killed as they had crawled about treating the wounded. Then Torrez heard the NVA patrols—the sickening screams of the victims before the gunshots. When a patrol got close to his position, he put down his aid kit and picked up an M-60 machine gun. He waited until three NVA soldiers were within spitting distance when he opened fire, cutting down all three of them. He then systematically sprayed the area from which they came. Torrez went back to treating the men, but whenever he would hear a sound that might be a prowling NVA soldier, he would cut loose with the machine gun. At daylight, Forrest and Tully sent a two-platoon patrol back into the area. A chopper came over and was calling "Ghost 4-6" on the radio. One of the survivors was an officer, Torrez recalls, and he operated the radio while Torrez located and then threw a smoke grenade. Once the position was fixed, the chopper guided the patrol to the position. A daylight sweep revealed even more wounded; the total pulled out of that area was thirty-five. Torrez eventually was awarded the Distinguished Service Cross for his heroism that night.

The two 5th Cavalry companies, after tending to the evacuation of the wounded, swept on toward the northwest and ALBANY. Tully said the battle area was a scene of carnage. Everywhere were dead and wounded. American and North Vietnamese soldiers lay within a couple of feet of each other. The advancing cavalry units also found a number of American soldiers who had their hands tied behind their backs and bullet holes in the backs of their heads. While 1/5 was advancing from the southeast, Diduryk's company began screening out from ALBANY. What Bravo's troops found matched the horror of the discoveries being made by the 1st of the 5th—except that there was the nauseating spectacle of American bodies blown to bits by American artillery or scorched by American napalm. The only balm was the thought that maybe the poor souls were already dead when the concentrations hit or the napalm splashed.

Over on COLUMBUS, members of Ed Boyt's Charlie Company, 2/5 Cav, were just heating their morning coffee when a young black soldier staggered into their sector of the perimeter. He asked for coffee and a cigarette, telling them he was from Charlie Company, 7th Cavalry, and had been in a big battle. Then Boyt noticed he had a gaping wound in his chest and the peculiar pallor of those who are gravely wounded. He gently sat the kid down, gave him some coffee, and summoned the battalion surgeon, Dr. Frank Lenoti, who hustled over, bandaged the wound, administered some morphine, and called for a medevac. Boyt recalls that when Lenoti called back to Camp Holloway to get a status report, he learned that the young man had died of shock on the flight.

The screens by Diduryk and the sweep in from the east by Tully and Forrest indicated that the NVA were no longer a threat to ALBANY or anywhere else in the immediate vicinity. The entire force was turned to for a giant and macabre police call over the length of the column, picking up dead and wounded, gathering up equipment, both American and North Vietnamese, and ensuring that the NVA bodies on the battlefield were in fact dead. One of Tully's platoons encountered a wounded North Vietnamese who, when offered assistance, attempted to throw a hand grenade. He was summarily shot. Daylight also brought aircraft into the perimeter to evacuate the wounded and then, finally, to begin hauling out the dead. The task started with just Hueys carrying out the bodies; finally, a Chinook was brought in and was stacked full, and still there were more American dead to take out. Extracting on one of the first aircraft available was a photographer—Rick Merron of the Associated Press—who had ridden in the night before with Diduryk's company.

All this time, from the contact at noon on the 17th, division headquarters was unaware of the severity of the battle. There was a single report from the 3rd Brigade to the division TOC early in the afternoon that listed a contact by the 2/7 in which half a dozen NVA were reported killed, with two casualties. Early on the 18th, brigade headquarters submitted a report that the battalion had sustained one killed and forty-eight wounded. Later a report was submitted listing 303 NVA killed. Knowles told a reporter later that he was elated when he got that report. Sometime in the early morning, Merron staggered into the press tent at division headquarters, wanting to use the phone to call Saigon. He was white as a sheet and nearly hysterical. He said, "There's been a massacre out there. I've never seen so many dead in all my life." And he wasn't talking about Vietnamese dead.

There was no direct connection to Saigon out of the press tent, but the II Corps information officer, Air Force Captain Larry Brown, had a phone, and soon Merron was dictating a wild, nearly incoherent story about a bloody ambush in the Ia Drang. The press picked up on the ambush story and the stigma stuck, no matter what anyone said or did thereafter. When Merron came back to the Cav's press tent to arrange transportation to Saigon for the film he had shot on the LZ overnight, Knowles was waiting for him and conducted a hasty debrief. Knowles also had a warrant officer in the division casualty branch at Camp Holloway, a sort of private tipster who he had primed to call him when casualties started coming in. Almost concurrent with the Merron report, the warrant called from Holloway with news that a dozen dead had arrived and more were coming in.

Knowles literally sprinted down the slopes of the II Corps compound to his chopper and flew off to the 3rd brigade. The fact that the brigade had not reported the severity of the contact was more than just vexing to Knowles. As he told Neil Sheehan of *The New York Times* later that afternoon, "We had considerable rapid reaction forces in the area that could have been used if the brigade commander and myself had decided it was necessary." He went on to say that he had not, however, been given the chance to make the decision on the necessity of reinforcements. A brigade staff officer said, long after the battle, that Brown had specifically told him not to make any more reports to division headquarters until he, Brown, personally gave his okay. He never did, the officer said.

The real question was whether Brown had done all he could. He always contended that it was impossible to make a decision on reinforcement because of the lack of a coherent report from ALBANY. Yet Frank Henry and his Air Force FAC remained lucid enough to call in air strikes to break the back of the NVA attacks, and Henry also was aware enough to tell Diduryk how to exit the aircraft when he landed. There was no lack of reinforcement available to Brown. When he dispatched Captain Tully's company from COLUMBUS, he had the full 2nd Battalion, 5th Cavalry sitting idle on CO-LUMBUS. It will always be a matter of speculation whether another full battalion in the battle area would have chased away the NVA execution squads and thus saved those American lives. Even Hal Moore's battalion, exhausted as it was, would have eagerly climbed on aircraft and flown into COLUMBUS to take over security if the 2/5 had been committed. Brown's decisions on the level of reinforcement always will be subjected to second-guessing. It is one of the prices those in command inevitably have to pay.

The survivors of ALBANY were still poking around the battlefield looking for dead and wounded when Brown decided to detach the two 1st of the 5th companies and return them to their parent battalion. This was around 2:00 P.M. The two companies trudged back to COLUMBUS and formally reverted to Ackerson's control.

The count on enemy casualties varied, depending on which after-action report was being read. McDade's after-action report listed 303, but that figure did not include the casualties inflicted on the NVA by Forrest and Tully's companies. The division's after-action report, summarizing all casualties inflicted by every unit, put down 403 by body count and estimated 100 more that couldn't be counted. A fair indication of casualties is the number of weapons captured after a fight; in this battle, a lot of weapons were taken. The volume of NVA equipment recovered from the battlefield was staggering: 212 assault rifles and carbines; thirty-nine light machine guns; three heavy machine guns; six (82-mm) mortars, and eight rocket launchers. So whatever the actual numbers of enemy dead and wounded, there was little question that the 8th Battalion of the 66th Regiment was shattered by its confrontation with the American forces. And, unlike LZ XRAY, where so much of the damage was done by artillery, rockets, and Tac Air, many of the NVA corpses found by the search parties met their doom by rifle and machine-gun fire. It had been a hip shoot and the NVA lost—at least in the sense that they were gone and the Americans were still on ALBANY. But the cost to the 1st Cavalry was horrendous. Among the units in contact, Charlie Company suffered most cruelly, with forty-one dead. Alpha had thirty-three killed, and Delta lost virtually all of its Antitank Platoon and part of its Mortar Platoon. The division's final report listed 151 killed in action, which included those who were wounded and later died of those wounds, 121 wounded in action, and four missing in action. The MIA figure may be suspect, however. In April 1966 Hal Moore, by then the commander of the 3rd Brigade, went back to ALBANY. He secured the area and conducted a very thorough search which turned up the remains of eight men. He called in graves registration specialists, who identified at least four of the men as Americans. They gathered up the remains and flew them to the mortuary in Saigon. Moore said the 3rd Brigade now had its record intact—no men were left behind on a battlefield. And, more important, some mothers finally knew what had happened to their sons.

13

WINDING
IT DOWN

The press had gotten a whiff of blood and was in force in Pleiku on November 18, baying for scalps. Division held a press conference the night of the 18th at the II Corps headquarters building. Knowles presided and had E. C. Meyer, the 3rd Brigade's deputy commander, give a briefing on the action at LZ ALBANY. Then Knowles opened it to questions. They came, hot and heavy, with the recurring theme that it had been an ambush—that someone had screwed up. Backed against the wall by the verbal abuse, Knowles continued to deny that it was an ambush and that it was, in fact, a meeting engagement. At the rear of the room was NBC cameraman Vo Huynh, who had gotten himself to ALBANY late on the 17th, stayed overnight, and been present on the battlefield during the sweeps and screens. He was squatting against the back wall and every time one of the newsmen would start talking ambush, Huynh would shake his head no.

At the conclusion of the press conference, Huynh was sought out and asked why he was so sure it was not an ambush, and least one in which the NVA had prepared positions and were waiting for the Americans to stumble into its trap. Huynh, an inscrutable Vietnamese whose background was widely rumored to have included a stint as a Vietminh officer in the war against the French, said there were three reasons: first, the automatic weapons were not dug in; second, many NVA soldiers were thrust into battle still wearing their heavy forage packs; and third, there were rice bowls found scattered around the area by the Ia Drang. Huynh opined that the NVA commander had about twenty minutes' warning in which to set up a hasty attack on the oncoming cavalry column. Much later in the war, captured documents indicated that Huynh had been right on the money.

But except for internal division documents, such as the after-action report, it really didn't make any difference. The press carried it as an ambush, and that was that. The death toll in the battle exceeded anything experienced by an American unit since the Korean War. The battalion was shattered, but it regrouped rather quickly and, contrary to published reports later, it was back in combat in six weeks, leading the 3rd Brigade into the opening rounds of a campaign called "Masher—White Wing" on the Bong Son plain. And, it was still commanded by McDade. Shortly after the battalion was pulled back to Camp Holloway, Kinnard told Meyer to go down and talk to the men and see who, if anyone, was at fault at ALBANY. Meyer said he talked to about forty men and never got the sense that blame was being placed on McDade. Gwin says Meyer never talked to him, or he might have gotten another idea. The question, however, really was moot. Kinnard never had any intention of relieving McDade. He told Knowles that it would just compound the problem by bringing the spotlight even more on the battalion. Even so, Knowles wanted him gone. Shortly after the battle, Swede Larsen asked Knowles, "How come you still have that guy around?" Knowles told him, "Hey, boss, you're talking to the wrong guy. You need to talk to General Kinnard. If Harry Kinnard wants McDade here, I'm going to get all I can out of him." Knowles said later, "I would stay with Harry Kinnard to the bitter end. Harry would back you all the way, so you had to give him back 100 percent."

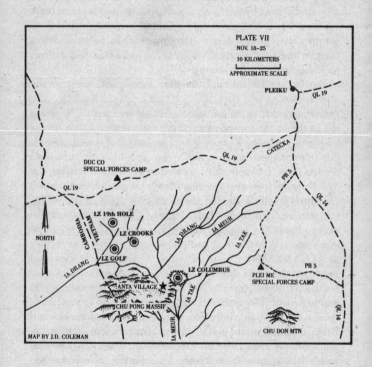

PLATE VII
NOV. 18–25

10 KILOMETERS
APPROXIMATE SCALE

PLEIKU
QL 19

DUC CO
SPECIAL FORCES CAMP.

QL 19

CATECKA

PR 5

QL 14

LZ 19th HOLE

NORTH

LZ CROOKS

IA DRANG

IA MEUR

IA TAE

LZ GOLF

IA DRANG

LZ COLUMBUS

PLEI ME
SPECIAL FORCES CAMP

PR 5

ANTA VILLAGE

IA TAE

CHU PONG MASSIF

IA MEUR

QL 14

CHU DON MTN

MAP BY J.D. COLEMAN

While the grim job of policing the battlefield was going on at ALBANY, Brown set in motion a maneuver designed to put artillery in support of the ARVN airborne battalions that were scheduled to begin movement south the next day from the Duc Co Special Forces Camp. He sent Bob Tully's battalion in an air assault to LZ CROOKS, about eighteen kilometers northwest of Columbus and only seven kilometers northeast of where the 32nd NVA Regiment was hiding. The LZ was secured without opposition and two of the companies began patrolling around it. Coming in immediately after the infantry were Charlie Battery, 2/17 Arty and Bravo Battery, 1/21 Arty. Because of the carnage on ALBANY, Brown had to postpone his plans of moving the artillery on COLUMBUS and had to settle with closing LZ FALCON to the east and bringing the two batteries of the 21st Artillery into COLUMBUS. The result of these moves was that, with the distance between CROOKS and COLUMBUS, neither were within mutual supporting artillery range of each other.

The problem wasn't critical at CROOKS, where small-unit probes the night of the 18th were easily beaten off by the battalion. A sweep of the perimeter on the morning of the 19th revealed two NVA killed and left behind. One cavalryman in Alpha Company was wounded.

The situation at COLUMBUS was a different story. There were two batteries of artillery there as well, and the 1/5 Cav, minus Charlie Company, was manning the perimeter. Company C was at Catecka on palace guard. COLUMBUS was organized as almost a rectangle with slightly rounded corners, with the long axis running north and south. Bravo Company had the south half of the rectangle; Alpha had the northwest quadrant, and Delta the northeast quadrant. Alpha and Bravo had closed on the landing zone about 5:00 P.M., after their march from ALBANY. Tully hurriedly set out three observation posts about one hundred meters beyond the perimeter and quickly organized his defense, giving all three rifle squads equal chunks of the perimeter to defend. Since the company had been occupying COLUMBUS prior to going to the relief of Forrest's company the day before, it was a fairly easy task to reoccupy the holes that had been dug previously. It was fortuitous for Bravo that there were holes available. It took about half an hour to get the company situated. At about 5:45, while the majority of the company was relaxing and eating their evening meal of C-rations, the observation posts on the south and east sides of the LZ began firing at the lead elements of a large enemy force. The warning enabled the company to drop its ration cans and scramble for weapons. The observation posts on the south and west made it back in, but the two-man post in a draw to the east was quickly overrun by the advancing enemy.

This was the H-15 Main Force Vietcong Battalion, a misnomer of sorts because the unit was filled primarily with NVA regulars who had come down the infiltration trail as squad and platoon packets. The battalion originally was to be a part of a two-battalion attack on COLUMBUS, but something called ALBANY happened to the 8th of the 66th en route to its attack position. So the H-15 would have to go it alone. The decision to attack at that particular time had to have been made because advance scouts had noticed the empty holes around the landing zone and presumed it would be easy pickings.

Ten minutes after the outposts had opened up, the entire south, southeast, and east sectors of the landing zone perimeter were brought under heavy small-arms and automatic weapons fire. The VC had located a heavy machine on a small knob about 150 meters due east of the LZ, just in front of the tie-in point between companies B and D. It was firing right down the throats of the defenders and apparently was dug in well enough to resist counter fires. The machine gun raked the front lines, the battalion command post, which was located on the eastern side of the LZ, and the Bravo Company Weapons Platoon. It was not silenced until Air Force napalm cremated its crew during strikes some time later.

The VC had not yet assaulted the perimeter, content with bringing heavy fire on the landing zone. They caught an H-13 still on the ground at the southeastern corner and set it on fire. A Chinook, unloading 105-mm howitzer ammunition adjacent to one of the howitzer batteries at the southwest corner, was hit by machine-gun fire just as it was taking off. The pilots lost power and had to set it down hard and then run for cover. The VC began firing mortars, aiming obviously for the RC292 antennas that marked the battalion headquarters as well as the howitzer batteries' fire direction centers. It was small consolation to soldiers manning the foxholes on the perimeter that the occasional rounds that burst close to their holes weren't really meant for them.

The mortar barrage was immediately followed by a three-pronged assault, probably by a reinforced company. The attacks came from the south, southeast, and east, with the main attack from the southeast. The attacks came like waves on the beach, washing up, then receding, only to re-form and come again. The sole fire support during the initial attacks was by the mortars on the LZ. The battalion mortar platoon was in an exposed location and subjected to direct fire from the heavy machine gun on the knoll to the east as well as to rocket fire from VC gunners who had maneuvered within range of the perimeter. Despite the withering fire, the gunners fired the equivalent of three basic loads at the attackers, even though the ammunition bearers had to sprint across a 100 meter open area to reach the resupply dump.

The Air Force came on station with A1E's and began making napalm and rocket runs at the VC positions outside the LZ. The attackers pulled back slightly and waited for nightfall. Then, under cover of darkness, they stepped up the firing and started another assault. This time the VC concentrated a full company at the southeastern edge of the perimeter and the attackers closed to within ten meters of the foxhole line before they were repulsed. The troopers of Bravo's 3rd Platoon, which took the brunt of the attack, fired until the barrels of their weapons glowed a dull red in the darkness. Specialist Four Brian Smedecker, a machine gunner with the 3rd Platoon, had his gun jam during the height of the assault. He calmly handed an M-16 to his assistant gunner and instructed him to fire it on full automatic until he fixed the gun. Then he ducked down in his hole and, working by touch, stripped the machine gun, corrected the malfunction, and put it back into action in time to play a role in halting the VC attack.

The situation became critical on Tully's side of the LZ. He had not held a reserve back, and, because so many men in the 3rd Platoon were wounded, he needed to reinforce that sector. His 1st Platoon, on the southwestern side of the landing zone, was not heavily engaged so Tully thinned their lines and brought over the equivalent of a squad. Battalion had less than a platoon held back as reserve for the entire fire base and Ackerson was reluctant to commit it too soon. The experience at XRAY had made commanders very wary of the capabilities of the NVA, and Ackerson did not want to strip his reserve prematurely.

Despite the yeoman's job by the mortars on the LZ, the brunt of fire support was from Tac Air and ARA birds. The night delivery of ordnance was complicated by an inability to accurately mark the front line trace. The defenders had placed a lighted T in the center of the landing zone, but it was almost useless as a guide for close-in support. Tully finally had to have his people throw trip flares just before the birds made their firing runs. The flares lasted just long enough for the pilots to get a bead on the target and were enough to get the job done. In later campaigns, the troops on the ground solved this problem by filling partially buried mortar or artillery canisters with a dirt and gasoline mixture and igniting them with a trip flare tied to the canisters.

By midnight, the VC broke contact. There was occasional sniper fire during the night, but no serious probes. On the morning of November 19, the companies swept out from their positions. Tully's platoons found twenty-seven dead VC soldiers within thirty meters of the Third Platoon area and ample evidence that perhaps as many as forty-six more died. The cost to Bravo Company was three killed and thirteen wounded and evacuated. It was the last major ground clash between the 1st Cavalry Division and the Field Front forces.

Later on the 19th, in a major move to the west, the 3rd Brigade pulled the 2/7 Cav out of ALBANY and airlifted the battalion to LZ CROOKS where it shared responsibility for a portion of the landing zone security with the 2/5 Cav. The latter unit also was running company-sized sweeps out of CROOKS, making very little contact.

The last vestiges of the battles in the Chu Pong–Ia Drang complex disappeared by 5:00 P.M. when Bravo Company 1/5 closed out COLUMBUS and lifted to a new LZ named GOLF where two batteries of the 21st Artillery were put in position to fire in support of the ARVN airborne battalions. This fitted in with the scheme of maneuver of the 2nd Brigade, which would be taking over the battle as of noon on the 20th. The two ARVN battalions, supported by the 52nd Aviation Battalion out of Camp Holloway, were slowly making their way along the Cambodian border toward the Ia Drang. Part of the ARVN agreement for a share of the action was to place the ARVN Marine brigade on roadrunner duties to keep Highway 19 open from An Khe to Pleiku. This relieved the need for resupply by air, since convoys could roll all the way from Qhi Nhon to Pleiku. John Stockton's 9th Cavalry, minus A Troop, was detached from division control and attached to the 2nd Brigade. It promptly was launched onto a landing zone called PAR, situated about halfway between Duc Co and LZ GOLF.

By noon of the 20th, Colonel William R. "Ray" Lynch had moved his forward command post to Duc Co to co-locate it with the headquarters of the ARVN Airborne Brigade. The 2nd Brigade still maintained its rear base at Catecka, which by now had become known as "Oasis." The 3rd Brigade headquarters began moving to An Khe along with the 1st Battalion, 7th Cavalry, and other attached and organic elements. For the 3rd Forward Support Element of Support Command, it was the first relief since the campaign had started on October 23.

Ray Lynch was as different from the other brigade commanders as night is from day. He was older; had come up through the National Guard system, which he joined in 1933; and integrated into the Regular Army when his guard unit, the 36th Infantry Division of Texas, was called to active duty. Lynch saw extensive combat in Italy, serving as battalion staff officer and company commander. He was a contemporary of and knew quite well the company commander, who was immortalized by Ernie Pyle—Captain Henry Waskow of Belton, Texas. It was during the Italian campaign that Lynch learned to love artillery, and his operations with the Cav always were marked by an extensive use of artillery in support of the infantry. Lynch had also commanded a battalion in Korea.

Late in the afternoon of the 20th, the 3rd and 6th battalions of the Airborne Brigade cornered a battalion of the NVA 32nd Regiment that had been too slow in heeding Field Front's order to retreat out of Vietnam to Cambodia. The four batteries on GOLF and CROOKS, using American advisors with the ARVN as forward observers, literally blew the NVA battalion apart. The ARVN had never seen artillery delivered in such massive doses and at such close ranges. The ARVN habitually deployed artillery in two-tube increments and rarely fired close support in tighter than two hundred meters. At GOLF, the fire direction center monitored a message directly from one of the paratrooper battalions. It said: "Artillery too close! But very nice! Keep shooting!" An advisor told a reporter long after the battle that the tough ARVN paratroopers could talk of little else for months afterward except that incredible artillery support. The incident led the ARVN Airborne Brigade to train forward observer officers to work with each rifle company. As for the battle itself, when the smoke cleared, the ARVN swept forward and the advisors told Lynch that they had found 127 bodies on the battlefield, most of them victims of cavalry artillery. The Cav had finally tangled, albeit with indirect fire, with the last regiment of the NVA division.

The 2nd Brigade was coming loaded for bear. The 2/12 Cav was trucked over from An Khe to Catecka, to be greeted that night by some 60-mm mortar rounds fired by local force VC. No one was hurt, but it was a reminder to Ingram's battalion that they were back in the Pleiku Campaign. Also coming back for a second go at the NVA was the 1/8 Cav. The 2nd Brigade's organic artillery battalion, the 1st Battalion, 77th Artillery, was brought in to replace the 1/21 Arty. Also coming in were the other two batteries of the 2/17 Arty, giving Lynch two full artillery battalions for his phase of the campaign. The 2/7 Cav was detached from brigade control at CROOKS and airlifted to Holloway, and, from there, moved by truck convoy to An Khe. When the Garry Owen troopers arrived back at An Khe, they found that Kinnard had arranged for the division band to be playing for them when they closed in to their battalion base. Also standing in the rain, saluting them as the convoy rolled into An Khe, was General Westmoreland.

From the 20th to the 24th of November, Lynch sent his four battalions on a series of company and platoon sweeps, searches, and patrols. There was occasional contact, generally with squad-sized units or smaller. Field Front had told its forces to get out of Vietnam and avoid contact and, by the 24th, it was becoming increasingly apparent that there were no more enemy soldiers in that part of South Vietnam.

It was during the 2nd Brigade's phase of the campaign that the saga of Private First Class Toby Braveboy was unveiled. A scout H-13 from the 9th Cav was flying low over the Ia Drang Valley near the location of ALBANY when he spotted a man in a clearing waving a T-shirt. The pilot, Chief Warrant Officer Marion Moore, made a low, slow pass and recognized the T-shirt waver as an American. He called his gunship partner, piloted by Captain Jerry Leadabrand, who flew low over the area and tossed out a box of C-rations. The meat ration within, turkey loaf, was appropriate since the next day was Thanksgiving. The scout team made numerous passes around the area to ascertain that there were no NVA patrols about, then Leadabrand brought his B-model Huey in and picked up the soldier. He had an ugly wound in his left hand and also wounds in his arm and leg.

The soldier was flown immediately to Camp Holloway, where he underwent emergency surgery on his hand. He was debriefed by intelligence officers and then flown to Qui Nhon for further treatment. The young man was a private first class rifleman from the 1st Platoon, Alpha Company, 2/7 Cav. He had the unlikely name of Toby Braveboy, and the even more unlikely hometown, given his saga of bravery, of Coward, South Carolina. He said that on November 17 he was walking point with his platoon when the NVA suddenly opened fire. He was wounded almost immediately, but was able to crawl to a small patch of brush. He stayed there until darkness and, starting to crawl about, found three of his buddies lying about, also wounded. "They all needed help," says Braveboy, "but with the Vietnamese all around us, I knew they would hear me if I yelled for help, so I started crawling." He was working his way toward the sound of some firing, and had come across another collection of wounded. That was when an NVA patrol found them. He said he had feigned death as they approached and executed a wounded American who was lying next to him, and had made the mistake of groaning.

Braveboy played dead for several hours, until the quietness indicated that the NVA patrols were gone; then he began pulling himself along the ground. He thought he was going toward his company, but actually he was headed almost due south of the contact. Braveboy, who had inherited his name from a Creek Indian ancestor, was a sandy-haired youngster with fair skin and few Indian features. He had no equipment except a pistol belt with a canteen and a bottle of water purification tablets. And, of course, he had no food. He kept moving all night and stopped at dawn in a small stream bed. He realized that he could survive for a while on water alone, so he stayed put. He wrapped his T-shirt around the gaping wound in his left hand (surgeons later were forced to remove the index finger) and watched enemy soldiers pass so close that "I could have picked up a rock and hit them with it."

He stayed huddled in the brush near the creek bank, suffering from cold at night, heat in the day, and an increasingly gnawing, empty belly. The mosquitoes and bugs drove him crazy, since he was bare from the waist up. Two days before his rescue, he had an encounter with a North Vietnamese who showed an uncharacteristic streak of mercy. "I heard footsteps, then four North Vietnamese soldiers walked by me," he recalls. "Three of them didn't see me, but the last one looked me right in the eye. He stopped and pointed his rifle at me. I raised my wounded hand and shook my head no. I'll never know why, but he lowered his rifle and walked away. He was so young, just a boy, not more than sixteen or seventeen."

Each day, helicopters from the Cavalry flew overhead looking for NVA units moving toward Cambodia, but Braveboy was fearful of standing up and exposing his position. Ironically, the hope of rescue from the air was counterbalanced by the threat of death from the air. Bombing missions swept over the area where the young American was stubbornly clinging to life. "I don't know how I survived the bombing," Braveboy said, "the bombs were landing all around me. All I could do was lay flat on the ground and pray they did not hit me." He was growing steadily weaker from hunger and loss of blood and had just about given up hope. That's when he decided to take a chance when he spotted the Cav scout bird. He unwrapped his hand and stood up, waving the bloody T-shirt as furiously as he could. "The shirt was dirty and bloody, but it was all I had to signal with. When he flew away, my heart sank, then he came back in very low. That's when I knew he had spotted me."

The word of Braveboy's rescue was flashed along command and public information channels. Almost immediately, the MACV information officer, Colonel Ben Legare, put out the word that there would be no interviews. This stung the cavalry-based correspondents, who had been in and out of jungle bases with the troops for a good part of the campaign. The Cav appealed the decision, but to no avail, and Braveboy was evacuated to Qui Nhon with no official interview. Except one. The ubiquitous Charlie Black, who was more like a member of the division than a newsman, just "happened" to wander into the medic tent at Holloway while Braveboy was waiting for his emergency surgery and "helped" the G-2 folks conduct the debriefing. He had an exclusive story, but typical of the way Charlie operated, it didn't appear in the Columbus paper until the mails had arrived. He never wired stories, relying instead on the Army Postal System.

By that time, there were a number of stories delivered electronically to stateside media, because Braveboy had no sooner arrived at Qui Nhon than Legare reversed himself and permitted interviews. This time, however, the people who benefited were the reporters who most of the field newsmen called ghouls. They interviewed wounded soldiers in the evacuation hospitals but wrote their stories with datelines that made it appear that the reporters had actually been in the battle. So notorious were a pair of these reporters that the latrines by the 1st Cavalry's press tents were named in their honor.

On the battlefield, 2nd Brigade troops were all over the landscape and finding nothing. The scout ships of the 9th Cav, who usually could be counted on to get fired at once in a while, were reporting nothing but silence. And from the ARVN sector, a belt of about eight kilometers from the Cambodian border in, there were similar reports. It was now apparent that the North Vietnamese division had abandoned all thoughts of either offensive or defensive combat with allied forces and had concentrated efforts in salvaging the remnants of the division in the sanctuary of Cambodia. That the enemy had fled to Cambodia was of little doubt. Smoke haze from hundreds of campfires was easily visible to aviators as they flew along the border. The temptation was strong to disregard the border and roll in hot with rockets and machine guns. But nobody did, and Field Front had an opportunity to count noses and heal wounds without the constant harassment of the Air Cavalry.

On the day after Thanksgiving, Lynch and Knowles met reporters at the brigade's rear base at Catecka and told them that there were no more North Vietnamese in the western plateau of Pleiku Province; that they had fled to the Cambodian sanctuary. The Pleiku Campaign was over. By noon on Saturday, November 27, all 1st Cavalry units had been extracted from the field and were back at the base camp in An Khe.

The Cavalry had completed its mission. How it had done so and how well can be told in small part by statistics. The devastation visited upon the North Vietnamese had been incredible. The division had killed 1,519 NVA by body count and estimated that another 2,042 were killed but couldn't be counted. It was estimated that an additional 1,178 were wounded, many of them seriously. And 157 captives had been taken. One of the last, a soldier captured by the 2nd Brigade, told interrogators that when his battalion, the 7th of the 66th, attempted to regroup along the base of Chu Pong after XRAY, less than 100 NVA soldiers could be found, and many of those were wounded. The division captured 897 individual weapons, and 126 crew-served weapons, and, of course, the entire contents of a regimental hospital.

But the cost to the 1st Air Cavalry Division was heavy. A total of 304 troopers lost their lives and 524 were wounded during those thirty-five days of the campaign. (In fact, almost the entire Panel III—East of the Vietnam War Memorial in Washington, D.C., represents the casualties of the Pleiku Campaign.) However, after Hal Moore's final police of the ALBANY battlefield, there were no more missing men carried on the rolls.

But there were other statistics that gave shape and form to

the meaning of the campaign. During those thirty-five days, the Cav's assigned and attached aviation units made "retail" delivery by air of 5,048 tons of cargo from the "wholesale" delivery terminus at New Pleiku. In addition, in the early days of the operation, before the Air Force wholesale operations got into gear, the Cav had made wholesale deliveries from Qui Nhon and Nha Trang of 8,216 tons of cargo. The division's three brigades made a total of sixty-seven artillery battery moves, all by air, and hundreds of infantry company air assaults. In a lesser-known part of the campaign, mostly as a result of the pacification missions south of Highway 19 by Bob Shoemaker's battalion, more than twenty-seven hundred refugees were flown from villages of high vulnerability to the Vietcong to areas of greater safety. And in all of this flying, the division had sustained hits on fifty-nine aircraft, three while caught on the ground during a sudden enemy attack. Of the fifty-six hit in flight, only four were shot down (one was a 9th Cavalry gunbird that was lost during the battle at XRAY with all four men aboard) and three of those aircraft were ultimately recovered.

One of the biggest logistical questions concerned the Cavalry's unproven ability to maintain aircraft over a prolonged period of combat. But after a stuttering start, the aircraft maintenance people, working both at the An Khe base as well as forward bases such as Camp Holloway and Stadium at Catecka, were able to keep the birds flying under very trying circumstances. At the end of the campaign, in fact, the aviation maintenance crews were actually putting back into the air more mission-ready aircraft than were being deadlined for combat, operational, or maintenance reasons. The major problem for the division was spare parts. The Army's system of resupply was not yet fully operational, so the Cav lived on what it had scrounged and brought with it in Conex containers and on a unique system of supply called "push packages." These were crates of spare parts that were assembled in stateside locations and sent by air in the weeks following the division's deployment. Between the stockpiling in country and in the States, the Cav was able to survive with sufficient spare parts until the regular resupply system was picking up the slack.

It was not only aviation mechanics that excelled during the campaign. The forward repair shops, co-located with the Forward Support Elements, handled a total of 410 job orders during the campaign, covering automotive, armament, engineer, signal, and quartermaster equipment. Of these 410 orders, 366 were completed at the forward sites and only 44 were evacuated to the rear. This included on-site repair of artillery pieces that were firing in support of XRAY. And the artillery fired plenty.

For a war billed as one of "low intensity," the firepower statistics are impressive: a total of 33,108 rounds of 105-mm howitzer ammunition was fired, fully one-fourth in support of LZ XRAY. In addition, there were 7,356 rounds of 2.75-inch aerial rockets. The amount of small-arms ammunition expended was awesome, consuming much of the tonnage flown to the forward bases by helicopters.

Once the campaign was officially terminated, dozens of congratulatory messages began arriving at General Kinnard's headquarters. The Chief of Staff of the Army telegraphed:

1. ON BEHALF OF ALL MEMBERS OF THE UNITED STATES ARMY, I SALUTE THE INTREPID OFFICERS AND MEN OF THE 1ST CAV DIV (AM) FOR THEIR SUPERB ACTION IN THE BATTLE OF THE IA DRANG VALLEY.
2. YOUR SKY SOLDIERS AND THEIR BRAVE VIETNAMESE ALLIES CARRY THE HOPES OF FREE MEN EVERYWHERE AS THEY REPEL THE HEAVY ENEMY ATTACKS.
3. THE ARMY AND THE NATION TAKE PRIDE IN YOUR DISPLAY OF COURAGE, DETERMINATION, AND FIGHTING SKILL. THE BRAVE AND RESOLUTE PER-

FORMANCE OF THE 1ST CAV DIV (AM) IN THIS BAT-
TLE IS IN KEEPING WITH THE FINEST TRADITIONS OF
THE AMERICAN SOLDIER.

Others who sent messages were Admiral U.S. Grant Sharp,
commander in chief of the Pacific, and General Wallace M.
Greene, commandant of the U.S. Marine Corps. And of
course General Westmoreland was ecstatic about the success
of the Cav in the highlands. But it was the man who cham-
pioned airmobility and dragged the Army kicking and
screaming into a new mode of warfare, Secretary of Defense
Robert McNamara, who had had the final word.

He visited the 1st Cavalry headquarters at An Khe, was
treated to a dog and pony show on the campaign, and viewed
the vast display of booty the sky troopers had captured. Then
he pronounced the airmobile division a success. He also said
that the Army would have other airmobile divisions, a "shoot
from the hip" announcement that probably shocked the Army
staff. But within three years, the 101st Airborne Division had
been converted to an airmobile division, a configuration it
still holds today. He called the results of the campaign an
"unparalleled achievement," and he declared to a small army
of media: "Unique in its valor and courage, the Air Cavalry
Division has established a record which will stand for a long
time for other divisions to match."

General Kinnard noted that remark when he wrote in his
recommendation for a Presidential Unit Citation for the division, "the only higher accolade possible is the award of the
Presidential Unit Citation." In the Rose Garden of the White
House on September 15, 1967, a grateful government concurred. The First Cavalry Division became the first (and only)
division in Vietnam to be awarded the Presidential Unit Citation and only the fifth division in the history of the U.S Army.
On this anniversary of the birthday of the 1st Cavalry Division, and the anniversary of the Cav's landing in Vietnam two
years previously, President Lyndon Johnson summoned Gen-

eral Kinnard, now a Lieutenant General, and the former division command sergeant major, Chester Westervelt, to hang the citation streamer on the division's battle flag.

In his remarks, President Johnson said, "America's history books are filled with the names of places that are far removed from America's shores, where her strength and her will were tested, and where it triumphed. We know most of those places very well: the Argonne—Anzio—Okinawa—the Pusan Perimeter....Now they will add the Ia Drang Valley in the central highlands of Vietnam."

14

IN THE FINAL ANALYSIS

The campaign was over and the accolades were in. So what did it all mean, statistics aside? Some of the results of the campaign had impact only on the conduct of the war, and while that was vitally important up until American forces left Vietnam in 1972, many things didn't matter much after that. But the longest-range and most fundamental impact of the campaign had to be that the future of the airmobile division was assured; indeed, the future of tactical mobility in the army. No longer were helicopters considered merely flying jeeps and trucks. Firing platforms using the rotating airfoil had been proven in combat and gave fresh impetus to designs for better gunbirds. The AH-1G Cobra, the first rotary-wing aircraft in the world designed specifically for armed combat, was introduced in early 1967 and followed by a whole new generation of attack helicopters. The ubiquitous Huey lasted into the mid-1970s before it was replaced by the Blackhawk, again a bird designed specifically for its mission—that of lifting troops into battle.

As was noted in the preceding chapter, the Army still has an airmobile division on its rolls—the 101st Airborne Division (Airmobile)—much to the disgust of old Cav veterans, now that the Army has seen fit to turn the Air Cav into a very ordinary armored division.

The techniques developed by the 9th Cavalry Squadron—the scout ship/gunship combination in screening enormous areas of an area of operations; the use of aero-rifle platoons to develop situations to the point where conventional infantry units could be profitably committed—meant that the Army had a true cavalry again. This was a cavalry whose differential speed advantage over ground vehicles was analogous to the earlier differential of a horse soldier over a foot soldier. These techniques endured throughout the Vietnam War and are still fundamental to the employment of the air cavalry troops in the Army structure today.

In still another functional area of combat, that of command control, the results were very gratifying. The division had moved major forces over very large areas under diverse and fast-changing command relations without experiencing any serious problems of communications and control. Here, again, the careful preparations during the months of testing and development paid off. Such equipment as the people pod forward command post at Pleiku, which was flown in by a Flying Crane, worked extremely well. The division's communication system, which had been downsized during the air assault testing days, worked extraordinarily well and soon became the standard in Vietnam.

The transport of the M-102 howitzer by helicopter to fire bases miles from any road was a concept only practiced in stateside maneuvers until the Cav began doing it as a matter of course in combat. It goes without saying that in nearly every battle and firefight in which the Cav engaged following the relief of Plei Me was predicated on having at least one battery of artillery in a supporting position. For a couple of years, helicopters, starting back with the H-19s and H-34s, had shuttled troops into landing zones, but their support was habitually limited to road-bound artillery, or to the early model gunships or Tac Air. There could have been no triumph at LZ XRAY had there not also been an LZ FALCON or LZ COLUMBUS, where the artillery poured tons of hot steel onto the attacking NVA.

Then, too, another form of artillery, the aerial rocket artillery, matured and came of age. Remember that in the beginning it was an experiment in substituting these aerial flying platforms for the conventional 155-mm medium artillery battalion. During the campaign ARA supplemented and, in many cases, substituted for tube artillery. As commanders became acquainted with the firepower potential of aerial rocket artillery and with its flexibility, accuracy, and immediate response, it was increasingly called upon. And its role continued to expand in Vietnam.

These things likely would not have occurred, at least not at the pace they did, had the 1st Cavalry stubbed its toe in the Pleiku Campaign. So the most important result was the successful combat test of the airmobile concept and of the "First Team."

The division racked up a number of impressive firsts during the campaign. Of primacy was the fact that it was the first battle between a North Vietnamese regular army division and an American division. That, of course, has to be qualified somewhat. At no time in the campaign did the Communists actually employ a full division, although they planned to do so when the XRAY battle erupted. On the Cavalry side, only one brigade, with no more than four battalions, was committed at once. But the potential for full divisional contact was certainly present.

For the first time in the Vietnam War, there was an immediate, prolonged, and relentless pursuit of the enemy. For the NVA, it was an entirely new adventure. And their serious, nonpropagandistic, written critiques on how to deal with airmobility indicated that this campaign had a profound effect on the tactical thinking of Hanoi.

For the first time, a large Army unit operated continuously over difficult terrain that was devoid of roads, relying primarily on aircraft in every aspect of its operations, including logistic support.

And, for the first time in Vietnam, an American unit

gained contact with the enemy and generally maintained it over a prolonged period. It is true that in many cases commanders, still unsure of themselves and their units and not yet totally conversant with the full potential of airmobility, let NVA elements slip from their grasp by failing to reinforce adequately or on time. But the lessons learned enabled commanders to do a better job of it the next time out. In the next big campaign of the Cav, Masher-White Wing, north of Bong Son, in January and February 1966, the division gained and maintained continuous contact over thirty-five days in all kinds of weather and in every conceivable type of terrain. That was the legacy of the Pleiku Campaign.

The semicontinuous contact also generated a great deal of solid tactical intelligence, based on such tangibles as actual contact with and sightings of the enemy, prisoner interrogations, and captured documents. The resulting intelligence was of great operational value to the division, multiplying its firepower advantage and focusing its maneuver. It also permitted higher headquarters to fill any gaps in strategic intelligence. But there were times when the intelligence picture, while crystal clear at the battalion and brigade level, was seemingly murky at higher headquarters. Later operations taught everyone more about how to react to combat intelligence, but the Pleiku Campaign was the precursor for all follow-on activities.

Harry Kinnard's decision to arm his division with M-16s might have been the difference between victory and defeat during several of the battles of the campaign. When Hal Moore stood in front of the press and, later, General Westmoreland, and said, "Brave men and the M-16 won this victory," he set off a chain reaction of procurement for the Army that lasted until every unit in Vietnam had the weapon. The M-16 has taken a lot of bad raps, but in 1965, in the Cav, in the Ia Drang, the troopers believed implicitly in the superiority of the weapon over anything the Communists had in the field.

The landmark study of S. L. A. Marshall during World War II revealed that only about four or five of the riflemen in a rifle squad actually ever fired their weapons, citing fear, uncertainty, apprehension about the "kick" of the rifle, lack of training, and other factors. A follow-up study in Korea showed only a slight improvement in the use of the M-1 in combat. And the M-14 was nothing but an improved version of the M-1, big, heavy, cumbersome, using weighty ammunition and with only a couple weapons per squad armed to fire full automatic. But in the firefights on the western plateau, particularly at XRAY, there was evidence that nearly every rifleman was firing his weapon. The singular lack of recoil made it a joy to fire, on single shot or full automatic. American soldiers love to fire on full automatic; there is something soul-satisfying about "switching your iron to rock and roll" and sending a torrent of lead out at an enemy. Whether or not you hit him is sometimes irrelevant. Soldiers, regardless of countries of origin or political philosophies, don't have to be hit with bullets to respect them. The snap and crack of rounds going overhead is strong incentive toward keeping one's head down. Which prevents him from firing at you. Which allows a fire team to maneuver, then a squad, then a platoon. And that's how victories on the battlefield are fashioned when the war is between infantrymen.

General Kinnard, writing about the campaign in *Army* magazine, said, "To appreciate the significance of this campaign, one needs only to contemplate the probable impact if we had lost by the same margin that we won. Given the situation that existed in Vietnam in October, 1965, I believe this victorious campaign was of major military importance and probably of major international importance as well."

Those words were published in 1967. The luster of that campaign has not dimmed because of the fact that the United States subsequently chose not to win in Vietnam.

The defeat the NVA suffered at the hands of the 1st Air Cavalry on the western plateau forced a change in their overall strategy. Although General Nguyen Chi Thanh's strategy of the offensive was not wholly discredited, there appeared to be a moderating of Hanoi's desire to close with and kill Americans, regardless of costs. Certainly, the Tay Nguyen Campaign, the plan to conquer the western highlands, took a stunning setback and was not resurrected during its planned time frame of 1965–66. Thanh still had two more field fronts (divisions) to play with for his Long Xuan Campaign in the northern part of South Vietnam, but what happened there was a considerable distance from Pleiku Province, and that, of course, is another story entirely.

Communist after-action reports invariably are written by political officers who are less concerned about tactical accuracy than political and psychological impact. Thus the published reports of the battles in the highlands by the NVA contained the usual communist hyperbole. One account claimed that the NVA had killed a thousand Americans at XRAY and ALBANY, and shot down a hundred helicopters. General Giap, writing a year or so later, as quoted in Patrick McGarvey's *Visions of Victory*, said of the Air Cav:

> It has never been able to achieve surprise or to destroy a single section of the Liberation Armed Forces. Troops of the Air Cavalry Division are even weaker than ordinary U.S. Infantry troops because they lack the mechanized support of artillery units. Units of the Air Cavalry Division have been battered by the Liberation Armed Forces in Plei Me, Binh Dinh and elsewhere.

Giap's contention that the Cav had no artillery probably would come as a distinct shock to the veterans of the 66th and 33rd Regiments who survived the Pleiku Campaign.

Some writers, in examining the campaign, say the U.S. would have been better served if the Cav had not been as successful as it was in the highlands. This would have insured that the American high command did not get overly optimistic and end up making the wrong changes in tactics and strategy. Other writers, citing the same victory for the cavalry, claim it was delusive; that it failed to produce any significant changes in leadership, strategy, or doctrine.

Whatever the point of view, nearly all critics agree that, ALBANY notwithstanding, the 1st Air Cavalry Division had won a stunning victory in Pleiku province. The opening round of the Tay Nguyen Campaign had been stopped cold. The Plei Me Special Forces camp still stood, as did all the other Special Forces Camps in the highlands. Eventually, because there was no way to plug up the Ho Chi Minh Trail, the never-ending packets of replacements refilled the depleted ranks of the 33rd and 66th Regiments and they returned to the highlands to fight again. But there isn't a veteran of the Pleiku Campaign alive today who doesn't believe to the bottom of his heart that if the Cav had been permitted to pursue Field Front into Cambodia, those regiments would have been wiped from the face of the earth.

And that is one of the things that still haunts us today. What would have been the course of history in Southeast Asia if the 1st Air Cavalry Division's first campaign had been, as Harry Kinnard so desperately wanted it to be, on the Ho Chi Minh Trail? Given the results that came out of the Pleiku Campaign, the mind boggles at the very thought!

EPILOGUE

In any work of contemporary history there inevitably arises the question: "Whatever happened to so-and-so?" In the case of the 1st Air Cavalry Division, some pretty good things happened to the career officers and noncommissioned officers. In fact, the ink had hardly dried on the congratulatory messages from the President when the Cav became *the* division to be associated with. Service with the Cav became pretty much a desirable "ticket punch" for officers on the way up. So it is not surprising that those who served during the pioneer stages did very well in their careers.

Not everyone whose name appears in this book was contacted and interviewed within the past couple years. Many stories were part of the records of the events. However, the following is what is known of some of the participants.

Major General Harry Kinnard retired in 1970 as a lieutenant general and as commander of the Army's Combat Development Command.

Brigadier General Richard Knowles retired in 1974 as a lieutenant general and deputy commander of the Eighth Army in Korea.

Brigadier General John Wright also retired as a lieutenant general.

Colonel George Beatty retired as a major general, and Colonel Elvy Roberts retired as a lieutenant general after returning to Vietnam in 1969 to command the Cav.

The noncavalry guys at Plei Me who were traced included Major Charlie Beckwith, who retired as a colonel after gaining some degree of fame as leader of Delta Force in Iran; Dr. Lanny Hunter, who is now a physician in New Mexico; Major Louis Mizell, a retired lieutenant colonel; Air Force Major Howard Pierson, a retired lieutenant colonel, and Dick Shortridge and Hank Lang, both retired lieutenant colonels.

The acting commander of the 1st Brigade, Lieutenant Colonel Harlow Clark, died tragically in a helicopter accident at An Khe in March 1966. One of the battalion commanders in his brigade, Lieutenant Colonel Robert Shoemaker, retired as a four-star general and commander of the Army's Forces Command. Two other battalion commanders who fought under Clark, Earl Ingram and James Mix, retired as full colonels.

In the Cavalry Squadron, Lieutenant Colonel John Stockton retired as a colonel; Major Robert Zion did also, as did Captain John Oliver. Captain Chuck Knowlen retired as a lieutenant colonel. One of the principals in the hospital fight was Captain Gene Fox, who retired as a colonel and now lives in Arlington, Virginia. Two who were at LZ MARY, Captain Theodore Danielsen, retired as a lieutenant colonel in the summer of 1987, and Lieutenant John Hanlon, was medically retired soon after the action with paralysis of his lower limbs. He now lives in Memphis, Tennessee. His platoon sergeant, Kenneth Riveer, retired as a master sergeant and also lives in Memphis. The division's assistant G-3, Lieutenant Colonel John Hemphill, went on to command the 2/8 Cav and ultimately retired as a major general.

Two members of 2/8 Cav who were traceable were Lieutenant Franklin Trapnell, who now is a full colonel stationed at Fort Benning, and Sergeant First Class Steve Coulson, who retired as a master sergeant in Charlotte, North Carolina.

The commander of the 3rd Brigade, Colonel Thomas W.

Brown, finally got his brigadier's star, but several years after all of his contemporaries had been promoted to brigadier and major general. He retired as a brigadier general in San Antonio, Texas.

Lieutenant Colonel Harold G. Moore retired as a lieutenant general in the mid-1970s. His fondest desire is to be able to return to XRAY and walk the ground of the battlefield in conjunction with the NVA commander, Major General Chu Huy Man, who is now a Senior General in the Peoples Army of Vietnam.

Nearly all of the captains who commanded companies or were staff officers at LZ XRAY retired as full colonels. These were John Herren, Ramon Nadal, Robert Edwards, Edward Boyt, and Gregory Dillon. Major Bruce Crandall survived being shot down in his second tour in Vietnam; he retired as a colonel. Captain John Mills retired as a lieutenant colonel. Lieutenant Joe Marm is still on active duty as a colonel. The commander of the 2/5 Cav, Lieutenant Robert Tully, retired as a colonel and now resides in Florida.

Two of the captains who commanded companies in the Ia Drang were killed in action when they returned to Vietnam as majors for their second tours. Myron Diduryk was killed by a sniper while serving as S-3 for a 1st Cavalry battalion north of Saigon in 1970, and Walter "Buse" Tully was killed in 1969, when he was checking the perimeter of his battalion in the Americal Division.

Of the company-grade officers in the 2nd Battalion, 7th Cavalry who survived, two went on to the grade of colonel. Joel Sugdinis retired a few years ago, but John Fesmire is still serving on active duty. S. Lawrence Gwin left the Army after his obligation was up and now lives in Massachusetts. The commander of Company A, 1st Battalion, 5th Cavalry, Captain George Forrest, retired as a lieutenant colonel and now is an assistant football coach at Morgan State University in Baltimore.

Lieutenant Colonel Robert McDade retired as a colonel

and now lives on Long Island. The commander of the 1/5 Cav, Lieutenant Colonel Frederick Ackerson, also picked up one more grade before he hung it up. The one lieutenant colonel in the 1st Cavalry Division who probably went further up the ladder than anyone was E.C. "Shy" Meyer. He went on to command the 2nd Battalion, 5th Cavalry, on his first tour, came back to command the 2nd Brigade in 1970, and later became the division chief of staff. He retired in 1979 as a four-star general and Chief of Staff of the U.S. Army.

Of the correspondents who covered the Cav, probably none was better known to the men of the division than Charlie Black. He came back to the division to cover its activities at least five more times. Charlie died of a heart attack on October 18, 1982, in Phenix City, Alabama. Vo Huynh is now the senior cameraman for the NBC team that covers the White House. Joe Galloway is Washington Bureau Chief for *U.S. News and World Report*, and Bob Poos is a free-lance writer in Washington, D.C. Of the Associated Press reporters who took many of the photos that appear in this book, Peter Arnett now is in Moscow (USSR) for Cable News Network, Horst Faas still shoots pictures for the AP, and Rick Merron died in an accident in New York harbor several years ago.

APPENDIX I

FORMATION OF THE 1ST CAVALRY DIVISION (AIRMOBILE)

This table shows the structure of the 1st Cavalry Division as it was constituted in 1965 and the source organizations. Either the 11th Air Assault Division or the 2nd Infantry Division were the principal contributors of the infantry, artillery, and support units. The new division's aviation units came from separate aviation units from throughout the Army's structure.

DIVISION UNIT	SOURCE UNIT
Headquarters and Headquarters Company, 1st Cavalry Division (Airmobile)	HHC, 11th Air Assault Division (Test)
HHC, 1st Brigade	HHC, 1st Bde., 11th Air Assault
1st Battalion (Airborne) 8th Cavalry	1st Battalion (Airborne) 188th Infantry
2nd Battalion (Airborne) 8th Cavalry	1st Battalion (Airborne) 511th Infantry
1st Battalion (Airborne) 12th Cavalry	1st Battalion (Airborne) 187th Infantry

HHC, 2nd Brigade	HHC, 2nd Brigade, 2nd Infantry Div.
1st Battalion, 5th Cavalry	1st Battalion, 38th Infantry
2nd Battalion, 5th Cavalry	2nd Battalion, 38th Infantry
2nd Battalion, 12th Cavalry	1st Battalion, 23rd Infantry
HHC, 3rd Brigade	HHC, 3rd Brigade, 2nd Infantry Div.
1st Battalion, 7th Cavalry	2nd Battalion, 23rd Infantry
2nd Battalion, 7th Cavalry	2nd Battalion, 9th Infantry
HHB, Division Artillery	HHB, 11th Air Assault Division Artillery
2nd Battalion, (Airborne) 19th Artillery (105 mm)	6th Battalion, 81st Artillery
2nd Battalion, 20th Artillery (Aerial Rocket)	3rd Battalion, 377th Artillery
1st Battalion, 21st Artillery (105 mm)	5th Battalion 38th Artillery 2nd Infantry Division
1st Battalion, 77th Artillery (105 mm)	1st Battalion, 15th Artillery 2nd Infantry Division
HHC and Band, Support Command	HHC and Band, Support Command 11th Air Assault Division
8th Engineer Battalion	127th Engineer Battalion
13th Signal Battalion	511th Signal Battalion
15th Medical Battalion	11th Medical Battalion
15th Supply and Service Battalion	408th Supply and Service Battalion
15th Transportation Battalion (Aircraft)	611th Aircraft Maintenance and Service Battalion
27th Maintenance Battalion	711th Maintenance Battalion
15th Supply and Service Battalion	165th Aerial Equipment Supply Detachment
15th Administrative Company	11th Administrative Company
545th Military Police Company	11th Military Police Company
191st Military Intelligence Detachment	11th Military Intelligence Detachment
371st Army Security Agency Company	Company C, 313th Army Security Battalion
HHC 11th Aviation Group	HHC, 11th Aviation Group, 11th Air Assault Division

HHC 227th Assault Helicopter
Battalion
Company A, 227th Assault
Helicopter Battalion
Company B, 227th Assault
Helicopter Battalion
Company C, 227th Assault
Helicopter Battalion
Company D, 227th Assault
Helicopter Battalion

HHC 228th Assault Support
Helicopter Battalion

Company A, 228th Assault
Support Helicopter Battalion
Company B, 228th Assault
Support Helicopter Battalion
Company C, 228th Assault
Support Helicopter Battalion

HHC 229th Assault Helicopter
Battalion
Company A, 229th Assault
Helicopter Battalion
Company B, 229th Assault
Helicopter Battalion
Company C, 229th Assault
Helicopter Battalion
Company D, 229th Assault
Helicopter Battalion

11th Aviation Company

1st Squadron, 9th Cavalry

HHC 227th Assault Helicopter
Battalion, 11th Air Assault Div.
Company A, 227th Assault
Helicopter Battalion
Aviation Company, 6th Special
Forces Group
Aviation Company, 7th Special
Forces Group
110th Aviation Company (Aerial
Weapons)

HHC 228th Assault Support
Helicopter Battalion, 11th Air
Assault Division
132nd Aviation Company
(Assault Support)
133rd Aviation Company
(Assault Support)
203rd Aviation Company
(Assault Support)

HHC 229th Assault Helicopter
Battalion, 11th Air Assault Div.
Company A, 4th Aviation
Battalion
Company A, 5th Aviation
Battalion
194th Aviation Company

131st Aviation Company
(Aerial Weapons)

11th Aviation Company, 11th
Air Assault Division

3rd Squadron, 17th Cavalry, 11th
Air Assault Division

APPENDIX II

The following is a reproduction of a translation by intelligence officers of a captured NVA 32nd Regiment battle order directing the ambush of the ARVN relief column en route to Plei Me from Pleiku City. Translators' comments are in brackets.

> T-R-A-N-S-L-A-T-I-O-N
> TOP SECRET (NVA Classification)
> COMBAT ORDER FOR AN AMBUSH
> BY THE 32ND REGIMENT
>
> PREPARED AT REGIMENTAL
> HEADQUARTERS/PLEI-LUO-CHIN
> AT 1500 HOURS, 12 OCT 1965
>
> PLEIKU
> PLEI THE [YA815080]

MAP: SCALE 1/100,000   MADE IN 1962

1. After the initial attack on PLEI ME the GVN will likely send a relief column. The relief column will probably be composed of one ARVN Battle Group and one Armored Battle Group from the

24th STZ. There will probably be one or two US battalions in reserve. The relief force could come by air or by road, which ever is most suitable. They could arrive at the battle area in one or two days. Their battle formation could operate up to one kilometer from the road. They could have the infantry and armor elements interposed with each other; as an example an Armor element leading with the infantry 500m to one kilometer behind. After the ARVN are ambushed they will pull back to the O-Gri area to regroup. ARVN forces behind the ambushed element will probably move to the area of PO Post (20-14), O-Gri (22-18) and KLAN (26-22).

2. In order to defeat the ARVN forces and those American forces engaged, all general activities must be coordinated throughout the battle area. To widen the liberation zone and develop guerrilla movement, the Field Front Headquarters orders the 32d Regiment (minus 7th Company, 966th Battalion) with two anti-aircraft companies, to destroy the ARVN infantry and armor units moving on Provincial Road #21 [T.N.-Provincial Route 5] from Phu My [AR750275] to Plei Me [ZA150065].

a. The sector from O-Gri to Chu Von is the main sector (for the ambush).

b. Units are responsible for attacking any enemy units that are airlanded in their zone. The ARVN air landings will probably be at PO and PIA Posts.

c. We will destroy the ARVN forces outside of Phu My [AR750275] and O-Gri by weapons fire, mines and explosives.

d. We will attack the ARVN forces concentrated at the junction of Phu My and O-Gri.

e. We must be prepared to conduct an attack along with the 33d Regiment.

3. The 33d Regiment has the mission of attacking and encircling Plei Me thus causing the enemy to send a relief force which will be destroyed by the 32d Regiment.

4. Based on the missions outlined above, the 32d Regiment has the following missions:

a. Set up an ambush to destroy the ARVN units on Road 21 [P.R. 5].

b. The ambush will be conducted using the terrain from Hill 538 (16-14-4) to Hill 601 (20-18-9) (4 kilometers).

c. The 334th and 635th Battalions will be at position #1. The 966th Battalion will be at position #2.

5. The 635th Battalion, with one machinegun platoon from the regimental machinegun company and with two 57mm recoilless rifles and two 90mm rocket launchers (B-40) from the 966th Battalion will deploy on the west side of Hill 538 and Hill SIU (18-14-9); and has the following missions:

a. Occupy one part of the regimental area and block one part of the road into the regimental area. This section of the regimental road is from Hill 538 to the north side of the "lone tree" hill.

b. The battalion will conduct violent attacks on the enemy, attacking from many points in order to separate the enemy forces.

c. The battalion will occupy Hill 538 and the "lone tree" hill in order to channelize the enemy down the valley and destroy them.

d. The 635th Battalion will organize its fire-power to destroy tanks and infantry and to shoot down any enemy aircraft bringing reinforcements.

e. The #1 combat formation will be in reserve [T.N.-exact translation and thus meaning could not be determined. Could mean one company will be held in reserve].

f. The left portion of the combat line of the 334th Battalion located on the north side of the "lone tree" hill, remains under the command of the 334th Battalion.

6. The 334th Battalion with one platoon of the regimental machinegun company, one platoon of the regimental 75mm recoilless rifle company, the regimental mortar company and one 90mm rocket launcher (B-40) from the 966th Battalion; will deploy on the west side and the southwest side of the hill at coordinates 20-16-7 and has the following missions:

a. Occupy one part of the regimental area.

b. Blocking one section of the road in the regimental area, within the area from the south side of Hill BLOU to the north side of Hill 601.

c. Use violent attacks to cut off the enemy forces in the rear.

d. Cut off the enemy counterattack elements in order to hold the battlefield under friendly control.

e. Attack at many points to separate enemy formations.

f. Seize Hill BLOU, Hill 600, and Hill NGON-HO (18-18-1).

g. Destroy and capture all enemy troops within the battle area.

    h. The battalion will organize its firepower to destroy enemy tanks, and infantry and to shoot down aircraft bringing enemy reinforcements.

    i. The #1 combat formation will be a reserve [T.N.-exact translation could not be determined.]

8. 1st Anti-Aircraft Company deploy on the west side of the IA DRANG River. Mission is to shoot down enemy aircraft and protect the 334th Battalion during its operations.

9. The Regimental Anti-Aircraft Company will deploy on the south side of Hill SIU. Mission is to shoot down enemy aircraft and protect the 635th Battalion and Regimental Headquarters.

10. The regimental 75mm recoilless rifle company (minus one platoon) is the reserve unit for attacking tanks of the enemy armored regiment. The company must first seize SIU village and then destroy enemy tanks on the north side of Hill 538. After the infantry has assaulted enemy elements on the road, the 75mm recoilless rifle company will withdraw and be in reserve for destroying tanks.

11. The Regimental Engineer Company has the following missions:

    a. CAU TRUC Regimental Headquarters [T.N.-Cau Truc is NVA military terminology which could not be translated. It could mean "protect" or "secure"].

    b. XOI 2 TRUC to protect the regiment during its operations [T.N.-This is NVA military terminology that could not be translated].

     c. Establish two controlled mine fields at O-Gri and PO Post.

     d. Establish two deception areas at Hill 516 and on the east side of NGON-HO Hill.

12. Regimental Headquarters will be located on the west side of Hill SIU.

13. Time of completion and preparation of operation.

14. Report time.

15. Report by direct means.

REGIMENTAL COMMANDER
s/ TO DINH KHAN
t/ TO DINH KHAN

FIELD GRADE POLITICAL OFFICER
     s/NGUYEN CHUC
     t/NGUYEN CHUC

     CHIEF OF STAFF
[Paper torn off at this point]

APPENDIX III

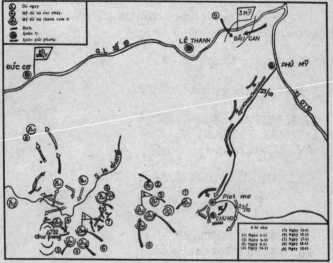

SƠ ĐỒ HOẠT ĐỘNG PLÂY - ME

This map of the Pleiku Campaign battle area was part of an NVA after-action report on the battles in the western highlands. The map was captured when the apparent headquarters of Vietcong forces in South Vietnam was overrun by troops of the 196th Light Infantry Brigade. Ironically, the commander of the 196th was Brigadier General Richard T. Knowles, who had commanded the 1st Air Cavalry maneuver units during the Pleiku Campaign. Although no translation was provided, a careful study of the map reveals the movements of the NVA forces (black arrows) and the activities of the American and ARVN forces.

APPENDIX IV

This is a transcript of the exact narrative recited by President Lyndon B. Johnson on Thursday, September 14, 1967, when he presented the Presidential Unit Citation to the 1st Cavalry Division (Airmobile).

By virtue of the authority vested in me as President of the United States and as Commander-in-Chief of the Armed Forces of the United States I have today awarded

THE PRESIDENTIAL UNIT CITATION (ARMY)
FOR EXTRAORDINARY HEROISM
TO
THE 1ST CAVALRY DIVISION (AIRMOBILE)
AND ATTACHED UNITS

The 1st Cavalry Division (Airmobile) and attached units distinguished themselves by outstanding performance of duty and extraordinary heroism in action against an armed enemy in the Republic of Vietnam during the period 23 October 1965 to 26 November 1965. Following the attack on a Special Forces camp at Plei Me, in Pleiku Province, on 19 October

1965 by regular units of the Army of North Vietnam, the 1st Cavalry Division (Airmobile) was committed to action. The division was initially assigned the mission of protecting the key communications center of Pleiku, in addition to providing fire support both for an Army of the Republic of Vietnam (ARVN) armored column dispatched to the relief of the besieged camp, and for the camp itself. The 1st Cavalry Division (Airmobile), having recently been organized under a completely new concept in tactical mobility, and having arrived in the Republic of Vietnam only a month earlier, responded quickly with an infantry brigade and supporting forces. Using air assault techniques, the division deployed artillery batteries into firing positions deep within enemy-held territory and provided the vital fire support needed by the ARVN forces to accomplish the relief of the Special Forces camp. By 27 October, the tactical and strategic impact of the presence of a North Vietnamese regular army division in Pleiku Province necessitated a change in missions for the 1st Cavalry Division. The division was given an unlimited offensive role to seek out and destroy the enemy force. With bold thrusts, elements of the division pursued the North Vietnamese regiments across dense and trackless jungles of the west-central highlands, seeking the enemy out in his previously secure sanctuaries and giving him no quarter. In unfavorable terrain and under logistical and tactical conditions that would have stopped a unit with less capability, motivation and esprit, the cavalrymen repeatedly and decisively defeated numerically superior enemy forces. The superb training, unflinching devotion to duty, and unsurpassed gallantry and intrepidity of the cavalrymen, individually and collectively, resulted in numerous victories and succeeded in driving the invading North Vietnamese division back from its positions at Plei Me to the foot of the Chu Pong Massif. There, in the valley of the Ia Drang, the enemy was reinforced by a fresh regiment and undertook preparations for more incursions into Pleiku Province. The 1st Cavalry Division deployed by air its men and weapons to launch an attack on this enemy staging area, which was 35 kilometers from the nearest road and 50 kilometers from the nearest logistical base. Fully utilizing air mobility in applying their combat power in a series of offensive blows, the men of the division completely defeated the numerically superior enemy. When the enemy finally withdrew his broken forces from the battlefield, the offensive capability of the North Vietnamese Army in the II Corps tactical zone had been blunted. The outstanding performance and extraordinary heroism of the members of the 1st Cavalry Division (Airmobile) and attached units, under the most hazardous and adverse conditions, reflect great credit upon themselves, the United States Army, and the Armed Forces of the United States.

GLOSSARY

ADC.   Assistant Division Commander.

AK-47.   Standard NVA assault rifle.

Alpha.   The letter A in the Army phonetic alphabet. Thus A Company could also be known as Alpha Company. The phonetic alphabet was used to spell out words in radio conversations.

A1E.   Skyraider fighter-bomber.

AO.   Area of Operations.

ARA.   Aerial rocket artillery.

ARVN.   Army of the Republic of Vietnam; pronounced *Arvin*.

Arty.   Abbreviation for artillery.

AT.   Anti-tank.

Battery.   The basic building block unit in the artillery, i.e., firing battery; also is the smallest unit in the artillery in which the commissioned leader is considered a commander.

Birddog.   O-1 aircraft, used by both Air Force and Army as spotters.

Blivet.   Rubberized, air-transportable fuel container.

Blues.   Rifle platoon of the 1st Squadron, 9th Cavalry.

Bravo.   The letter B in the Army phonetic alphabet.

C-130.   Air Force Hercules transport aircraft.

Caribou.   Army twin-engine transport aircraft.

C and C.   Aircraft in which a troop or unit commander circles a battle area to direct the conduct of the fight. The letters mean command & control. The troops also called it a Charlie-Charlie.

CG.   Commanding General.

Charlie.   The letter C in phonetic alphabet; also slang for Vietcong.

Chopper.   Another term for helicopter.

Chinook.   The official name of the CH-47 tandem rotor transport helicopter. Also known to soldiers as a "Hook."

CIDG.   Civilian Irregular Defense Group; these were indigenous populations recruited to serve with Special Forces units.

CINCPAC.   Commander in Chief, Pacific.

Claymore.   Antipersonnel mine that spews out 700 steel balls in 60-degree arc; lethal up to 50 meters.

COMUSMACV.   Commander, U.S. Military Assistance Command, Vietnam.

Company.
The basic building block unit for all non-artillery and noncavalry units in the Army; it is the smallest unit in which the commissioned leader is a commander.

CP.
Command Post.

CS Grenade.
Tear gas grenade.

CTZ.
Corps Tactical Zone, numbered I through IV north to south. The zones were as much administrative as tactical and the ARVN use of the term "corps" caused the American forces to invent euphemisms for a corps-level command structure, e.g., Task Force Alpha.

Delta.
The letter D in the phonetic alphabet; also Delta Teams were long-range patrol teams in 5th Special Forces.

Divarty.
Division Artillery; the term usually means the headquarters, could also mean all of the artillery in the division.

Division.
The Army's major maneuver element; ranging in strength from 18,000 to 24,000 men, depending on the type; commanded by a two-star general.

DMZ.
Demilitarized Zone; created by Geneva Convention along 17th parallel.

DTOC.
Division Tactical Operations Center.

Dustoff.
Medical evacuation helicopter; a term used in non-1st Cavalry units.

Eagle Flight.
A reaction force circling in aircraft while awaiting a target.

Echo.	The letter E in the phonetic alphabet.
EM.	Enlisted man (men).
F-4C.	Air Force fighter-bomber, also known as a Phantom.
F-105.	Air Force fighter-bomber.
FAC.	Forward Air Controller; an officer of the air control team, directing air strikes, from the ground or air.
FDC.	Fire Direction Center; at battery level in the artillery; mortar platoon level in the infantry.
Flare.	As a noun, it is an illumination device; as a verb, it is the landing attitude of an aircraft.
FM.	Frequency modulation, also known as Fox Mike; used in most tactical radios.
FO.	Forward observer. Usually provided by the supporting artillery batteries to the rifle companies to adjust artillery fire by radio or other means; may also be sent from mortar platoons to rifle platoons to direct mortar fire.
Frag.	Fragmentation grenade; also used to denote a fragmentory order for a unit action or movement.
G-1.	Personnel officer at division level or higher.
G-2.	Intelligence officer at division level.
G-3.	Operations and training officer at division level.

G-4.	Logistics officer at division level.
GI.	Term for American soldier, carried over from World War II.
Green Berets.	Popular name for the Special Forces, taken from the color of their distinctive headgear.
H-13.	The Army's light observation helicopter.
HE.	High explosive ammunition.
H&I.	Harassing and Interdiction fires.
Hog.	The armed Huey B-model with various configurations of outboard mounts for rockets and machine guns.
HQ.	Headquarters.
Huey.	HU-1, the utility helicopter that was the workhorse of Vietnam. The name arose from the original designation of the aircraft—HU-1 (Helicopter, Utility). The Army's official name, Iroquois, just never caught on.
How.	The letter H in the phonetic alphabet.
India.	The letter I in the phonetic alphabet, also was the designator of the radio telephone operator for a leader, i.e., Bullwhip-6 India, would be the radio operator for the commander of the 9th Cavalry Squadron.
JCS.	Joint Chiefs of Staff.
JUSPAO.	Joint United States Public Affairs Office.
KIA.	Killed in action.
Klick.	Slang for kilometer.

L-19. Army nomenclature for Bird Dog aircraft.

Logging. Practice of sending logistics helicopters to troop units—the airmobile equivalent of the kitchen and supply trucks of WWII and Korea.

LP. Listening post.

LRRP. Long range reconnaissance patrol unit.

LZ. Landing zone.

M-16. U.S. caliber 5.56mm, the basic rifle of the infantryman.

M-60. U.S. caliber 7.62mm, platoon and company machine gun.

M-67. The 90-mm recoilless rifle that was the basic weapon for the anti-tank platoon of the combat support company of each battalion. It generally was left in base camp and the platoon organized as infantry.

M-72. Light anti-tank weapon, called a LAW. Fired a 66-mm projectile from a disposable launcher. Used as a bunker buster in Vietnam.

M-79. The 40-mm grenade launcher that looked like a stubby, sawed-off shotgun.

MACV. Military Assistance Command Vietnam, the highest U.S. command authority in the Republic of Vietnam.

Medevac. Term used in the 1st Cavalry for aerial medical evacuation. *See also* Dustoff.

Medic. Medical aid man.

MOH. Medal of Honor, the highest award for valor in the U.S. Army.

MR. Military Region. Both North and South used MRs to denote geographical areas.

M-102. The 105-mm howitzer used by 1st Cavalry artillery units. It had a slightly longer range than the older model, M-101A1, and was substantially lighter, permitting airlifting by Huey.

Napalm. Jellied gasoline used in air strikes.

NCO. Noncommissioned officer, a sergeant, sometimes referred to as noncoms.

Net. Short for radio network. All tactical radios operated within a defined network on a designated frequency.

NVA. North Vietnam Army. Generic term for any soldier or group of soldiers from the North.

Order of battle. Listing of units committed to a theater of operations. Obtaining a correct OB on the enemy was a major intelligence operation.

OP. Observation post.

Organic. Military term for hardware items— vehicles, aircraft, weapons—that belong to a specific unit. All other materiel comes to units on a mission basis and the commander sometimes has limitations in its employment.

Phantom. F-4 fighter plane.

PIO. Public information officer.

PF. Popular Forces. Native military forces locally recruited and employed within their home districts by district chiefs.

Police. Military term for clean-up of an area. Implies a clean, thorough search of the battlefield.

POW. Prisoner of war.

PRC-25. Backpack FM radio—basic communications for nearly every level of command within the division except aviation.

Prep. Short term for preparatory fires on a landing zone.

Quickfox. A brevity code developed in the 11th Air Assault Division to assist in the air-ground coordination.

Recon. Reconnaissance.

REDCON. Readiness Condition.

RF. Regional Forces. Native military forces recruited and employed by province chief within a province. Along with PF, were popularly known as "RuffPuffs."

RPD. Soviet (North Vietnamese) caliber 7.62-mm light machine gun.

RPG. Soviet rocket-propelled grenade that fired an 82-mm warhead. Basically an antitank weapon, the NVA also used it as an antipersonnel weapon.

RTO.   Radio telephone operator.

RVN.   Republic of Vietnam.

S-1.   Personnel officer at brigade or battalion.

S-2.   Intelligence officer at brigade or battalion.

S-3.   Operations and training officer at brigade or battalion.

S-4.   Supply officer at brigade or battalion.

Sapper.   Soldier training to attack fortifications.

Satchel Charge.   Explosive package fitted with a handle for ease of handling or throwing.

Sitrep.   Situation report.

SKS.   Soviet carbine.

Skyraider.   *See* A1E.

Slick.   Term for the Huey troop transport, so named because lacked the outboard weapons mounts that the gunships had.

Smokey the Bear.   Air Force flare ship, usually a C-123, but occasionally a C-47.

Strikers.   Slang for members of the Strike Force, a military force recruited by the American Special Forces. *See* also CIDG.

Strip Alert.   State of readiness for a reaction force that generally meant they were either next to the aircraft or actually sitting in the aircraft that parked along an airstrip.

Tango.   The letter T in phonetic alphabet.

TOC.	Tactical operations center.
20 Mike-Mike.	The 20-mm Gatling gun carried in fighter aircraft that fires up to 4,000 rounds a minute.
Tube artillery.	Artillery that fires projectiles from a gun barrel or tube, as opposed to rocket artillery.
USAF.	United States Air Force.
USARV.	U.S. Army Vietnam; the Army component headquarters that controlled logistics.
Victor.	The letter V in the phonetic alphabet.
VC.	Vietcong, also known as Victor Charlie.
Whiskey.	The letter W in phonetic alphabet.
WIA.	Wounded in action.
WP.	White phosphorus; also known as Willie Peter, a hold-over term from WWII and Korea.
Xray.	The letter X in phonetic alphabet.
XO.	Executive officer. The assistant to the commander of units below division level. Corresponds to the chief of staff at higher level headquarters.
Yankee.	The letter Y in phonetic alphabet.

SELECTED BIBLIOGRAPHY

Beckwith, Colonel Charlie A., and Knox, Donald. *Delta Force*. New York: Harcourt, Brace, Jovanovich, 1984.

Dawson, Alen. *55 Days—The Fall of South Vietnam*. Englewood Cliffs, N.J.: Prentice-Hall, 1977.

Fall, Bernard B. *Last Reflections on a War*. Garden City, N.Y.: Doubleday, 1967.

Karnow, Stanley. *Vietnam—A History*. New York: Viking Press, 1983.

McGarvey, Patrick J. *Visions of Victory*. Stanford, Calif.: Hoover Institution on War, Revolution & Peace, 1981.

Maclear, Michael. *The Ten Thousand Day War*. New York: St. Martin's Press, 1981.

Mertel, Colonel Kenneth D. *The Year of the Horse*. Jericho, N.Y.: Exposition Press, 1967.

Palmer, Dave Richard. *Summons of the Trumpet*. San Rafael, Calif.: Presidio Press, 1978.

Palmer, General Bruce, Jr. *The 25 Year War: America's Military Role in Vietnam*. Lexington, Ky.: University of Kentucky Press, 1984.

Pike, Douglas. *PAVN: Peoples Army of North Vietnam*. Novato, Calif.: Presidio Press, 1986.

Robinson, Anthony. *Weapons of the Vietnam War*. New York: Gallery Books, 1983.

Stanton, Shelby L. *The Green Berets*. Novato, Calif.: Presidio Press, 1985.

————. *The Rise and Fall of an American Army*. Novato, Calif.: Presidio Press, 1985.

————. *Vietnam Order of Battle*. New York: U.S. News Books, 1981.

Summers, Colonel Harry G., Jr. *Vietnam War Almanac*. New York: Facts On File Publications, 1985.

Van Dyke, Jon M. *North Vietnam's Strategy for Survival*. Palo Alto, Calif.: Pacific Books, 1972.

Westmoreland, General William C. *A Soldier Reports*. Garden City, N.Y.: Doubleday, 1976.

U.S. Government Publications

Cash, John A. "Fight at Ia Drang" In *Seven Firefights in Vietnam*. Washington, D.C.: Office of the Chief of Military History, U.S. Army, 1970.

First Cavalry Division (Airmobile), *Combat Operations After-Action Report, Pleiku Campaign, An Khe, Vietnam, 1966*.

Tolson, Lieutenant General John J. *Airmobility, 1961–1971*. Washington, D.C.: Department of the Army, Government Printing Office, 1973.

Periodicals and Unpublished Monographs

Binzer, Vaughn. "Plei Me and Men of October," *VFW Magazine*, October 1985, 41–43; 56–57.

Black, Charles. "Trial by Fire!" *Argosy*, March 1966, 19–25.

Boyle, Major William P., and Samabria, Major Robert. "The Lure and the Ambush." Unpublished monograph, December 1965. On file in the Office of the Chief of Military History, U.S. Army, Washington, D.C.

Gwin, S. Lawrence. "A Day at Albany." Unpublished monograph, Boston, 1983. On file in the Office of the Chief of Military History, U.S. Army, Washington, D.C.

Kinnard, Lieutenant General Harry W. O. "A Victory in the Ia

324

Drang: The Triumph of a Concept." *Army*, September 1967, 71–91.

Oles, Robert T. "Winning One for Garry Owen." *Soldier of Fortune*, April 1983, 42–52.

Sheathelm, Glen H. "The Ia Drang—Almost Forgotten." Unpublished paper, Muskegeon, Mich., 1983. Author's Collection.

Triplett, William. "Ia Drang," *VVA Veteran*, October 1986, 18–22.

INDEX

They go where no one else will go.
They do what no one else will do.
And they're proud to be called ...

TWILIGHT WARRIORS

INSIDE THE WORLD'S SPECIAL FORCES

MARTIN C. AROSTEGUI

From deadly Scud hunts in the Gulf War to daring hostage
rescue missions at London's Iranian Embassy, Special
Forces go where no other army would dare—fighting for
their countries and their lives on the world's most dangerous
missions. Now, journalist and counterterrorism expert
Martin C. Arostegui tells their story—a fascinating true
account of bravery, daring, and the ultimate risk.

TWILIGHT WARRIORS
Martin C. Arostegui
0-312-96493-5____ $6.99 U.S.

It was a war within a war—and it took no prisoners…

COVERT OPS
The CIA's Secret War in Laos

James E. Parker, Jr.

For the first time, veteran James Parker, codename "Mule," reveals the story of the covert war in Laos—a bloody battle that raged behind the face of the Vietnam War. As Parker takes you inside the hell and devastation of war, he provides a first-person account of the people who courageously fought until the bitter end.

COVERT OPS
(Previously published in hardcover as *Codename Mule*)
James E. Parker, Jr.
0-312-96340-8___$5.99 U.S.___$7.99 Can.